COMMON BEES OF EASTERN NORTH AMERICA

COMMON BEES OF EASTERN NORTH AMERICA

OLIVIA MESSINGER CARRIL
AND JOSEPH S. WILSON

PRINCETON UNIVERSITY PRESS

PRINCETON AND OXFORD

Published by Princeton University Press
41 William Street, Princeton, New Jersey 08540
6 Oxford Street, Woodstock, Oxfordshire OX20 1TR

press.princeton.edu

Library of Congress Cataloging-in-Publication Data
Names: Messinger Carril, Olivia, 1976– author. | Wilson, Joseph S., author.
Title: Common bees of eastern North America / Olivia Messinger Carril, Joseph
    S. Wilson.
Description: Princeton : Princeton University Press, [2021] | Series: Princeton field
    guides | Includes bibliographical references and index.
Identifiers: LCCN 2020046594 (print) | LCCN 2020046595 (ebook) | ISBN
    9780691175492 (paperback) | ISBN 9780691218694 (hardback) | ISBN
    9780691222806 (pdf)
Subjects: LCSH: Bees—East (U.S.)—Identification. | Bees—Canada, Eastern—
    Identification.
Classification: LCC QL567.1.A1 C36 2021 (print) | LCC QL567.1.A1 (ebook) | DDC
    595.79/9097—dc23
LC record available at https://lccn.loc.gov/2020046594
LC ebook record available at https://lccn.loc.gov/2020046595

British Library Cataloging-in-Publication Data is available

Editorial: Robert Kirk and Abigail Johnson
Production Editorial: Karen Carter
Text Design: D & N Publishing, Wiltshire, United Kingdom
Jacket/Cover Design: Ruthie Rosenstock
Production: Steven Sears
Publicity: Matthew Taylor and Caitlyn Robson
Copyeditor: Lucinda Treadwell

Jacket/Cover Credit: Cover image by Joseph S. Wilson

This book has been composed in Scala Pro (main text) and Scala Sans Pro (headings
and labels)

Printed on acid-free paper. ∞

Printed in China

10 9 8 7 6 5 4 3 2 1

Dedications

Olivia

To my teachers, who built for me a foundation from which to see the bigger picture. Who shared the joy of getting lost in the details. Who pushed me to try and dared me to fail. The ones who showed me how to learn. And inspired me to teach.

Joe

To Lindsey, who first introduced me to the fascinating and complex world of bees.

Bee to the blossom,
moth to the flame;
Each to his passion;
what's in a name?

—HELEN HUNT JACKSON

CONTENTS

INTRODUCTION

Though they are miniscule across a large landscape, bees are essential pollinators throughout a wide range of ecosystems—from the fields of opportunistic weeds we see in abandoned urban lots, to cultivated and tended botanic gardens, to the wildflowers that flourish in uninhabited and remote open spaces. When we think about the busy bees, most of us picture the non-native honey bee (an introduced labor force from farms and fields overseas), but the honey bee represents the smallest fraction of North America's hard-working pollinators. The most effective pollinators are native bees—those that evolved in concert with the natural ecosystems of this continent. North America's native bees are diverse, widespread, and beautiful. While many species are rarely encountered, a handful are abundant and commonly seen in natural and urban settings alike. Identifying these diminutive flower visitors can be difficult even for the trained professional, yet knowing what species of bees make up a community can reveal a varied and highly connected network of individuals working together—sharing, and yet competing for floral resources.

There are an estimated 20,000 to 30,000 bee species on the planet. Around 20,000 of these species have been named and described. While bees have now been documented in every country, there are many ecosystems and habitats that have not been thoroughly sampled; in these areas the potential for discovering new species is high. In the U.S. and Canada there are somewhere between 3,500 and 4,000 species; conservatively then, 10% to 18% of the world's bees occur in these two countries. Species, as a taxonomic unit, are grouped together into genera according to morphological characteristics they have in common. There are about 111 genera in North America (north of Mexico), with 65 east of the Mississippi River. In the East, the 65 genera comprise 770 species. This guidebook is an introduction to some of the most frequently seen species in the eastern regions of North America, focusing on habitats east of the Mississippi River. Although it does not cover all 770 species, our hope is that it will provide the bee enthusiast with a tool to aid in the discovery of the rich bee fauna that exists all around us—a community of energetic insects visiting the flowers in our gardens and facilitating their transformation from blossoms to fruits and vegetables, and seeds.

IS THIS A BEE?

While bees are common across most landscapes, differentiating between a bee and something else is devilishly difficult when watching an insect in flight. This difficulty is due, in large part, to two facts: (1) Bees and wasps are close relatives and still share many genes, which results in many structural similarities in how they look, and (2) many other kinds of insects have evolved to resemble bees in order to fool potential predators into thinking they are able to sting.

Bees and certain groups of wasps in particular can be tricky to distinguish. Generally, wasps, yellow jackets, and hornets (both of which are kinds of wasps) have less hair, have a slimmer waist, and have more slender legs with spines on them. Bees, in contrast, usually have more hair, a thicker waist, and stouter, shorter legs; most also

Compared with bees, wasps often have less hair, a skinnier waist, and skinnier legs with spines on them.

Mud Dauber Wasp

Paper Wasp

RIGHT:
Bees, like this Svastra, often have more hair than wasps, a thicker appearance, and thicker legs (often with pollen-collecting hairs on them).

Yellow Jacket

have pollen-collecting hairs on their legs. There are, of course, exceptions, and some bees are nearly bald, while some wasps are robust and relatively hairy. Some wasps can be separated from bees on the basis of the silvery hairs on their faces; this is not a character that applies to all wasps, but it can be useful for ruling out some. In addition most nonparasitic wasps lack branched hairs anywhere on their bodies, while bees always have branched hairs somewhere.

One (somewhat) reliable way to differentiate between bees and their wasp cousins is to pay attention to behavioral cues. Bees and wasps have markedly different diets. Bees provision their nests with pollen, but wasps provision with meat (often other insects). Bees, therefore, spend more time on flowers collecting pollen while wasps merely stop at the flower for a sip of nectar before returning to the hunt. These dietary differences have led to the evolution of some physical differences as well, such as pollen-collecting hairs on bees and spiny legs on wasps to assist in carrying prey. Just as there are exceptions to using physical characteristics for identification, there are some exceptions to employing these dietary preferences as identification guides. For example, there are some wasps that feed their offspring pollen and at least one group of bees that is known to feed its progeny dead animal flesh (neither of these exceptions occurs in eastern North America).

While flies are not closely related to bees, many have evolved to look like bees, at least at first glance. Fortunately, there are simple ways to distinguish flies from bees. First, flies (especially those that look like bees) have larger eyes than bees (exceptions would include male honey bees and some male bumble bees). The eyes of the fly fill most of its head. Second, most flies have short antennae, while bee antennae extend at least to the back of the head. These two distinguishing characteristics are often enough to tell the two apart. Other differences are seen in the legs and wings—flies tend to have smooth skinny legs while bees have thicker legs, often with pollen-collecting hairs, and flies have two wings while bees have four. Again, there are exceptions to these simple rules, but in most cases, they will suffice to separate bees from flies.

Bee-mimicking flies, like this hover fly, have larger eyes and shorter antennae than bees. They also have skinny legs and only two wings while bees have thick legs and four wings.

AN OVERVIEW OF BEE BIOLOGY

THE BEE LIFE CYCLE Because we see bees flying among flowers on a warm day, one might assume that most of a bee's life is spent tiptoeing through the tulips, so to speak. In fact, the greater part of a bee's life is spent out of sight, sealed up inside a nest that was built by its mother. Most bees live for just one year. For six to nine weeks of that year they can be seen among the flowers; the rest of the year is passed in relative darkness, inside the nest cell, undergoing a variety of developmental changes. With a life history more commonly associated with butterflies and beetles, bees are holometabolous, meaning they go through a complete metamorphosis. They begin life as an egg, which subsequently develops into a larva (similar in appearance to a grub or maggot). This bee larva morphs into a pupa; a pupa may even be enclosed in a cocoon. The bee completes its life cycle after pupating, finally emerging from the nest as a winged adult.

WHERE DO BEES LIVE? Unlike the ubiquitous honey bees that live socially in large hives, most bees are solitary, meaning a single female bee builds a nest, by herself, for her offspring. A majority of North American native bees nest in holes in the ground, dug by the female that intends to use it. Other bees nest in preexisting holes like abandoned beetle burrows in dead trees, tiny holes in rocks, or even in snail shells. Some cavity-nesting bees bees excavate their own tunnels in rotting wood, pithy-

ABOVE:
A Nomia *entering her ground nest.*

RIGHT:
A Megachile *carrying a leaf to line her nest located in a hole in a piece of wood.*

centered plant stalks, or even solid wood. And a few bees construct nests on the outside of rocks or branches using pebbles and gravel mixed with resin, mud, or plant material to build small enclosures. A female bee constructs a nest, then provisions the brood cells within it with pollen and nectar for her offspring. Internal nest architecture is variable among bees, and may differ markedly even among species of the same genus.

WHAT DO BEES EAT? Adult bees drink nectar from flowers and eat some pollen. Most female bees have specialized pollen-collecting hairs on their legs or abdomen called **scopa**. (Note: The placement of these hairs or even their color can help in bee identification.) However, one genus (*Hylaeus*) collects pollen and nectar in its crop, carrying its harvest home internally. This genus has no scopal hairs. Cleptoparasites also lack scopal hairs; see below for more information. Pollen-collecting bees stock their nest cells with a mixture of pollen and nectar to sustain their offspring as they develop.

Many bees collect pollen from a wide assortment of flowering plants, not limiting themselves to one taxonomic group. These bees are referred to as generalists, or polylectic bees. Dietary preference is on a spectrum, however, with some generalists visiting seemingly any flowering plant, while other generalists limit themselves to a narrower selection of plants. At the opposite end of the spectrum are specialists, or oligolectic bees: Those that are more particular about the flowers from which they collect pollen. Just as there is a range of foraging preferences among generalists, specialists may visit one genus or one family of plants when collecting pollen to feed to their offspring, or they may forage from a wider array of closely related plants, though still fewer plants than generalists do.

A Diadasia *species that specializes on cactus flowers, foraging in a prickly pear flower.*

Cleptoparasites

Among bees, there exist genera known as cleptoparasites that have evolved to usurp the pollen of another bee for their offspring instead of collecting their own. They find their way into the nests of their hosts and lay an egg discretely. Some adult cleptoparasites kill the host egg when they find it in the nest. In other groups, when the parasitic egg hatches, this foreign larva kills the host larva. Either way, the cleptoparasitic larva ingests the pollen meant for the larva of the host bee (hence the name "clepto," emphasizing the stealing of the pollen).

Due to their unique life history, cleptoparasites often look different from pollen-collecting bees. They are usually much less hairy than pollen-collecting bees, and are thus more likely to be confused with wasps. In many, there are body parts with red coloring. While their major body parts are the same, some structures are more developed than in nonparasitic bees, while other structures are less so. The specific characteristics and appearance of these structures are discussed in the sections of this book devoted to cleptoparasitic genera.

AN OVERVIEW OF BEE ANATOMY

The adult bee body is geared toward very specific tasks. In males, the task is procuring a mate, while in females it is building a nest and providing offspring with the pollen and nectar they need to mature to adulthood. As with all insects, the adult form has a head, with antennae and mouthparts, a thorax, with six legs, and an abdomen. Most insects, bees included, also have a pair of wings, compound eyes, and ocelli.

A Nomia *showing the three parts of a bee's body: the head (with antennae), the thorax (which includes the wings and legs), and the abdomen.*

There are a few words commonly used to identify bee structures that aren't encountered in regular conversation that should be defined here. These words will be used throughout the book.

A **carina** is a thin raised line on a hardened body part. In essence, it is a razor thin ridge.

Dorsal refers to the topmost surface. **Ventral** is the underside.

Posterior refers to the back side of a structure, while **anterior** refers to the front side.

Basal refers to the beginning of a segment (the base), and **apical** refers to the tip (the apex) or end of a body part.

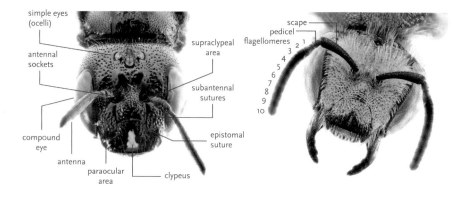

A Ceratina *face showing the location of the large compound eyes, the simple eyes (ocelli), the antennal sockets and the antennae, the clypeus, epistomal suture, and subantennal sutures. The paraocular area and supraclypeal area are also marked. In some bees, the epistomal suture is strongly angled on each side and may even create lobes in the paraocular area that extend into the clypeus.*

A *female* Agapostemon *face with the antennal segments. Closest to the bee's head is the scape, followed by the pedicel, which tends to be shorter than any of the flagellomeres. Next are 10 or 11 flagellomeres; typically, males have 11 flagellomeres and females have 10.*

The **head** is made up of a series of plates that come together at seams, called sutures. The number and shape of the sutures can be important for bee identification. Bees have two sets of eyes. There are two **compound eyes**, on the sides of the head, that are used to see color, shape, and movement. On the top of the head are three simple eyes **(ocelli)** that sense light and dark. The ocelli also help the bee orient with the sun. Between the two compound eyes are the **antennal sockets** from which emerge the **antennae**. The antennae are composed of multiple segments, with the **scape** at the base followed by the **pedicel** and several flagellar segments called flagellomeres (males have 11 flagellomeres and females have 10). Areas of the face are named to aid in identification. The **gena** is the area behind the eye, before the head curves posteriorly. The **preoccipital region** refers to the area behind the gena, once the head has curved to the back, and the curve itself is called the **preoccipital ridge**. The **malar space** is the area between the lower margin of the compound eye and the base of the mandible. The **foveae** are shallow depressions on the faces of some bees next to the upper inner margin of the compound eye, which may be filled with thick hair or may be bare. The **clypeus** is the more or less hexagonal plate that makes up the lower portion of the bee's face. Between the clypeus and the compound eye is a triangular region called the **paraocular area**. Between the antennae is a region called the **supraclypeal area**. The **frons** is the space above the antenna, running up to the **vertex**, which is the top of the head.

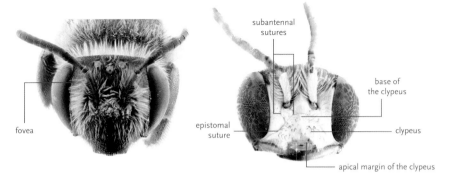

An Andrena *face showing the foveae, which are shallow depressions next to each compound eye. In* Andrena *the foveae are filled with thick appressed hair.*

The shape of the clypeus and the grooves around this more or less hexagonal plate can be diagnostic for telling different bee groups apart.

RIGHT: *A* Halictus *face showing various parts of the head that can aid in identification. These include the gena, preoccipital ridge, malar space, clypeus, frons, and vertex. The length of the malar space is measured from the bottom of the compound eye to the base of the mandible, and is the shortest distance between the two; its width is the same as the width of the base of the mandible.*

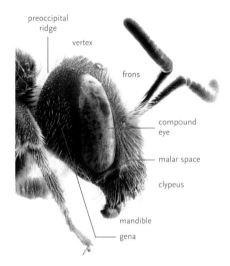

The **mouthparts**, including the mandibles, are often tucked under the bee's head and are hard to see. If these mouthparts are extended, however, they contain useful information for bee identification. There are two mandibles, hinged just below the compound eyes. The apex of the mandibles at the front of the face contains the bee's "teeth." The overall shape, width, and number of teeth are distinctive between genera, as are the grooves and ridges on the outermost surface of each mandible. Finally, there is the tongue, or proboscis, which is made up of a number of smaller pieces. When not being used to construct a nest, or probe flowers, it is folded up under the body. The **labrum** is the plate, hinged to

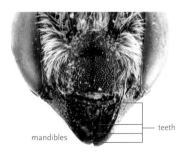

A Megachile *face showing the mandibles with the teeth, which can be useful for identification.*

the clypeus, that, when folded under, covers the other mouthparts. The tongue itself is called the **glossa**. The glossa can vary significantly in shape, from long and pointy to short and lobed; it may be brushy or smooth. The **galea** are two sheaths on either side of the glossa that more or less close over it when it is retracted. Connected to the top of the glossa are the **labial palpi**. They can range in number from one to six, and the length and number of these is one of the main ways to distinguish between long- and short-tongued bees.

The **thorax** is also made up of joined plates (sclerites). The shape of the edges of the plates and the degree to which they are polished are important identifying features. The dorsal surface, the largest plate making up the thorax of the bee, is the **scutum**. Two shallow grooves are usually visible on either side of the center of the scutum. These are called **parapsidal lines**. On either side of the scutum are two small covers for the connecting point of the wings, referred to as **tegula**. The lateral edges of the scutum may be drawn out into points referred to as **axilla**. Behind the scutum is the **scutellum**, a small curved plate. Behind the

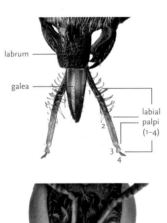

The tongue and some of the mouthparts of a Chelostoma, a long-tongued bee. Notice that the labial palpi have the first two segments elongated and flattened—they are much longer than the second two segments, which are angled to the side just slightly. A few bees have more than four labial palpi. Also shown in this picture is the labrum, which is a long plate that folds up underneath the clypeus. When folded up it is hard to see unless you look underneath the bee (this is unfortunate because the shape of the labrum can aid in identification). The galea are two sheaths that fold around the glossa (the tongue), which is hidden between them in this picture.

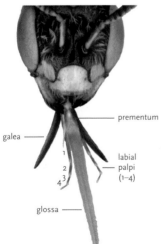

The tongue and some of the other mouthparts of a Perdita, a short-tongued bee. While the tongue does not look particularly short, the first and second segments of the labial palpi (one set on either side of the bee) are the same length as the second two (numbered 1–4). Compare this with the long-tongued bee tongues in the previous image. Also shown is the prementum (the beginning of the glossa), the glossa, and the galea (two parts, one on either side).

(Photos courtesy USDA-ARS Pollinating Insects Research Unit)

scutum

tegula

scutellum

metanotum

propodeum

propodeal pit

ABOVE: *Dorsal view of
the thorax of a* Halictus. *Major plates used in
identification are labeled.*

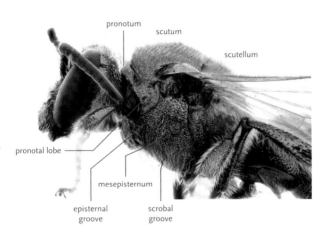

pronotum

scutum

scutellum

RIGHT: *Side view of
the thorax of an*
Augochloropsis. *Major
plates used in identification
are labeled.*

pronotal lobe

mesepisternum

episternal
groove

scrobal
groove

scutellum is a dorsal plate called the **metanotum**. Posterior to the metanotum
is the **propodeum**, which has two faces, one dorsal, and one posterior (facing
the abdomen). The propodeum is, in truth, the first segment of the abdomen.
At its center is the **propodeal pit**, a noticeable indentation in the surface of the
exoskeleton. From the side, the structure supporting the front of the scutum can
be most clearly seen. It is called the **pronotum**, and the lateral-most protrusion on
this plate is called the **pronotal lobe**. The ridge that runs from the pronotal lobe
up to the dorsal surface of the bee is the dorsolateral angle of the pronotum, and
is useful for identifying some bees, as is the pronotal collar, a ring of material that
may extend from the dorsolateral angle toward the head. The edge that separates
the transition from the anterior face of the thorax to the lateral face is termed the
omaulus. Behind the pronotum is the **mesepisternum**, which has two grooves
in its surface that are of interest. They are referred to as the **episternal groove**,
and the **scrobal groove**, with the former occurring above (dorsal to) and forward
(anterior of) the latter. The scrobal groove runs perpendicular to the episternal
groove, when the episternal groove is present.

The fore- and hindwings of a Halictus. *The forewing is the larger wing, and nearer the head. Important veins and spaces are colored. In blue are, moving from the body out, the prestigma, the stigma, and the marginal cell (mc). The tip of the marginal cell is sometimes squared off, and the entire cell may be extremely short, or very long and tapering. The stigma is the dark area on the bee's wing adjacent to the marginal cell. While it is very noticeable on this wing, it is sometimes very small. The prestigma is often narrow, but in some bees it is very wide. Different bee genera may have one, two, or three submarginal cells. The submarginal cells are named (first, second, and third) from the one closest to the body and working out. The relative widths of these cells in relation to each other is an important feature of many bees. In green is the basal vein (b). In this bee it has a distinct arc; other bees have a straight basal vein. The red vein at the outside edge of the wing is called the second recurrent vein (2r). Its shape and how much curve it has are also important. Closer to the body is the first recurrent vein (1r). Where it intersects with the submarginal cells can be telling. At the front edge of the hindwing are tiny hooks (hamuli) that attach the hindwing to the forewing. Finally, there are two important lobes at the back edge of the hindwing: the jugal lobe (entirely missing in some bees) and the vannal lobe.*

The **wings** are made up of veins and cells. Although most bees have the same cells, the shape and size of those cells and veins in relation to each other can be used to identify the bee.

The **legs** are configured as three pairs: forelegs at the front, midlegs in the middle, and hind legs in the back. These legs are each composed of a series of segments, and the size and shape of each can be important for identification. Many female bees carry pollen on their hind legs; the placement and style of the **scopal hairs** they use to hold the pollen grains can vary substantially between genera, and even species.

The **abdomen** also consists of many small segments. When working with bees, it is helpful to know that males have seven exposed abdominal segments while females have

The hind leg of an anthidiine, which carries pollen on the underside of its abdomen. Identified from the end closest to the body (the base) to the apex, the distinct sections are the coxa, the trochanter, the femur, the tibia, and the tarsal segments (the segment closest to the tibia is the basitarsus and is often much longer than the others). There may be an additional little pad between the tarsal claws known as the arolium (not shown). On the tibia, there is often a basitibial plate at the end closest to the femur. At the apex of the tibia are the tibial spurs, which vary in length, shape, and sometimes number. Every hair, spine, and specially curved surface hints at the life history of the bee.

A male Hoplitis, *with the tergal segments (sometimes called tergites) numbered. Because the segments telescope in on each other, the last several may be hard to see. Many important distinguishing features are found on the first one, which has two parts—the front (anterior) side, which faces the thorax, and the top (dorsal) side, which faces up.*

six exposed, with the seventh hidden. Considering that insects at large are made up of a series of segments, which are homologous across groups, it is technically the case that the first segment of the abdomen is incorporated as the last section of the thorax (the propodeum, discussed above). Thus, it can be difficult to accurately name bee body parts—is it more helpful to refer to the natural breaks in the structure of the body? Or to the anatomical structure from which they are derived? For this reason, some scientists refer to the abdomen as the metasoma, and the thorax as the mesosoma. For simplicity, we refer to the abdomen as the

The sternal segments of a female bee. These are in general difficult to see because they run underneath the edges of the tergal segments. The back rims of the sternal segments sometimes have features on them that are important for distinguishing between species.

last large body segment of the bee, and to distinguish between each segment, we follow the format used by other bee taxonomists and number each segment, beginning with 1 for the segment closest to the thorax. The dorsal, or top, surface of the abdomen is a series of plates called **tergites**, or **tergal segments**. And thus the first tergal segment is called T1. The apical edge of each tergite rests over the base of the tergite that comes after it. On the ventral surface, or underside, of the abdomen are matching plates called **sternites** or **sternal segments** that also overlap each other. The resulting effect is similar to a collapsing camp cup or a pocket telescope, where each section folds into and under the one before it.

Of particular interest in the collection of tergal segments is T1, because it has an anterior surface, which faces the thorax, and also a dorsal surface that points upward. The transition of this surface from anterior to dorsal often comes with interesting ridges or carinas and other features that can be used for identification. Also important are the hair bands on the tergal segments. The color, length, and placement of hair bands can contribute much to bee identification. At the apex of T5 in females is the **prepygidial fimbria**, which is a dense band of hairs, quite different in texture from other abdominal hairs, running its width. At the apical end of the abdomen is the **pygidial plate**, a flat plate, often surrounded by an easily seen ridge. On T6, on either side of the pygidial plate are the **pygidial fimbria**, dense hairs thought to be used in nest construction. The pygidial plate is on T6 in females, and on T7 in males (not as easily seen in males).

The sternal segments follow the same numbering system as the tergal segments. Some female bees collect pollen on scopal hairs on the underside of their abdomens instead of on their legs. The color, length, and positioning of these sternal scopal hairs can be important to bee identification.

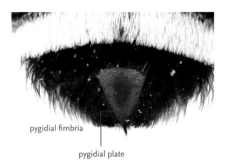

pygidial fimbria

pygidial plate

The pygidial plate of a Eucera.

DETERMINING THE SEX OF A BEE Distinguishing male bees from female bees is a simple matter for most specimens, though there are some cases where it requires a closer look. If scopal hairs are large and full of pollen, so that they can be easily seen on the abdomen or legs of the bee, the female designation is easy. Scopal hairs may be on the femur, or the tibia; be sure to look for long hairs in both areas of the hind leg when using this feature. However, if scopal hairs are not robust or otherwise easy to see, other features can be used. Males have 13 antennal segments, while females have 12. What's more, the 13 antennal segments are often elongated, so that the antennae extend further on males than on females of the same species. In many genera, males have more yellow on the face and legs compared with their female counterparts. Males usually have one more visible tergal segment (seven) than females (six). However, sometimes tergal segments retract, so that the bee may appear to have fewer than the true six or seven; as a result this character is not always an easy way to distinguish male from female bees. Finally, and perhaps easier to see, female bees possess a sting, which male bees do not.

BODY FORMS Bee bodies can look very different from each other when the hair is removed and they are seen as silhouettes. Some are stout and stocky, while others are long and slender. These body forms are named after the most common genus that exhibits that form. **Andreniform** bees have the form of an *Andrena*: slender, with an oval abdomen that rounds or tapers at either end. **Euceriform** or **anthophoriform** bees

Andreniform   Euceriform or anthophoriform   Megachiliform

Bees are often described based on the overall shape of their bodies. Andreniform bees are slender, with an oval abdomen that rounds or tapers at either end. Euceriform or anthophoriform bees have a robust head, thorax, and abdomen and are often very hairy. Megachiliform bees have a thick round head, stout thorax, and wide abdomen.

have the form of *Anthophora* or *Eucera*: robust head, thorax, and abdomen, and often very hairy. **Megachiliform** bees have the form of *Megachile* or Anthidiini: thick round head, stout thorax, and wide abdomen.

USING THIS BOOK

This book will address species commonly found east of the Rocky Mountains, with a particular focus on bees east of the Mississippi River. A few rare species that occur only in Texas, the Midwest, or Florida have also been included. Because there are more than 750 bee species in the East, it is not possible to include all of them in this book. Instead, we focus on the common and the unique species. Remember that bee identification requires patience, even for trained bee scientists. This book should, however, serve as a springboard to recognizing the bees you see and will help you appreciate the incredible diversity of bees that live in eastern North America.

There are several ways to tackle the challenge of identifying small bees. The most reliable way to determine a bee's identity is to capture it using a net or some other tool, euthanize it, and pin it. Species determination can then be done using a microscope, taxonomic keys, and/or a reference collection. This level of effort and equipment may be beyond the capability of many, as microscopes, pins, and storage containers are expensive, and access to reference collections is limited.

Should the bee enthusiast choose to make their own collection, there are a number of sources listed at the end of this book that outline how to collect, euthanize, and preserve specimens.

Alternatively, bees can be photographed as they root around, unaware, in flowers. Many characters that can aid in the identification of a bee to genus level, and even to the species level, can be seen from crisp images taken with modern digital cameras or even with smartphones. It is best to take photos of the bee from several angles, and to include as many of the body parts as possible. Wing venation is useful in determining or distinguishing between some closely related genera. Legs can offer additional clues, especially in females where different species carry pollen on different sections of the leg. The abdomen is important because the number, color, length, and position of stripes can be telling. The thorax may be shiny or densely punctured and may have interesting

Taking photos of a bee from several angles can aid in identification.

projections or other sculpted contours that are important. And finally, the general shape of the face, the facial markings, the presence or absence of hair, and the position (and length) of the antennae are important identifying features. Setting a camera to a continuous shooting mode (also called burst mode, sports mode, or continuous high-speed mode) can help—in the age of digital photography, redundant and out-of-focus images can easily be deleted after being viewed. For the serious bee photographer, we recommend a 100 mm or greater lens and 10 megapixels or more (so that photos can be zoomed while shooting, or cropped afterward).

Another way to take photos of bees for identification purposes is to collect them using a net, transfer them carefully to a small container, and chill them in the refrigerator or a cooler for at least five to ten minutes, and up to several hours. The bees will enter torpor and can be photographed without the risk of blurring the image and can be turned and staged for optimum photographic capture of their various identifying features. After a short time they will return to normal and will fly away. In addition, specimens can be briefly netted and placed in transparent vials for viewing with a loupe or hand lens before being released.

With practice, common bees can be identified in the field without the aid of photos. Familiarity with what is in a given area is particularly helpful, so time and dedication are key. It can be daunting as a beginner to know where to start with bee identification. We recommend that beginners start at the beginning: familiarize yourself with bee terminology and read the sections in this book that highlight bee family characteristics.

This book can be used to aid in identification in several ways.

— Flip from page to page looking for a matching group of bees and then read the detailed identification characteristics to determine if the bee is a match, cross referencing with genera and species listed as similar.

— Use the taxonomic key at the back to arrive at the correct family and genus.

— Use the "quick reference" guide for bees that appear fairly distinctive.

We have sorted the bees included here taxonomically, so that successively larger groups share more characteristics. For example, all members of the Andrenidae bee family have two subantennal sutures. Within this family, all bees in the subfamily Andreninae have (in addition to two subantennal sutures) thick facial fovea. And within the subfamily Andreninae, all members of the genus *Andrena* have (in addition to subantennal sutures and thick facial fovea) a hind basitarsus that is more than half as long as the hind tibia. You will find family descriptions and tribe descriptions that highlight characteristics shared by the genera within.

Our summaries for genera are divided into the following sections:

1 **AN OVERVIEW** that lists general life history characteristics for the genus, including specialist or generalist tendencies, nesting preferences, and what is known of the genus' characteristic sociality.

2 **IN THE WORLD**, which outlines the distribution and abundance of species.

3 **CLEPTOPARASITES**, listing known cleptoparasites for each genus—likely to be seen in concert with their host species.

4 **IDENTIFYING FEATURES** of the genus, including similar genera that might deserve a look for comparative purposes.

At the back of the book can be found selected references for the reader who seeks to learn more about behavior, ecology, or identification of that genus. Note that many of these publications, especially newer ones, will likely require purchasing. Also at the end is a glossary with definitions and descriptions of terminology used throughout the book.

For each species, we list body size, phenology, floral hosts, range, and nesting habits followed by identifying characteristics *in addition to* those listed for the genus. For each description, we highlight the characters most useful for distinguishing the bee from other species, but do *not* include full body descriptions. We begin each description at the front of the body and move through to the abdomen (Head, Thorax, Wings, Legs, Abdomen). If there are no distinguishing or notable features on a body part, we do not include it. Unless stated otherwise, characters listed apply to both male and female bees of that species. We also list similar species, which may or may not be described in detail in this book.

Each bee species that is featured in this book has an accompanying range map, shaded from light green to dark green. Because the actual ranges for most bees are not well understood, we modeled the suitability of habitats in eastern North America for supporting each bee, based on verified locality records, correlated with temperature and rainfall patterns, across 1 km grid squares. For example, in the sample map here, the light green color for *Bombus auricomis* in Alabama suggests a lower probability here that the appropriate habitat for this species occurs. In contrast, Illinois is a dark green, meaning that the habitats associated with this more northern state are

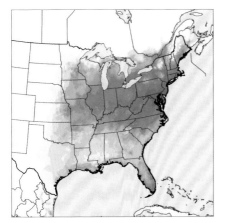

more likely to support this bee. The drawback to this approach is that it relies on verified historical locality records, and so it may be less accurate for rarer species, or for species whose ranges are experiencing contemporary shifts, for example, in response to climate change.

An example of the distribution maps shown throughout the book. Darker shades of green indicate a higher likelihood that the habitat is suitable for an individual bee species and lighter shades indicate a lower likelihood.

A QUICK REFERENCE GUIDE TO BEES OF EASTERN NORTH AMERICA

BEES THAT ARE COMPLETELY RED

Nomada
(page 218)

BEES THAT ARE YELLOW AND BLACK

Anthidiini
(page 140)

Nomada
(page 218)

Perdita
(page 98)

Bombus
(page 202)

Xylocopa
(page 162)

Ptilothrix
(page 173)

Habropoda
(page 196)

Anthophora, some species (page 192)

BEES THAT ARE METALLIC GREEN OR BLUE

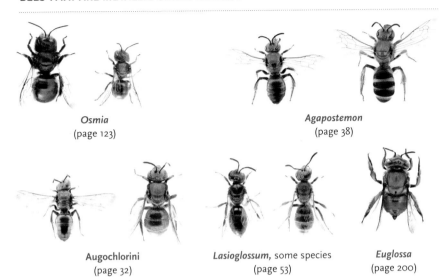

Osmia
(page 123)

Agapostemon
(page 38)

Augochlorini
(page 32)

Lasioglossum, some species
(page 53)

Euglossa
(page 200)

BEES THAT HAVE A BLACK THORAX AND RED ABDOMEN

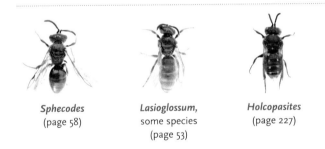

Sphecodes
(page 58)

Lasioglossum,
some species
(page 53)

Holcopasites
(page 227)

BEES THAT HAVE LONG ANTENNAE

Male Eucerini
(page 175)

Male *Lasioglossum*
(page 53)

BEES THAT ARE DARK WITH LIGHT HAIR BANDS ON THE ABDOMEN

Halictus
(page 44)

Lasioglossum,
some species
(page 53)

Eucerini,
some species
(page 175)

Megachile,
some species
(page 132)

Osmiini,
some species
(page 112)

Many parasitic bees
(pages 130, 222, 224)

Colletes,
some species
(page 67)

Andrena,
some species
(page 82)

Lithurgopsis
(page 156)

Melitoma
(page 171)

Calliopsis
(page 94)

Perdita
(page 98)

Nomia
(page 62)

Hesperapis
(page 104)

Melitta
(page 107)

BEES WITH A TRIANGULAR OR POINTY ABDOMEN

Coelioxys
(page 130)

BEES THAT ARE EXTREMELY LARGE (BIGGER THAN THE TOP JOINT OF THE THUMB)

Bombus
(page 202)

Centris
(page 198)

Xylocopa
(page 162)

Dieunomia
(page 60)

Eucera (Xenoglossa)
(page 181)

BEES THAT ARE MINISCULE

Perdita
(page 98)

Lasioglossum,
some species
(page 53)

Ceratina
(page 165)

Hylaeus
(page 74)

BEES THAT ARE VERY HAIRY

Apidae,
many species
(page 159)

Colletes,
some species
(page 67)

Andrena,
some species
(page 82)

Osmia,
some species
(page 123)

BEES THAT ARE SMALL AND DARK

Ceratina
(page 165)

Panurgini
(page 96)

Hylaeus
(page 74)

Osmia,
some species
(page 123)

Osmiini,
some species
(page 112)

Dufourea
(page 63)

Calliopsis
(page 94)

Macropis
(page 105)

BEES THAT ARE LARGE AND DARK

Melissodes,
some species
(page 184)

Megachile,
some species
(page 137)

Osmia,
some species
(page 123)

BEES THAT CARRY POLLEN ON THEIR ABDOMEN

Megachilidae
(page 109)

HALICTIDAE

Halictidae are small to medium-sized bees, ranging from bright metallic green to matte-black. Most species are abundant where they occur, with numerous individuals of the same species occupying an area. The majority of Halictidae in the U.S. nest in the ground, but a few can be found nesting in rotting wood. Many Halictidae are polylectic, or generalists, though a few genera (*Dufourea*, *Dieunomia*) include species that are specialists. A number of species exhibit some form of sociality, ranging from communal nesting, where multiple individuals share a nest entrance, to modest sociality (primitively eusocial), with a division of labor, and a queen and her subordinate daughters and sisters aiding in rearing the subsequent generations.

IDENTIFICATION: Few features unite the Halictidae, but the arcuate basal vein on the wing is strong in most of the genera and can be a good character for verifying the family in most cases. Pollen is collected on the tibia of nonparasitic females. There is one subantennal suture. The tongue is short. Despite the complexity of family level characters, many of the genera are distinctive in appearance and can be easily identified.

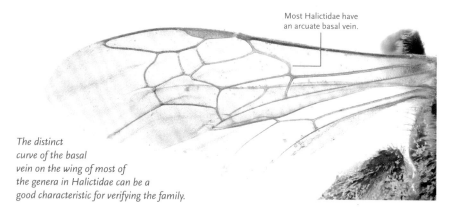

Most Halictidae have an arcuate basal vein.

The distinct curve of the basal vein on the wing of most of the genera in Halictidae can be a good characteristic for verifying the family.

TAXONOMY: The Halictidae are the second most speciose group in the United States. In North America there are 18 genera in the Halictidae, and in the eastern parts of the U.S. and Canada there are 10 genera. These genera are divided into three subfamilies, and several tribes, outlined below:

— SUBFAMILY HALICTINAE

Includes the most commonly seen and abundant Halictidae in North America. Females are andreniform. Males are elongated with slender abdomens and long antennae. On the wing, the basal vein is strongly arcuate.

— AUGOCHLORINI: On the abdomen, in females, the apical margin of T5 is strongly notched. Distinctly green or coppery in color.

Augochlora, Augochlorella, Augochloropsis

— **HALICTINI:** On the abdomen, in females, the apical margin of T5 has no notch in it. May be matte-black, black and red, gunmetal green or blue, or brilliant green.

Agapostemon, Halictus, Lasioglossum, Sphecodes

T5 of Augochlorini has a little notch in the middle.

— SUBFAMILY NOMIINAE

Includes the agriculturally important *Nomia melanderi* (alkali bee), which pollinates alfalfa. Differs in wing venation from the Halictinae in that the marginal cell is rounded and doesn't taper much (the top and bottom margins remain parallel to each other). The middle of the three submarginal cells is significantly smaller than the first and third submarginal cells. The two genera look little alike, and both are unique among halictids in appearance.

Dieunomia, Nomia

T5 of Halictini has no apical notch.

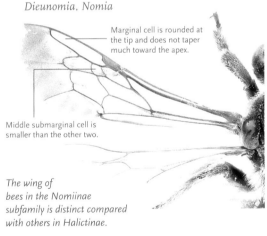

Marginal cell is rounded at the tip and does not taper much toward the apex.

Middle submarginal cell is smaller than the other two.

The wing of bees in the Nomiinae subfamily is distinct compared with others in Halictinae.

Antennal sockets are low on the face, close to the clypeus.

— SUBFAMILY ROPHITINAE

In eastern North America only *Dufourea* is represented. It is seldom seen but can be identified by the wide clypeus and low antennal sockets. All members of this genus are specialists.

Bees in the subfamily Rophitinae have antennal sockets placed low on the face.

— ROPHITINI

Dufourea

Within these 10 genera there are around 175 species.

AUGOCHLORA

— **SUBFAMILY:** Halictinae
— **TRIBE:** Augochlorini

OVERVIEW: *Augochlora* are blue-green (occasionally copper-colored) bees of medium to small size; though there is only one species in the East, it occurs widely across the region. All *Augochlora* are generalists, or nest above or below ground, often in aggregations of several hundred individuals.

IN THE WORLD: More than 100 species, with just one of those in eastern North America. All *Augochlora* are found in North, Central, and South America, and they are most abundant in Central and South America.

CLEPTOPARASITES: In the U.S., maybe *Sphecodes.*

IDENTIFYING FEATURES: Medium-sized bright green to coppery bees; petite. **HEAD:** The inner margins of the compound eyes appear notched just above the level of the antennal sockets. The paraocular area dips into the clypeus, creating a slightly raised protrusion beside the compound eye. The mandible is dark, becoming green only at bases in females. Mandible is bidentate. **THORAX:** The margin of the propodeum is smooth, not carinate. **WINGS:** The apex of the marginal cell is rounded or squared off, appearing as a blunt rather than a sharp point. The basal vein is strongly curved. **ABDOMEN:** Green in both males and females. In females, T5 is notched in the middle and S1 has a strong central keel. In males, the apical margin of S4 is straight.

SIMILAR GENERA: *Agapostemon* is similarly bright green, but has a strong ridge (carina) running around the propodeum that is not seen in *Augochlora*. Additionally, the inner margin of the *Augochlora* eye is notched, which is not the case in *Agapostemon*. *Augochlora* also looks similar to other Augochlorini genera, which share with *Augochlora* the characteristics that distinguish it from *Agapostemon*. They can be distinguished from each other by differences in the marginal cell, the clypeus, and the shape of the tegula (see those genera for clarification).

— *Augochlora pura*

SIZE: Small; 8 mm. **PHENOLOGY:** April through September; may be earlier and later along the Gulf Coast. Females appear before males in the spring. **FLORAL HOSTS:** Polylectic. **RANGE:** Maine to Florida, west to Minnesota and Texas. **NESTING:** Solitary, usually in dead or decaying wood. Multiple females may overwinter together. Males can be seen sleeping in groups of half a dozen individuals in holes near female nests, or hovering near dead wood where females are nesting. Females forage in mornings and work in nests in afternoon and evening. May be multivoltine with two to three generations per year.

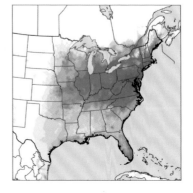

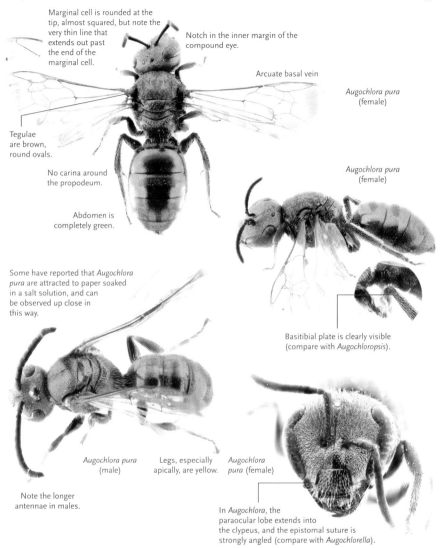

Marginal cell is rounded at the tip, almost squared, but note the very thin line that extends out past the end of the marginal cell.

Notch in the inner margin of the compound eye.

Arcuate basal vein

Augochlora pura (female)

Tegulae are brown, round ovals.

Augochlora pura (female)

No carina around the propodeum.

Abdomen is completely green.

Some have reported that *Augochlora pura* are attracted to paper soaked in a salt solution, and can be observed up close in this way.

Basitibial plate is clearly visible (compare with *Augochloropsis*).

Augochlora pura (male)

Legs, especially apically, are yellow.

Augochlora pura (female)

Note the longer antennae in males.

In *Augochlora*, the paraocular lobe extends into the clypeus, and the epistomal suture is strongly angled (compare with *Augochlorella*).

IDENTIFICATION: One of the more commonly seen bees in eastern North America; occasionally land on human skin to lick sweat. Females and males are bright metallic green, though in some regions males may appear bluer than females. In males, the apical margin of the clypeus is yellow. As this is the only eastern species in this genus, other characters are included in the genus description above.

SIMILAR SPECIES: There are three other species of *Augochlora* that are occasionally found in Texas. *Augochlora aurifera* occurs along the Mexican border. *Augochlora nigrocyanea* (a mostly black species) occurs in south central Texas. And *Augochlora azteca* can be found rarely in southern Texas.

AUGOCHLORELLA

— **SUBFAMILY:** Halictinae
— **TRIBE:** Augochlorini

OVERVIEW: *Augochlorella* are small to medium-sized bees, brilliant green to copper-green. These bees can be solitary or social, depending on climate. All *Augochlorella* are ground-nesting, often occurring in dense aggregations. They are polylectic.
IN THE WORLD: 16 species total. All are restricted to North, Central, and South America. Most abundant in Central and South America. In the U.S. and Canada there are 7 species. East of the Rocky Mountains there are 3 species.
CLEPTOPARASITES: *Sphecodes.*
IDENTIFYING FEATURES: Small, petite green bees. **HEAD:** The inner margin of the compound eye is notched, just above the level of the antennal sockets. On the clypeus, between the subantennal sutures and the compound eye (i.e., the lateral portion of the epistomal suture), the epistomal groove is right-angled, but the paraocular area is not lobed. In males, the second flagellar segment is significantly shorter than the first. **THORAX:** The propodeum is smooth, with no sharp ridge delimiting its border. **WINGS:** The marginal cell is pointed. The basal vein is strongly curved. **ABDOMEN:** Green in both males and females. In males, the apical margin of S4 is concave.
SIMILAR GENERA: *Agapostemon* is similarly bright green, but has a strong ridge running around the propodeum that is not seen in any of the Augochlorini. Also, the inner margin of the *Augochlorella* eye is notched, which is not the case in *Agapostemon*. *Augochlorella* looks similar to other Augochlorini genera. They can be distinguished from each other by differences in the marginal cell, the clypeus, and the shape of the tegula (see those genera for clarification).

— *Augochlorella aurata*

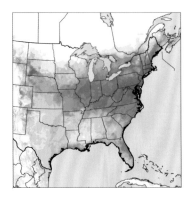

SIZE: Small; 5–8 mm. **PHENOLOGY:** April through October. **FLORAL HOSTS:** Polylectic. **RANGE:** Southern Canada south through Florida, west to Colorado and Texas. **NESTING:** Ground-nesting bee. Eusocial or semisocial at lower elevations, and solitary at higher elevations and northern latitudes.
IDENTIFICATION: *Augochlorella aurata* is one of the most abundant bees seen in eastern habitats, including forests, agricultural fields, and urban environments. It is shiny metallic green, perhaps with coppery highlights. In females, on the face, the bottom one-third of the clypeus is brown. Distinguishing features are listed in the generic description above and in the comparison with similar species below.
SIMILAR SPECIES: There are two other uncommon *Augochlorella* found in the eastern U.S.: *A. gratiosa* and *A. persimilis*. *A persimilis* is never overly abundant but is

consistently found. It has a distinctive ridge behind the compound eye at the rear of the head (a preoccipital carina), and in females the bottom two-thirds of the clypeus is usually brown. *Augochlorella gratiosa* is not commonly seen but is more frequent further south in its range. It intergrades to some extent with *A. aurata*, making it difficult to distinguish between the two. For additional information and a key to the three species, see Coelho (2004).

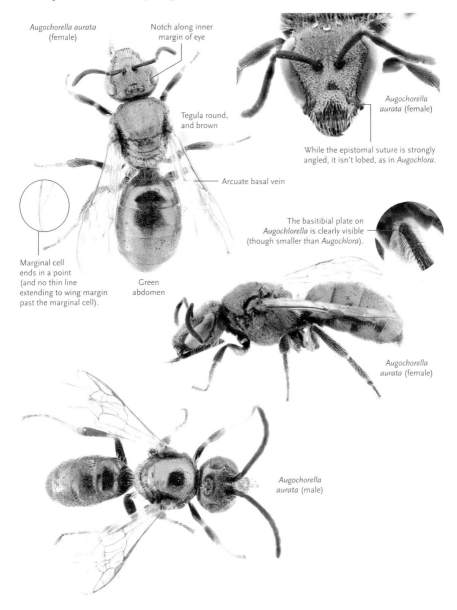

Augochorella aurata (female)

Notch along inner margin of eye

Tegula round, and brown

Arcuate basal vein

Marginal cell ends in a point (and no thin line extending to wing margin past the marginal cell).

Green abdomen

Augochorella aurata (female)

While the epistomal suture is strongly angled, it isn't lobed, as in *Augochlora*.

The basitibial plate on *Augochlorella* is clearly visible (though smaller than *Augochlora*).

Augochorella aurata (female)

Augochorella aurata (male)

AUGOCHLOROPSIS

— **SUBFAMILY:** Halictinae
— **TRIBE:** Augochlorini

OVERVIEW: Small to medium-sized brilliant green sweat bees. Nest in the ground, and are occasionally primitively eusocial, with at least a few daughters of late summer generations foraging while their mother remains home (other daughters venture off to start their own solitary nests). As such, population sizes grow over the course of the summer, and these bees are relatively abundant by midsummer to early fall. *Augochloropsis* are generalists, collecting pollen from any number of summer/fall flowering plants.

IN THE WORLD: Worldwide, there are around 140 described species, mostly occurring in Central and South America. In North America there are 3 species, and all can be found in the East; they are less common in western states.

CLEPTOPARASITES: *Sphecodes.*

IDENTIFYING FEATURES: Green bees, slightly larger than other green sweat bees in the East. **HEAD:** There is a notch in the inner margin of each compound eye. The epistomal groove does not angle sharply, as it does in other Augochlorini. **THORAX:** There is no carina outlining the propodeum. The pronotal lobe has a strong carina outlining it, which can be seen from a front oblique angle. The tegula is comma-shaped, metallic in color, with a clear indent on the inner margin. **WINGS:** Basal vein is arcuate. **LEGS:** In females, the basitibial plate is hardly visible at all. In both sexes the inner midtibial spur has wide parallel comblike projections. **ABDOMEN:** The first two tergal segments exhibit a thin row of sparse, stout hairs (this may wear off in older specimens).

SIMILAR GENERA: *Agapostemon* is also green but has a strong ridge running around the propodeum that is not seen in *Augochloropsis*. Also, the inner margins of the compound eyes of *Augochloropsis* are notched, which is not the case in *Agapostemon*. *Augochloropsis* look similar to other Augochlorini genera. They can be distinguished by the clear presence of a basitibial plate in females of those groups, as well as differences in the marginal cell, the clypeus, and the shape of the tegula (see those genera for clarification).

— *Augochloropsis metallica*

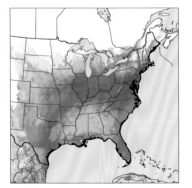

SIZE: Medium; 11 mm.
PHENOLOGY: March through November. **FLORAL HOSTS:** Broadly polylectic. **RANGE:** Maine and Ontario south through Florida, west to Colorado and Texas.
NESTING: Ground-nesting bee. Reports exist of this bee being solitary, communal, or social.
IDENTIFICATION: Bright metallic green, in some geographic areas with blue highlights to the green colorations. Less common than other

Notch on inner margin of compound eye

Augochloropsis metallica
(female)

Tegula is not
a perfect oval and
is slightly metallic.

Rows of bristles run
across T1 and T2.

With *Augochloropsis*, the
clypeus is only barely notched,
not as in other Augochlorini.

Marginal cell
ends bluntly.

green metallic halictids seen
in the East. Most features
listed in characters for the
genus. **HEAD:** In males,
mandibles and antennae
may be black, at least in part.
THORAX: Scutum shiny, with
small punctures that become
closer together toward the
head and laterally. Tegulae
green along inner margin,
brown toward outer margin.
WINGS: Marginal cell ends
bluntly. **LEGS:** In males, tarsi
are yellowish, but legs are otherwise
green. In females, basitibial plate is
greatly reduced. **ABDOMEN:** Green in both
males and females. In females T1–T3 with
deep, distinct punctures.

*Augochloropsis
metallica*
(male)

Tibiae are yellow, but
other leg segments
are green.

Rows of bristles at the apex
of T1 and T2, which have
deep distinct punctures.

Augochloropsis species have a fringe of
stiff hairs lining the apex of T1 and T2.

There are two subspecies of *A. metallica:*
A. metallica metallica, and *A. metallica
fulgida.* The differences between the two
are notable enough that they may be
designated as separate species at some
point. *Augochloropsis m. metallica* females
are not very polished on T2 and have a
distinct comb of flattened hairs across the

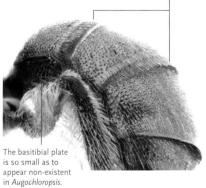

The basitibial plate
is so small as to
appear non-existent
in *Augochloropsis*.

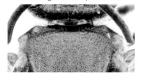

Augochloropsis metallica: note the more rounded lateral angles of the pronotum.

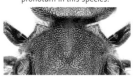

Augochloropsis sumptuosa: Note the points on the lateral angles of the pronotum in this species.

apical edge of T2. In males, the tergal segments are densely and finely punctate, and the propodeal triangle is roughened and not polished. *A. m. fulgida* is highly polished on T2, with large, well-separated punctures. The apical fringe of hairs on T2 does not look much different from other apical hairs on the abdomen. In males, the surface of the tergal segments, T2 included, are polished between punctures, and the propodeal triangle is polished. **SIMILAR SPECIES:** There are two other species of *Augochloropsis* in the East. *Augochloropsis anonyma* is found in Florida north to North Carolina. The body is a brilliant azure or purple. *Augochlora sumptuosa* is more widespread, found from Florida north to Delaware, and west to at least Colorado. On the sides of the pronotum of *A. sumptuosa* are wide projections, distinct from the more rounded (typical) shape of *A. metallica*. On the head, the vertex bulges, rising up above the ocelli noticeably when the face is viewed straight on.

AGAPOSTEMON

— **SUBFAMILY:** Halictinae
— **TRIBE:** Halictini

OVERVIEW: Small to medium-sized bees commonly seen from mid-spring through late fall. All *Agapostemon* species nest in the ground. May nest solitarily, communally with many females using one hole, or in dense aggregations. May even nest among aggregations of other bees, including *Halictus, Nomia,* and *Andrena.* Nests can be in lawns, vertical banks, or shallowly sloped hills. *Agapostemon* are generalists, found on a variety of flowers. Males sometimes swarm around larger blooming shrubs, especially in the fall. Many species are bivoltine or multivoltine. Fertilized females overwinter, emerging in early spring. After foraging and nesting, they die. Their offspring are the late summer/fall generation, with females of this generation emerging first, and males emerging in early fall to mate with the females that will overwinter again, fertilized. **IN THE WORLD:** *Agapostemon* are found only in North, Central, and South America. There are 14 species north of Mexico. Four of these are commonly seen east of the Mississippi River. **CLEPTOPARASITES:** *Nomada* and *Sphecodes.* **IDENTIFYING FEATURES:** *Agapostemon* all have a brilliant green head and thorax. **HEAD:** Green in both sexes, but lower half of clypeus yellow in males. No indentation along the inner margins of the compound eyes. **THORAX:** The perimeter of the propodeum is carinate, separating this genus from other metallic green Halictidae (see Augochlorini). **LEGS:** The hind tibiae are very long—at least as long as all the tarsal segments of the hind leg together. Males have four tarsal segments on the hind legs,

All *Agapostemon* have a strong ridge around the perimeter of the propodeum.

instead of the more typical five tarsal segments. **WINGS:** Basal vein is strongly curved. **ABDOMEN:** In females the abdomen is usually green (but see *A. virescens*). Male individuals can be identified by the yellow-and-brown or black stripes running across the abdomen.

— *Agapostemon sericeus*

SIZE: Small to medium; 9–11 mm. **PHENOLOGY:** At southern edge of range, almost year-round; may be multivoltine. In northern latitudes, April through November. **FLORAL HOSTS:** Polylectic. **RANGE:** Central eastern Canada south through central Florida, west to Kansas and Nebraska. Least common of the eastern *Agapostemon*. **NESTING:** Solitary; communal nests have not been seen.

IDENTIFICATION: THORAX: The punctures are all roughly the same size and the area between punctures is shiny; the propodeum lacks a distinct median triangular area with longitudinal ridges (this is hard to see). **ABDOMEN:** In males, the abdomen is yellow and matte-black or brown striped, the anterior face of T1 is dark brown to black, and S6 has some yellow on it.

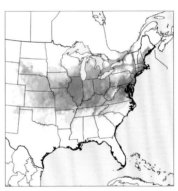

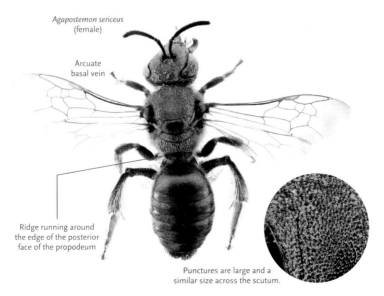

Agapostemon sericeus (female)

Arcuate basal vein

Ridge running around the edge of the posterior face of the propodeum

Punctures are large and a similar size across the scutum.

S6 lacks any raised ridge at its center. In females, the abdomen is bright metallic green, with white hair bands across each segment (may be thinner in older specimens).

SIMILAR SPECIES: *A. texanus* females are similar, but the thorax has two distinct sizes of punctures. In males of *A. texanus,* the abdomen maintains a metallic tinge especially near the sides, even with the yellow and black markings.

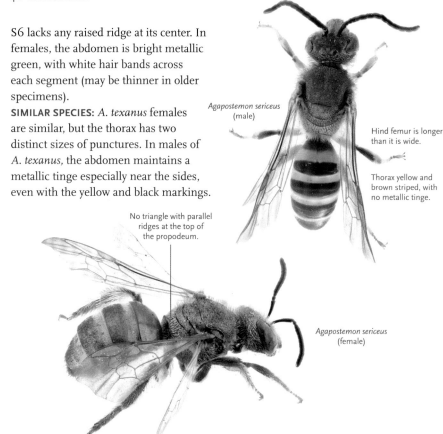

Agapostemon sericeus
(male)

Hind femur is longer than it is wide.

Thorax yellow and brown striped, with no metallic tinge.

No triangle with parallel ridges at the top of the propodeum.

Agapostemon sericeus
(female)

— *Agapostemon splendens*

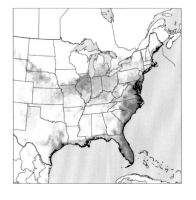

SIZE: Medium; 10–11 mm.
PHENOLOGY: April through October, with sightings in February through November in the South. **FLORAL HOSTS:** Broadly polylectic. **RANGE:** Maine to Florida, west to Texas and North Dakota. Most common *Agapostemon* in the southeastern U.S. and into the Gulf. Prefers lower elevations. **NESTING:** Solitary; communal nests have not been seen. May nest in sparse aggregations, usually in bare areas, and appears to nest mainly in sand. Sometimes found in vertical banks.

IDENTIFICATION: THORAX: Punctures are small, roughly uniform in size. In females, there is a distinct central wedge of longitudinal ridges on the dorsal section of the

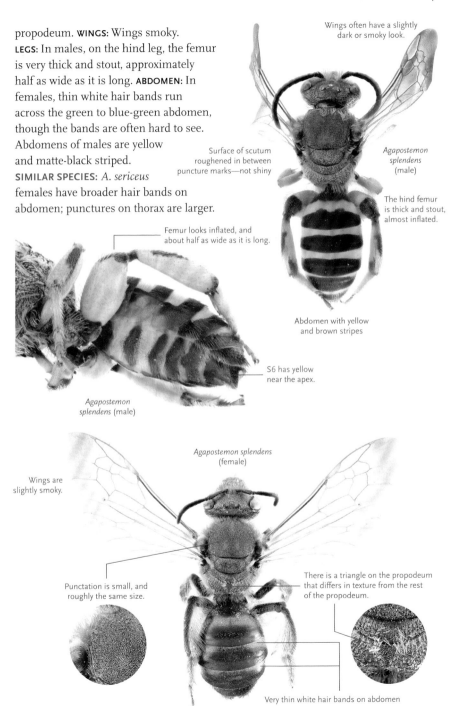

propodeum. **WINGS:** Wings smoky. **LEGS:** In males, on the hind leg, the femur is very thick and stout, approximately half as wide as it is long. **ABDOMEN:** In females, thin white hair bands run across the green to blue-green abdomen, though the bands are often hard to see. Abdomens of males are yellow and matte-black striped.
SIMILAR SPECIES: *A. sericeus* females have broader hair bands on abdomen; punctures on thorax are larger.

Wings often have a slightly dark or smoky look.

Agapostemon splendens (male)

Surface of scutum roughened in between puncture marks—not shiny

The hind femur is thick and stout, almost inflated.

Femur looks inflated, and about half as wide as it is long.

Abdomen with yellow and brown stripes

S6 has yellow near the apex.

Agapostemon splendens (male)

Agapostemon splendens (female)

Wings are slightly smoky.

Punctation is small, and roughly the same size.

There is a triangle on the propodeum that differs in texture from the rest of the propodeum.

Very thin white hair bands on abdomen

— *Agapostemon texanus*

SIZE: Small to medium; 9–11 mm.
PHENOLOGY: Roughly April through October; multivoltine. **FLORAL HOSTS:** Polylectic.
RANGE: Extremely widespread, occurring from southern Canada south through Costa Rica and from coast to coast. In the East, it is more common in the mid-Atlantic states than further south. **NESTING:** Solitary; may be communal in some cases. Nests in a variety of soil types, and may be in flat areas, or vertical banks. Can occur in aggregations with other individuals, or even with other bee species (i.e., *Halictus*).
IDENTIFICATION: Females have an overall hairy appearance, especially on the sides of the thorax, as well as covering the abdomen. This makes some of the hair bands on the abdomen less distinct than in other species. **THORAX:** In females, punctures of two sizes lie on a shiny surface. **LEGS:** In males, on the hind leg, the inner face of the tibia has a dark stripe or spot running from the femur to the basitarsus; often a mark on the outer surface as well. **ABDOMEN:** In males, the yellow-and-black striped abdomen may appear lightly metallic, especially laterally, and S5 and S6 are yellc In females, abdomen is green.
SIMILAR SPECIES: In the western U.S., females of *Agapostemon angelicus* and females of *A. texanus* are indistinguishable.

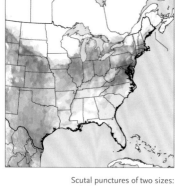

Scutal punctures of two sizes: shallow and numerous, with a few larger deeper pits interspersed.

Overall, the body of *Agapostemon texanus* is hairier

Arcuate basal vein

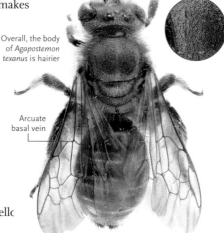

Agapostemon texanus (female)

Agapostemon texanus (female)

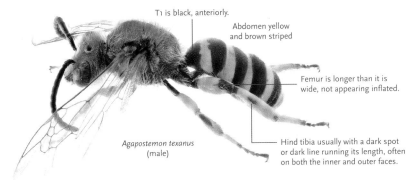

T1 is black, anteriorly.

Abdomen yellow and brown striped

Femur is longer than it is wide, not appearing inflated.

Agapostemon texanus
(male)

Hind tibia usually with a dark spot or dark line running its length, often on both the inner and outer faces.

— *Agapostemon virescens*

SIZE: Medium; 10–11 mm. **PHENOLOGY:** April through November. **FLORAL HOSTS:** Polylectic. **RANGE:** Widespread, occurring across the U.S., rare in the Gulf Coast states. **NESTING:** Usually nests in aggregations, and sometimes with multiple females using the same nest entrance. Nests may be in lawns, near gardens, or in disturbed areas.

IDENTIFICATION: THORAX: Covered in fine punctures, almost touching. **LEGS:** In males, the hind femur is long and narrow. The hind tibia is mostly yellow, with only small amounts of dark coloration at the joints. **ABDOMEN:** There are no yellow sterna in males, though the tergal segments are yellow with brown stripes. Also

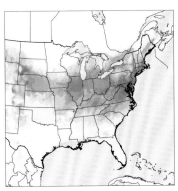

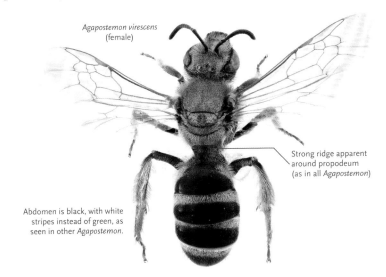

Agapostemon virescens
(female)

Strong ridge apparent around propodeum (as in all *Agapostemon*)

Abdomen is black, with white stripes instead of green, as seen in other *Agapostemon*.

in males, on S6 there is an oval-shaped depression with a ridge in the middle. In females, the abdomen is black, with white hair bands. This is the only eastern *Agapostemon* in which the female does not have a green abdomen.

SIMILAR SPECIES: Female *A. virescens* are a unique combination of green thorax and black-and-white abdomen; they are hard to confuse with other bees. Males may be confused with *A. texanus*. The difference in coloration of the hind tibia should distinguish.

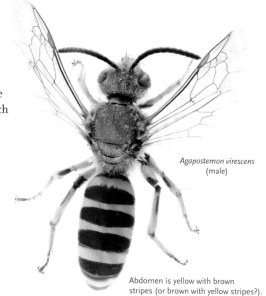

Agapostemon virescens
(male)

Abdomen is yellow with brown stripes (or brown with yellow stripes?).

Femur is longer than it is wide, not looking inflated.

HALICTUS

— **SUBFAMILY: Halictinae**
— **TRIBE: Halictini**

OVERVIEW: Small to medium, incredibly abundant brown to black bees. All *Halictus* nest in the ground, and many exhibit varying levels of sociality, even within the same species depending on the length of the flowering season. Because of their social lifestyles, *Halictus* species are often seen for a long period of the flowering season, rather than for a short window in the spring or summer. As such, they are all generalists. *Halictus* are one of a few bees that will land on humans and "lick" the salty sweat from their skin.

IN THE WORLD: Found on all continents except Australia. Most common in Northern Hemisphere. Nearly 300 species are known. In eastern North America there are 8 species.

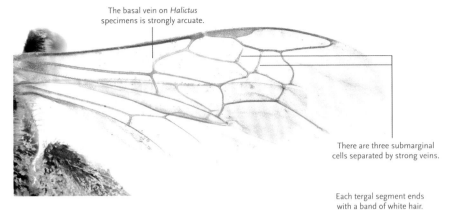

The basal vein on *Halictus* specimens is strongly arcuate.

There are three submarginal cells separated by strong veins.

Each tergal segment ends with a band of white hair.

CLEPTOPARASITES: *Sphecodes.*
IDENTIFYING FEATURES: Species may have light metallic green or copper hues, but the majority are matte-black/brown. Males are long and slender, with long antennae that reach to the back of the thorax. **HEAD:** The gena is usually thick, giving the head a bulky appearance. Male faces include yellow markings on the clypeus, and the legs may be yellow (or red) as well. **WINGS:** *Halictus* have the arcuate basal vein that is characteristic of many Halictidae. Veins that define the first, second, and third submarginal cells are strongly developed. **ABDOMEN:** The hair bands are apical, running across the end of each tergal segment. In worn specimens this may be less visible in the center, but the hair is usually still present on the sides.

We cover characteristics for identifying the five most common species here (*Halictus poeyi* is embedded in *Halictus ligatus*). Species not covered: *Halictus farinosus*, mostly a western species, uncommonly seen in the East and Midwest, and *Halictus tectus*, a recent invasive from southern Europe, currently known only from Washington, D.C., Maryland, and Philadelphia.

SIMILAR GENERA: *Halictus* look superficially similar to *Lasioglossum*. Though some *Halictus* species may exhibit lightly metallic colorations, they are never as prominently metallic as *Lasioglossum* subgenus *Dialictus*. The heads of *Halictus* individuals are thicker than those of *Lasioglossum*. The wings of *Lasioglossum* often have weak veins separating the submarginal cells, which is not the case with *Halictus*. And tergal hair bands in *Halictus* are apical, while in *Lasioglossum*, if present, they are basal. *Andrena* and *Colletes* may also bear some resemblance. The arcuate basal vein is useful in separating *Halictus* from these two.

— *Halictus confusus*

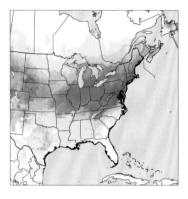

SIZE: Small; 7 mm. **PHENOLOGY:** March through October. **FLORAL HOSTS:** Polylectic. **RANGE:** Across the U.S. and Canada, as far north as northern Quebec, and northern Alberta. Also found in northern Europe and northern Asia. **NESTING:** Ground-nesting bee, often gregarious. Interconnected nests may have multiple entrances. **LIFE HISTORY:** Primitively eusocial with annual colonies. One generation of mated queens (foundresses) overwinter, emerging between March and May and digging a new nest in the ground. They produce a brood of workers and some males that are mature by midsummer. Some of these females retain the ability to make their own offspring, but some are sterile. All females nest together, with many passively provisioning nest cells for the queen's eggs, while others are bullied by the larger queen into helping with her offspring. If the queen dies, one of these reproductively mature daughters will take over egg-laying. In the fall, males and the next year's queens are produced.

IDENTIFICATION: Very common bee, especially abundant from June through October. In the early spring, individuals seen are likely queens that have overwintered—they appear worn with ragged wings and worn-down mandibles. Smaller individuals that appear around the summer solstice are usually this year's workers. Smallest of the *Halictus* species in the East, and the one most likely confused with *Lasioglossum (Dialictus)*. In both sexes, bees are moderately metallic blue or green, not matte-black.

HEAD: In females, the clypeus is not metallic, so appears darker than the rest of the face and protrudes slightly.

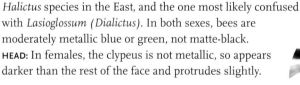

Halictus confusus (male)

The eyes slightly converge ventrally, and the supraclypeal area is elongated so that the whole face is longer than it is wide.

The clypeus appears slightly darker than the rest of the face, though in males, the lower margin is yellow.

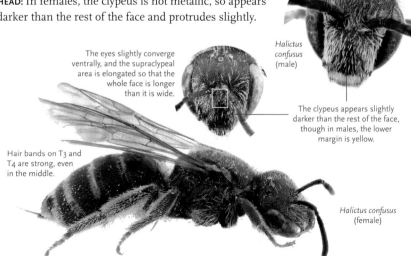

Hair bands on T3 and T4 are strong, even in the middle.

Halictus confusus (female)

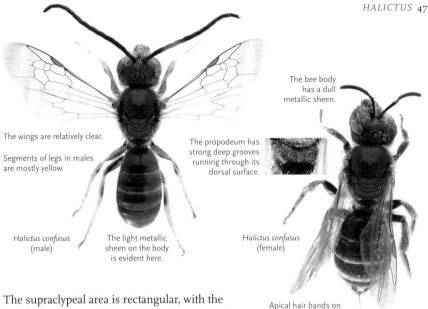

The wings are relatively clear.

Segments of legs in males are mostly yellow.

The propodeum has strong deep grooves running through its dorsal surface.

The bee body has a dull metallic sheen.

Halictus confusus (male)

The light metallic sheen on the body is evident here.

Halictus confusus (female)

The supraclypeal area is rectangular, with the subantennal sutures longer than the epistomal suture so that the face is longer than broad. In

Apical hair bands on *H. confusus* do not diminish in the middle on T3 and T4.

males, the face is oval-shaped and the underside of the antennae and lower margin of the clypeus are light yellow. **THORAX:** The dorsal surface of the propodeum is finely and unevenly striated. **LEGS:** In males, the trochanter and the femur on the forelegs are yellow. **WINGS:** The wings are clear with no smoky coloration. **ABDOMEN:** In females, apical hair bands across T3 and T4 are broad throughout, not narrowing in the middle (in older specimens this may be hard to see).

SIMILAR SPECIES: Other species of *Halictus* in the East may look similar at first, but only *Halictus tripartitus* (which overlaps with *H. confusus* only in prairie states) is also dull green. Between the two, the face of *H. confusus* is longer in females. In males, the color of the antennae and the foretrochanters are yellower in *H. confusus* than in *H. tripartitus*. Additionally, the striations on the propodeum are finer in *H. confusus*.

— *Halictus ligatus*

SIZE: Small; 7–10 mm. **PHENOLOGY:** March through October in northern states, year-round in Florida. **FLORAL HOSTS:** Polylectic. **RANGE:** Widespread across North America, with records as far north as southern Canada. **NESTING:** Ground-nesting bee, often in large colonies, in nests that have multiple entrances. **LIFE HISTORY:** Very similar to *H. confusus*; see above.

IDENTIFICATION: One of the most common summer bees in the eastern United States.

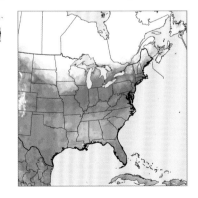

The wings are clear.

The tegulae and legs are yellow.

The lower half of the clypeus is yellow, as are the undersides of the antennae.

The thorax is matte-black in this species, but up close you can see that it is polished in between the punctures.

Halictus ligatus (male)

The ocelli are well below the vertex.

The head of female *H. ligatus* is wider than it is long.

Halictus ligatus females have a "tooth" on the gena.

Note also that the presence of that tooth makes the head extremely thick.

Halictus ligatus (female)

The head is wider than the thorax in females.

Halictus ligatus (female)

Even from above, the thickened gena is evident.

The thorax is shiny, polished between larger pits.

The apical hair bands on T1 and T2 aren't as thick on *H. ligatus* females as they are on other specimens.

Body is matte-black, without a metallic sheen, though the surface of the thorax is polished between punctures, which are small and close together. **HEAD:** In females, the head is large, wider than the thorax, and also thick, with a protuberance (tooth) occurring at the posterior ventral corner of the gena (near the back lower margin). This is stronger or weaker depending on the specimen, but is always present. In instances where the lower part of the face isn't visible, the thicker genal area is still evident, being much wider than the width of the compound eye. From the front, the face is wider than long, and the ocelli are well below the vertex. In males, the lower half of the clypeus is yellow, as are the mandibles, the underside of the antennae, and the tegulae. The face is relatively round, and the wings are clear (not brown or dusky). **THORAX:** Punctures on scutum are fine, but deep and distinct. **LEGS:** In males, the tibiae are reddish, with a yellow stripe, and the tarsi are

yellow. **ABDOMEN:** In females, apical hair bands on T1 and T2 are narrow, almost inconspicuous. In males, S2 and S3 have long hairs that stand up.
SIMILAR SPECIES: Most similar to *Halictus ligatus* is *H. poeyi*, a cryptic "sister" species that is best identified by its distinct genetic profile. More practically, in the southeastern U.S. (Florida, Georgia, South Carolina, Louisiana, Alabama, and Mississippi), *Halictus poeyi* is the more common of the two. *Halictus ligatus* and *H. parallelus* males also look similar. The wings of *H. parallelus* are darker, and the thorax is not as polished as in *H. ligatus*. The face of male *H. ligatus* is much wider than long, with the ocelli set well below the vertex, compared with all other eastern *Halictus* species.

— *Halictus rubicundus*

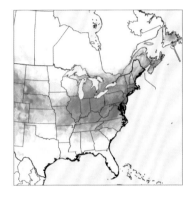

SIZE: Medium; 10–11 mm.
PHENOLOGY: March through November.
FLORAL HOSTS: Polylectic. **RANGE:** Widespread across North America, occurring throughout Canada and into Alaska. Also found in Europe. **NESTING:** Ground-nesting bee, nesting in a variety of soil types but appearing to prefer loosely packed earth. **LIFE HISTORY:** Primitively eusocial or solitary bee depending on the climate. In cooler climates (Alaska, northern Canada, northern Europe), the bees are solitary. In warmer climates, the bees are eusocial, with foundresses emerging earlier in the spring than solitary individuals farther north, to start their own nests. After rearing a single brood, the female (gyne) remains in the nest rearing a second brood, while the majority of her daughters commence gathering pollen for their mother's next batch of offspring. In the fall, next year's foundresses mate, and hibernate for the winter. **IDENTIFICATION:** Medium-sized matte-black summer bee; larger than most *Halictus*.
HEAD: In males, the eyes are angled inward, nearly converging, and the clypeus sticks out noticeably from the head; the bottom half of it is bright yellow. The mandible is nearly all black at the apex. Also in males, the antennae are entirely black; the only eastern species to have entirely black antennae. **LEGS:** In females, on the hind tibia, the hindmost of the two spurs has large irregularly shaped teeth. Female legs are light red in color. In males, the femur and the tibia are yellow to orange, though the femur has a dark spot on it.

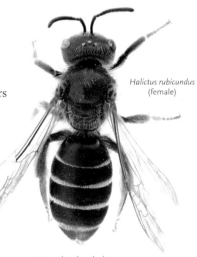

Halictus rubicundus
(female)

Narow hair bands that get even narrower near the center

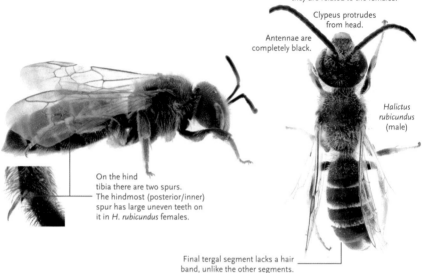

All male *Halictus* have very long antennae and narrow abdomens. It's hard to believe they are related to the females!

Clypeus protrudes from head.

Antennae are completely black.

Halictus rubicundus (male)

On the hind tibia there are two spurs. The hindmost (posterior/inner) spur has large uneven teeth on it in *H. rubicundus* females.

Final tergal segment lacks a hair band, unlike the other segments.

ABDOMEN: In females, the apical hair bands are narrow, especially near the center. In males, S4 has a brush of hair along the apex and the margin of S5 is concave. Also in males, the final tergal segment does not have a band of hair.

SIMILAR SPECIES: The black antennae of the males, and dark black body, combined with thin (nearly absent on older specimens) apical hair bands, are distinctive features on this bee. In the East it looks most similar to *H. parallelus*, but the redder legs and larger body size of that bee should help to distinguish between the two.

— *Halictus tripartitus*

SIZE: Small; 5–8 mm. **PHENOLOGY:** March through October. **FLORAL HOSTS:** Polylectic. **RANGE:** Mostly a western bee, but can be found throughout the prairie states, as far east as Missouri and southern Illinois. **NESTING:** Ground-nesting bee; appears to prefer packed earth. Nests are often connected in the ground even though they have separate nest entrances. **LIFE HISTORY:** Primitively eusocial with annual colonies. Select females (gynes) are mated in the fall and overwinter in a hole in the ground.

In the spring these foundresses begin new nests and forage for pollen until their first generation of sterile daughters are mature. These smaller workers forage for pollen for a second, late summer generation, which includes males, and next year's gynes. **IDENTIFICATION:** Small, lightly metallic bee. **HEAD:** The subantennal suture is short, about half the length of the epistomal suture, so that the supraclypeal area is square

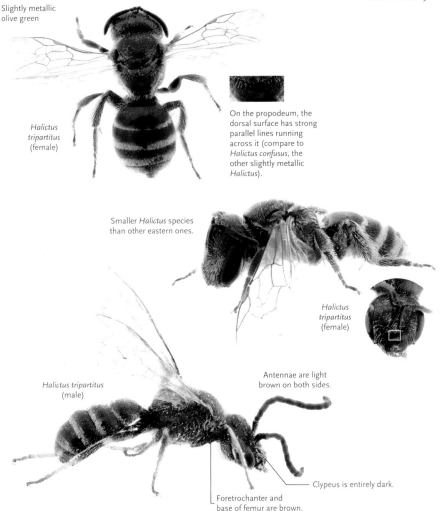

Slightly metallic olive green

Halictus tripartitus (female)

On the propodeum, the dorsal surface has strong parallel lines running across it (compare to *Halictus confusus*, the other slightly metallic *Halictus*).

Smaller *Halictus* species than other eastern ones.

Halictus tripartitus (female)

Halictus tripartitus (male)

Antennae are light brown on both sides.

Clypeus is entirely dark.

Foretrochanter and base of femur are brown.

in shape. The malar space is short, giving the head a very round appearance. In males, the antennae are brown, only slightly lighter on the bottom than the top. Also in males, the clypeus is entirely dark. **THORAX:** The pits on the scutum are small but distinct. The propodeum has deep, parallel striations. **LEGS:** In males, the trochanter and base of the femur on the foreleg are brown, while the apical two-thirds of the femur are light yellow.

SIMILAR SPECIES: For most of the East, a metallic *Halictus* specimen is *Halictus confusus*. In the Midwest, where both species occur, the shape of the faces of the females differs, with *H. confusus* females, and males to a lesser degree, having longer faces. Other differences include the color of the foretrochanters and antennae in males, and the striations on the propodeum.

— *Halictus parallelus*

SIZE: Medium; 10–13 mm.
PHENOLOGY: March through August.
FLORAL HOSTS: Broadly polylectic,
visiting a very large array of plants.
RANGE: United States, mainly east of the Rocky
Mountains. Likely also in southern Canada.
NESTING: Ground-nesting bee.
IDENTIFICATION: A larger *Halictus* with dark
wings. **HEAD:** In females, the vertex is elongated,
with the ocelli set far down on the face and not
near the top of the head. In males, the clypeus is
mostly yellow, and the undersides of the flagellar segments on the antennae are light
rusty red. In both sexes the eyes converge toward the bottom; this is more prominent
in males. **THORAX:** The scutum is dull between fine, close-together punctures. **LEGS:** In
males, legs are often rusty red. In females, the inner hind tibial spur has minute
evenly spaced teeth. **ABDOMEN:** Hair bands are thick, narrowing slightly at the center.
SIMILAR SPECIES: The red legs and large size of this bee can be diagnostic, but it can be
confused with *Halictus rubicundus*. The black antennae on the males
of *H. rubicundus* are a distinguishing feature. And in females
the thinner hair bands on *H. rubicundus* are distinctive.

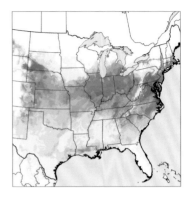

Ocelli are low on the face.

Halictus parallelus
(female)

Scutal punctures are
fine, and close together.

Wings, especially at
bases, are slightly
darker than those of
other *Halictus* species.

Thick hair bands,
but may be worn
in older individuals

Ocelli are
low on head.

Underside of antennae
is red/yellow, as is
most of the clypeus.

Halictus parallelus
(male)

Legs of males have
red hues to them.

LASIOGLOSSUM

— **SUBFAMILY:** Halictinae
— **TRIBE:** Halictini

OVERVIEW: Petite, generally metallic bees. Though their small size makes them less noticeable, by midsummer these are the dominant bees in many environments. Species range from being solitary to completely eusocial. Most nest in the ground, but some nest in rotting wood.

IN THE WORLD: Worldwide there are more than 600 species. In North America there are roughly 300 species, with more than 100 species in the eastern United States and Canada.

CLEPTOPARASITES: *Sphecodes.*

IDENTIFYING FEATURES: *Lasioglossum* are considered one of the most difficult groups to identify with confidence. Among the many hundreds of species, the distinguishing characteristics are minute, and, in many cases, grade into each other. *Lasioglossum,* in the broad sense,

consists of four subgenera that differ markedly in their appearance. Most common are *Lasioglossum (Dialictus)*. Though not as common as *L. (Dialictus)*, the subgenera *L. (Lasioglossum)*, *L. (Hemihalictus)*, and *L. (Sphecodogastra)* are also found throughout the East. The characteristics defining these subgenera bleed together. With few unique characters to identify subgenera, often a combination of many characters are required to separate them. All are united under the genus *Lasioglossum* by the following: First, as with many species within the family Halictidae, the wing has a distinct arcuate basal vein, often visible in photographs taken at the correct angle. There are two or three submarginal cells (usually three), and the veins separating them are often weak. *Lasioglossum* specimens are usually petite, small to medium-sized bees. All subgenera of *Lasioglossum* have basal hair bands (i.e., at the beginning of the tergal segment). These are strongest across the first two or three tergal segments. Many specimens are shiny and may (as in the case of subgenus *Dialictus*) or may not (most other subgenera) have a light metallic sheen to the body. A few species have red abdomens. We include representatives from *Lasioglossum* subgenus *Dialictus, focusing on the females.* Note that other *Lasioglossum* occur in the East that may have similar features to the ones included here. *Lasioglossum (Hemihalictus)* is not included here, though some species in this genus can be locally abundant. With few exceptions, *Lasioglossum* are challenging to identify and require multiple keys (see references) and a microscope. Many males are indistinguishable from each other.

— *Lasioglossum (Dialictus)*

SIZE: Small; 4–10 mm. **PHENOLOGY:** April through October, with peak abundance during July and August. **FLORAL HOSTS:** Polylectic. **RANGE:** Widespread across eastern North America. **NESTING:** Ground nester.

IDENTIFICATION: Often incredibly abundant, though the small size and diminutive habit make them easy to overlook. The head and thorax are a light aquamarine, olive green, or deep gunmetal blue color. This subgenus is unique among *Lasioglossum* in that the integument of the thorax has a metallic reflection. Some species have entirely red abdomens, or abdomens with one or two red tergal segments. Features used to distinguish between species include the size and distance between puncture marks on the thorax, the degree to which the scutum is polished, the texture of the propodeal rim, the density and depth of grooves underneath the head, the pattern of the hair on the anterior face of T1, and the shape of the tegula.

— *Lasioglossum coeruleum*   — *Lasioglossum longifrons*

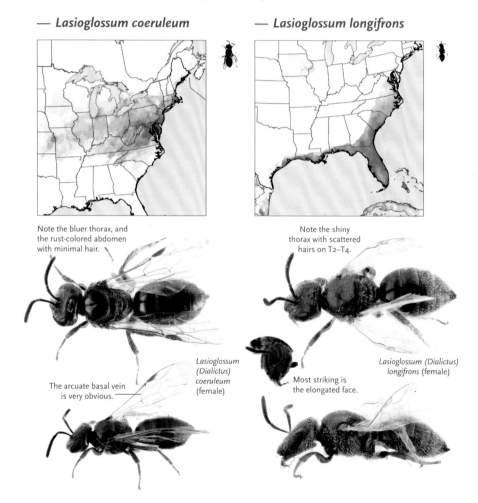

Note the bluer thorax, and the rust-colored abdomen with minimal hair.

Note the shiny thorax with scattered hairs on T2–T4.

Lasioglossum (Dialictus) coeruleum (female)

Lasioglossum (Dialictus) longifrons (female)

The arcuate basal vein is very obvious.

Most striking is the elongated face.

— *Lasioglossum pilosum*

— *Lasioglossum tegulare*

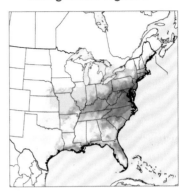

Lasioglossum (Dialictus) pilosum (female)

Note the relatively fuzzy abdomen, with many flattened hairs obscuring the surface.

Also, the edge of the dorsal rim of the propodeum is polished.

Lasioglossum (Dialictus) tegulare (female)

The most notable feature here is the tegula, which is hooked along the posterior edge.

— *Lasioglossum imitatum*

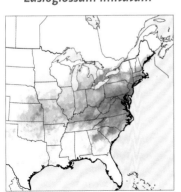

This bee is often extremely abundant when it occurs. T3 and T4 have flattened, evenly spaced hairs.

Lasioglossum (Dialictus) imitatum (female)

— *Lasioglossum zephyrum*

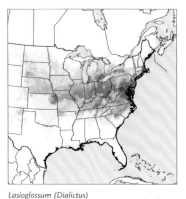

Lasioglossum (Dialictus)
zephyrum (female)

A common bee,
with light metallic
reflections on abdomen.
Punctation consists of
very tiny marks
on a roughened
thorax.

— *Lasioglossum illinoense*

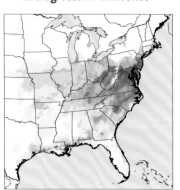

— *Lasioglossum nymphale*

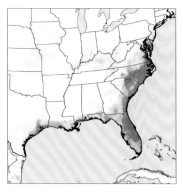

One of a handful of *Lasioglossum (Dialictus)*
species that have a red abdomen.

Lasioglossum
(Dialictus)
nymphale
(female)

Lasioglossum (Dialictus)
illinoense (female)

— *Lasioglossum albipene*

Lasioglossum (Dialictus) albipene (female)

Note the white hair on T3–T5 and the large punctations on the thorax. The veins in the wings are white.

— *Lasioglossum (Sphecodogastra) quebecense*

SIZE: Small; 7–8 mm. **PHENOLOGY:** March through May. **FLORAL HOSTS:** Generalist.
RANGE: Mostly northern species: Newfoundland, Nova Scotia, and northern Quebec west to Alberta and the Northwest Territories. South through Minnesota, Michigan, Tennessee, and Georgia at higher elevations. **HABITAT:** Common in woodlands and bottomlands.

IDENTIFICATION: Relatively large for a *Lasioglossum*. **HEAD:** Dark, about as long as wide, clypeus projecting slightly from face. In females, clypeus and supraclypeus with few punctations. In males, lower half of clypeus yellow, eyes converging strongly toward lower portion of face, antennal segments elongated.

THORAX: In females, scutum is roughened, with fine, shallow, widely spaced punctations. Posterior face of propodeum is delineated laterally by two strong carinae that run all the way to the dorsal face of the propodeum. In males, scutum is dull with denser punctation. The propodeum is marked by raised ridges running up its

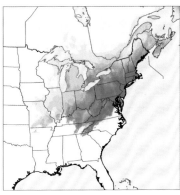

Carina outlines the edge of the posterior face of the propodeum.

Lasioglossum (Sphecodogastra) quebecense

Very fine apical hair bands run across at least the first three tergal segments.

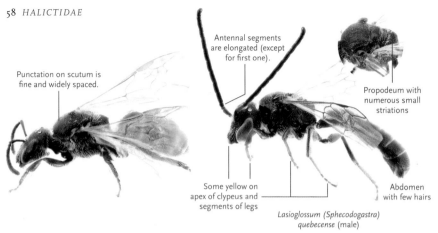

Antennal segments are elongated (except for first one).

Punctation on scutum is fine and widely spaced.

Propodeum with numerous small striations

Some yellow on apex of clypeus and segments of legs

Abdomen with few hairs

Lasioglossum (Sphecodogastra) quebecense (male)

posterior face, and across the dorsal face. **LEGS:** In males, legs are yellow. **ABDOMEN:** In females, thin hair bands run across the *apical* edge of each tergal segment (rare in *Lasioglossum*). In males, abdomen may include red tergal segments. The abdomen in males is also polished and with few hairs.

SPHECODES

— **SUBFAMILY:** Halictinae

— **TRIBE:** Halictini

OVERVIEW: *Sphecodes* are small to medium-sized cleptoparasitic bees. Females are usually black on the thorax, with a blood-red abdomen (sometimes with black stripes), while males are either red and black or all black. *Sphecodes* do not collect pollen. They parasitize ground-nesting bees, usually in the Halictidae family.

IN THE WORLD: Worldwide there are about 350 species, occurring on all continents, though rare in Australia. In the Americas, this genus ranges from southern Alaska south through Argentina. In the United States and Canada there are more than 70 species, with around half of them occurring in the East.

CLEPTOPARASITES: *Sphecodes* are cleptoparasites; typical hosts include *Halictus*, *Lasioglossum*, *Andrena*, and *Colletes* (all of which are ground nesters).

IDENTIFYING FEATURES: Small to medium-sized bees; easy to overlook at first glance though the bright-red abdomen is eye-catching. **HEAD:** Generally oval-shaped, wider than long with a short and broad clypeus. Antennae are entirely black. **THORAX:** Sculpturing is thick, with large indentations, and the integument in between is not polished. **WINGS:** The arcuate basal vein typical of many Halictidae is evident. **LEGS:** Females often have spines on their hind legs. **ABDOMEN:** In females, T5 usually has a white tuft of hair. The abdomen of females is almost always red; males are also often red, though they may have more extensive black markings.

SIMILAR GENERA: Several bee genera have red and black abdomens like *Sphecodes,* and may at first glance appear similar. A few *Lasioglossum* have a red abdomen, but the color on those bees is closer to orange, and the thorax is coppery. *Sphecodes* have wider heads than *Lasioglossum*. *Ashmeadiella* individuals with red abdomens may resemble female *Sphecodes*. Scopal hairs on the abdomen of female *Ashmeadiella* should distinguish them from *Sphecodes*; in addition, *Ashmeadiella* have two submarginal cells, while *Sphecodes* nearly always have three. Some *Andrena* also have red abdomens. The presence of pollen-collecting hairs on female *Andrena* should distinguish

Sphecodes have oval heads, much wider than long.

the two; *Sphecodes* also have much narrower, parallel-sided abdomens compared with *Andrena*, and *Andrena* lack an arcuate basal vein. Finally, *Sphecodes* males, with their red-and-black abdomens, may look similar to *Halictus* species—the unpolished exoskeleton, the wider face, and the shorter antennae should distinguish the two.

Sphecodes are difficult to identify to species. Of the roughly 35 eastern species, we highlight here one that is common and uniquely distinctive. For other species, positive identification is best done with a microscope and taxonomic keys (see references).

— *Sphecodes heraclei*

SIZE: Small; 7–11 mm. **PHENOLOGY:** Spring through late summer. **RANGE:** From Kansas to New Hampshire south to Florida. **HOSTS:** Likely *Andrena, Halictus, Lasioglossum*. **IDENTIFICATION:** Smaller *Sphecodes* that may be locally abundant. **HEAD:** A large "goose egg" behind the ocelli is evident as a polished, raised bump. Antennae are thick, with each segment constricted, giving a ridged look. Face often covered in thick white hair. **THORAX:** The scutal punctures are widely spaced, of large diameter, and deep. **ABDOMEN:** Ranges from blood red to matte-black; typically T1–T3 are red. **SIMILAR SPECIES:** There are two subspecies of *S. heraclei*. In Florida, *S. heraclei ignitus* is more common, and the thorax of that subspecies is marked by red patches on the thorax in addition to the abdomen. More common is *S. heraclei heraclei*, which occurs throughout eastern North America and is black on the thorax. Also, *S. heraclei* is the only eastern species of *Sphecodes* with a raised, polished protrusion behind the ocelli.

Behind the ocelli on the top of the head, *S. heraclei* has a polished bump that is very distinctive.

Sphecodes heraclei (female)

In Florida, the subspecies *S. h. ignitus* has red on the thorax as well as the abdomen.

Female cleptoparasitic bees have no scopal hairs.

DIEUNOMIA

— SUBFAMILY: Nomiinae

OVERVIEW: Large dark bees; easy to spot when they occur, but neither widespread nor abundant. Most are seen in the late summer and fall when Asteraceae bloom; they are all specialists on this plant family. Often nest in large aggregations, with nests deep enough that they can survive in plowed fields. Thus, many species in this genus are common in agricultural areas.

IN THE WORLD: Nine species total. All are restricted to the Americas. Most abundant in Central and South America. Eight occur north of the Mexican border; three are in eastern North America.

CLEPTOPARASITES: *Triepeolus* species, especially *T. distinctus*.

IDENTIFYING FEATURES: Sizable bees, usually with dark integument and auburn hair. HEAD: In males, the last segment of the antenna is flattened and broad. WINGS: Basal vein is not arcuate, as it is in many other Halictidae. LEGS: In females, scopal hairs occur thickly on the hind legs, but also extend onto the underside of the abdomen (S2–S5), almost wrapping onto the terga. In males there are often protrusions and extra structures on the mid- and hind legs that can be distinctive. ABDOMEN: In both sexes, when viewed from above, there is an indentation in the forward face of T1, causing it to appear like a V.

SIMILAR GENERA: *Andrena* species can look like *Dieunomia*, as both share a similar body shape (andreniform). The indentation on T1 is a key factor in telling the two apart, as is the facial fovea in female *Andrena*. Larger Apidae (e.g., *Xylocopa*) may also be confused with *Dieunomia*. Look for the distinct scopal hairs in females, and the flattened antennae in males, of *Dieunomia*.

— *Dieunomia heteropoda*

SIZE: Large; 18 mm. PHENOLOGY: July through October. FLORAL HOSTS: Specialist on plants in the Asteraceae, especially sunflowers (*Helianthus*). RANGE: Maine and Ontario south through Florida, west to Utah. NESTING: Ground-nesting bee. Appear to be solitary, but multiple females have been observed to use the same nest entrance in some cases. Often nest in aggregations of a hundred to several hundred. Nests can be recognized by mound of dirt, often in sandy areas, with nest entrance at the base of the mound. IDENTIFICATION: Large dark bee with exceptionally long wings that are often held up and out from body in a distinctive fashion. HEAD: The gena is thick, at least as wide as the width of the compound eye. THORAX: Wings

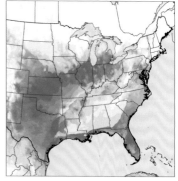

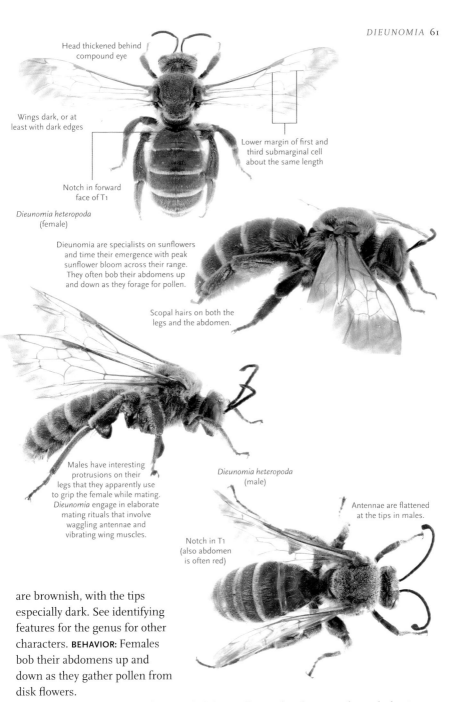

Head thickened behind compound eye

Wings dark, or at least with dark edges

Lower margin of first and third submarginal cell about the same length

Notch in forward face of T1

Dieunomia heteropoda (female)

Dieunomia are specialists on sunflowers and time their emergence with peak sunflower bloom across their range. They often bob their abdomens up and down as they forage for pollen.

Scopal hairs on both the legs and the abdomen.

Males have interesting protrusions on their legs that they apparently use to grip the female while mating. Dieunomia engage in elaborate mating rituals that involve waggling antennae and vibrating wing muscles.

Dieunomia heteropoda (male)

Antennae are flattened at the tips in males.

Notch in T1 (also abdomen is often red)

are brownish, with the tips especially dark. See identifying features for the genus for other characters. **BEHAVIOR:** Females bob their abdomens up and down as they gather pollen from disk flowers.

SIMILAR SPECIES: *D. triangulifera* is slightly smaller, and without smoky or dark wings (though may be clouded at the very tips). *D. nevadensis* is much smaller (about half the size), with a thinner face and clear wings.

NOMIA

— **SUBFAMILY:** Nomiinae

OVERVIEW: Medium to large dark bees with light pearlescent bands on their abdomen. A few species specialize, but the majority are generalists. Often nest in large aggregations with more than 1,000 nests in a few square meters. Sometimes multiple females will share one entrance, though inside the nest each female digs and provisions her own nest cells. Includes *Nomia melanderi*, the alkali bee, widely used in the West for pollinating alfalfa.

IN THE WORLD: More than 130 species are found worldwide; 9 of these can be found in North America (north of Mexico), with only 2 occurring in eastern North America.

CLEPTOPARASITES: *Nomia* is seldom parasitized by other bees; a few scattered reports of *Nomada* entering *Nomia* nests are all that have been observed.

IDENTIFYING FEATURES: Medium-sized bees with pearlescent hair bands on abdomen; stunning bee, but seldom seen. **HEAD:** Face is round, about as wide as long, but tapering slightly as inner eye margins converge. Face may be covered with dense white hairs. **THORAX:** Deep black, with widely spaced, distinctive pits. **WINGS:** Basal vein is not as distinctly arcuate as in many other Halictidae. **LEGS:** In females, scopal hairs are thick and stout on the femur and tibia. **ABDOMEN:** Wide, unpitted shiny ivory-colored bands take up the apical quarter to third portion of each tergal segment.

SIMILAR GENERA: This genus is alone in having ivory bands on the tergal segments. Should these not be visible, the converging compound eye margins are somewhat similar to the eye margins of *Colletes*. Wing venation should be distinguishing (see *Colletes*), in addition to the slenderer body of *Colletes*.

— *Nomia nortoni*

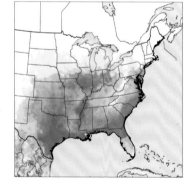

SIZE: Large; 16–18 mm.
PHENOLOGY: July through November. **FLORAL HOSTS:** Polylectic with some preference for Asteraceae. **RANGE:** Rare in Maryland south through Florida, becoming more common west toward Texas. **NESTING:** Ground-nesting bee. Though solitary, multiple females have been observed to use the same nest entrance. Often nest in aggregations.

IDENTIFICATION: Large black bee with pearl-white or ivory integumental stripes at the apex of each tergal segment. Bands are sometimes tinged with a blue or green sheen. **HEAD:** In males, the antennae are narrowed to points toward the apex. **THORAX:** Large deep pits occur laterally against a shiny black surface. **WINGS:** Brownish, darkening toward the tips. **LEGS:** In males, the femur and tibia are inflated and much enlarged. See genus identification for more characteristics.

The femur and tibia are hugely inflated.

Nomia nortoni (male)

Even males have pearly bands on the abdomen.

Antennae are narrowed to fine points in males.

Nomia is the only bee genus with pearly bands on the integument. There usually aren't many pits in this shiny area.

SIMILAR SPECIES: Only one other *Nomia* occurs in the eastern U.S., *N. maneei,* and it is more common than *N. nortoni* near the coast. Overall, *N. nortoni* is larger, with denser pits on T1–T3.

Nomia nortoni (female)

DUFOUREA

— **SUBFAMILY:** Rophitinae

OVERVIEW: Small black bee, seldom seen, but may be locally abundant. The only genus in the Rophitinae subfamily to be found in eastern North America. *Dufourea* are all specialists, often on just one genus of flowering plant. Ground-nesting species.

IN THE WORLD: One hundred and seventy species total. Found throughout the Northern Hemisphere, but most common in the western United States. Around 70 species in North America, with 5 occurring in the East (though some are exceedingly rare).

CLEPTOPARASITES: Unknown in the eastern U.S.

IDENTIFYING FEATURES: HEAD: Antennae are very low on the face accompanied by a very short clypeus. Only one subantennal suture. **WINGS:** There are two submarginal cells; nearly all other Halictidae covered in this book have three. The basal vein is not arcuate, as it is in many other Halictidae. **LEGS:** Males often have modifications and projections on the hind legs.

SIMILAR GENERA: Across all *Dufourea,* there is some resemblance to smaller *Andrena,* but the shape of the face, with the low antennae, and single antennal suture should be distinctive. Small *Halictus* may also resemble *Dufourea.* Two versus three submarginal cells, and the low antennae should distinguish the two.

— *Dufourea novaeangliae*

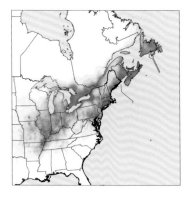

SIZE: Small to medium; 9 mm.
PHENOLOGY: July through August. **FLORAL HOSTS:** Specialist on *Pontederia* (pickerel weed). **RANGE:** Northeastern United States (Maine to Virginia, east to Missouri and Wisconsin) and southern Ontario. **NESTING:** Ground-nesting bee. Found only in the immediate vicinity of water (ponds, streams, etc.), where its host plant grows. Generally nests in sandy soils, in the shade, and may be found in aggregations.
IDENTIFICATION: HEAD: Longer than wide. Clypeus sticks out from head appreciably. In females, the head has long, prominent, flattened hairs on tongue parts, though these are hard to see, even under a microscope. **LEGS:** Mid-basitarsus is rounded outward, so it is not parallel-sided. In males, the hind trochanter has a point on it, a distinct angle not found in other eastern *Dufourea*. **SIMILAR SPECIES:** Also found in the eastern U.S. and eastern Canada are *Dufourea marginata*, *D. monardae*, *D. harveyi*, and *D. maura*. The plant on which the female bee forages for pollen is the best indicator of which *Dufourea* species it is, as the distinguishing characters between species are challenging. *Dufourea monardae* can be locally abundant in the East; it visits only *Monarda fistulosa* for pollen. *Dufourea marginata* is a rare species, most abundant in Ontario, Wisconsin, and Illinois. It visits Asteraceae (especially *Helianthus*) for pollen. *Dufourea harveyi* is rarely collected in the East (specifically, only Michigan), occurring mostly west of Colorado, where it is a specialist on *Potentilla*. *Dufourea maura* is primarily a western species, occurring as far east as North Dakota and Nebraska, with isolated records at Isle Royale National Park in Michigan. It is a specialist on *Campanula rotundifolia*.

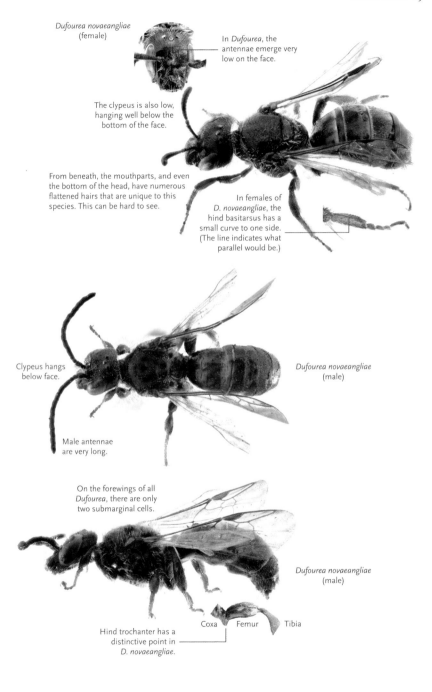

Dufourea novaeangliae
(female)

In *Dufourea*, the antennae emerge very low on the face.

The clypeus is also low, hanging well below the bottom of the face.

From beneath, the mouthparts, and even the bottom of the head, have numerous flattened hairs that are unique to this species. This can be hard to see.

In females of *D. novaeangliae*, the hind basitarsus has a small curve to one side. (The line indicates what parallel would be.)

Clypeus hangs below face.

Dufourea novaeangliae
(male)

Male antennae are very long.

On the forewings of all *Dufourea*, there are only two submarginal cells.

Dufourea novaeangliae
(male)

Coxa   Femur   Tibia

Hind trochanter has a distinctive point in *D. novaeangliae*.

COLLETIDAE

Colletidae are widely distributed around the world, consisting of diverse genera that range in appearance from miniscule, hairless black bees to large fast-flying fuzzy bees. Despite the worldwide variety, in North America just two genera are common: *Colletes* and *Hylaeus*. All are solitary, though many species of *Colletes* nest in aggregations of several hundred. The family includes both ground and cavity nesters, and nests are lined with a cellophane-like secretion. Within Colletidae are bees that are narrow specialists, as well as bees that broadly generalize.

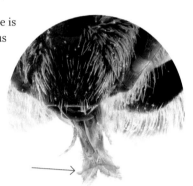

Bees in Colletidae have unique "tongues," with a short glossa and often a bilobed, or forked, tip.

IDENTIFICATION: Identifying a bee as a Colletidae is often harder than identifying the bee at the genus level, as the generic characters are easier to see without a microscope. Memorizing the features that distinguish, especially, *Colletes* and *Hylaeus* will be most useful. Colletidae are united in that they all have a short glossa, which is generally thick (wider than long). At the end it is either abruptly truncated, or more often bilobed (forked). Note that unlike Andrenidae, Colletidae have one subantennal suture. Little else unites this family, morphologically. Behaviorally, all North American Colletidae line their nests with a cellophane-like material that is unique to this family, though some genera nest in the ground while others nest in hollow twigs.

TAXONOMY: There are about 2,500 species of Colletidae, found on every continent (reaching peak diversity in South America and Australia), in 54 genera. In the U.S. there are five genera split into three subfamilies; in the eastern U.S. and Canada can be found three of those genera, two of which are covered here.

— SUBFAMILY COLLETINAE

In North America, there is just one genus, *Colletes*. A medium-sized bee, very common in the spring and fall (many specialize on early- and late-blooming flowers). Females resemble *Andrena* in body shape. On the wing, the second recurrent vein is strongly curved. The inner margins of the compound eyes converge toward the lower portions of the face.

— SUBFAMILY HYLAEINAE

There is just one genus in this subfamily in North America, *Hylaeus*. They are miniscule, black, hairless bees. Most species have yellow markings on the face. On the wing, there are two submarginal cells. There are no scopal hairs in females, as they ingest pollen and nectar and regurgitate both in nest cells.

— SUBFAMILY DIPHAGLOSSINAE

There are three relatively rare genera in this subfamily of large fuzzy bees in North America. All have pointed, bifid glossa. One of these rare genera is found in the eastern U.S. It is not pictured in this book.

— CAUPOLICANINI

There is one species of *Caupolicana* in the East, *C. electa*, found from North Carolina, west to Alabama, and south through Florida. *Caupolicana* differ from other Diphaglossinae by the extremely long first flagellar segment. The species *C. electa* is a large bee with a ruddy-tan thorax, as well as the first segment of the abdomen, the rest of which is black, with light white stripes. It is rarely seen, flying at dawn and dusk, and listed as Rare and Endangered in Florida. There is another genus, *Ptiloglossa*, found in this tribe as well. It occurs in western states.

Within the Colletidae genera there are 64 species.

COLLETES

— SUBFAMILY: Colletinae

OVERVIEW: Medium-sized bees, generally with white, gray, or brown hair on a black integument. All species are ground-nesting, and all line their nests with a clear membranous material that is waterproof. The membrane is formed by secretions from the Dufour's gland in the abdomen. Drops of the oily substance are secreted from the gland, and a female bee quickly ingests them, then regurgitates them onto the wall using her forked, paintbrush-like tongue. The membranous "envelope" contains mostly liquid provisions, heavy with floral nectar. Eggs are attached to the wall, so that they are suspended above the liquid. Cells are constructed at night.

For most species there is one generation per year, with most bees flying early in the spring or in the late fall. A few species have two generations per year, especially at the southern extent of their range.

IN THE WORLD: Worldwide there are more than 500 species, occurring on all continents except Australia. In North America there are approximately 100 species, ranging from Florida through Alaska. Thirty-seven species can be found in the East.

Note that the inner margin of the eyes slants inward, so that the eyes appear to converge.

CLEPTOPARASITES: *Epeolus.*

IDENTIFYING FEATURES: HEAD: The compound eyes of *Colletes* slant toward each other, and are closer together at the bottom of the head than at the top. **THORAX:** The front

Colletes, like all Colletidae, have a short "tongue." In the case of *Colletes*, it is also forked.

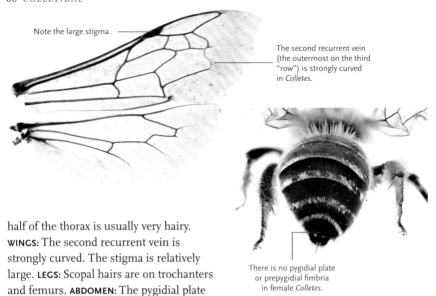

Note the large stigma.

The second recurrent vein (the outermost on the third "row") is strongly curved in *Colletes.*

There is no pygidial plate or prepygidial fimbria in female *Colletes.*

half of the thorax is usually very hairy. **WINGS:** The second recurrent vein is strongly curved. The stigma is relatively large. **LEGS:** Scopal hairs are on trochanters and femurs. **ABDOMEN:** The pygidial plate and basitibial plate are much reduced. Also, there is no pygidial nor prepygidial fimbria.

Distinguishing between the species of *Colletes* occurring in North America is difficult and requires a microscope. A handful of common *Colletes* are included here; note that the features associated with these species are not unique to them. Other species, not included here, may also share these characteristics; nonetheless, the characters are useful for distinguishing between the common bees included in this book. **SIMILAR SPECIES:** *Andrena* can superficially resemble *Colletes. Andrena* faces are more oval-shaped, with the inner margins of the eyes more or less parallel instead of converging, as in *Colletes. Andrena* have less hair on the front half of the thorax. *Colletes* carry pollen lower on their hind legs. And on the face of *Colletes,* there is no facial fovea near the compound eyes, nor are there two subantennal sutures. Larger species of *Halictus* may superficially resemble *Colletes,* but they have more robust heads, are usually smaller, and the wing venation is quite different.

— *Colletes compactus*

SIZE: Small to medium; 9–13 mm. **PHENOLOGY:** Midsummer (July) through November; most common in the fall. **FLORAL HOSTS:** Appears to specialize on fall Asteraceae. **RANGE:** Occurs as far north as Newfoundland, south to Tennessee and North Carolina. **NESTING:** Ground-nesting, sometimes occurs in small aggregations of 10 or fewer.

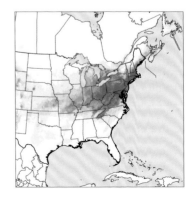

Note the bulge in the second recurrent vein.

The fine punctations on T1 and T2 are about the same density.

T1

T2

Colletes compactus (female)

Colletes compactus (female)

A line of dark hairs occurs right next to the inner margin of each compound eye.

The malar space here is longer than in *Colletes inaequalis*; it is about half as long as it is wide.

Colletes compactus (female)

Dark hairs are intermixed with light on the dorsal surface of the thorax, especially the posterior margin of the scutum and the scutellum.

The male has less dark hair than the female.

The malar space is exceptionally long in males.

Colletes compactus (male)

IDENTIFICATION: Robust bee with fuzzy gray head and thorax, black-and-white abdomen. **HEAD:** Black hair lines the edges of the compound eyes. In males, the malar space is long. In females it is about half as long as it is wide, but still longer than in many other *Colletes* species. In males, there is a depression in the middle of the clypeus, shining, and with few pits; this may be hidden by hair. In females, there is no depression, but the clypeus is bare. **THORAX:** Black hair lines the scutum and is common on the scutellum. In females, pits on the scutum are close together, but more sparse posteriorly. Integument in between is dull anteriorly. In males, the scutum is shiny with few pits. **ABDOMEN:** The pits on T2 are as dense as they are on T1, but not more dense. In females, S6 has two median parallel ridges running from the apex to the base of the segment. **SIMILAR SPECIES:** There are two subspecies of *Colletes compactus*. *Colletes compactus hesperius* is found from the Rocky Mountains west, while *C. compactus compactus* occurs east of the Rocky Mountains. This species can be hard to distinguish from other *Colletes* unless using a microscope.

— *Colletes inaequalis*

SIZE: Small to medium; 9–13 mm.
PHENOLOGY: Early March through May—one of the earliest bees seen in the spring. **FLORAL HOSTS:** Polylectic, but appears to have a preference for early flowering trees, including apples (*Malus*) and maples (*Acer*). **RANGE:** Southern Canada south to Georgia, and west to Washington State. Typically seen in more forested regions. **NESTING:** Ground-nesting bee with a preference for sandy habitats. Nests may be in aggregations, with males hovering over them; they have been found with as many as five bees sharing a nest entrance.

Colletes inaequalis
(female)

There is a shiny line down the middle of the clypeus.

The malar space here is small, twice as wide as it is long.

Hair on the scutum and scutellum ranges from light brown to dark gray.

Colletes inaequalis
(female)

Thick stout black hairs on T6

Pits on T1 and T2 are deep and widely spaced.

Colletes inaequalis

Colletes inaequalis has a long and skinny hind basitarsus, while other *Colletes* have a thicker, broader hind basitarsus.

Other *Colletes*

Colletes inaequalis
(male)

The propodeum is dull, and roughly sculptured.

Note the deep, widely spaced pits on T1.

IDENTIFICATION: Gray to brown bee; fuzzy thorax contrasts with strong white-and-black stripes on the abdomen. HEAD: In females, the malar space is about half as long as it is wide. The clypeus is shiny centrally, but there are also pits, which are evenly spaced, close, and deep. THORAX: The portion of the propodeum that faces the abdomen is dull, not shiny or polished; this can be difficult to see through the hair. LEGS: Hind basitarsus is much longer than wide. ABDOMEN: In females, T2–T5 have thick white hair bands at the apex of each segment. Sparse hairs can be found on T1, which has deep dense punctures. On T6, black stout hairs can be seen.

SIMILAR SPECIES: Two other species of *Colletes* seen in the East look similar to *C. inaequalis*: *C. thoracicus* and *C. validus*. *Colletes thoracicus* is almost indistinguishable from *C. inaequalis*; in general *C. inaequalis* has dense and deep punctures set far apart, while *C. thoracicus* is shiny, with few punctures, and none of them are deep. *C. validus* has malar spaces that are nearly twice as long as wide in males, and one and a quarter times as long in females. Of the three, *C. inaequalis* is the most commonly seen, and the earliest to emerge each spring.

— *Colletes latitarsis*

SIZE: Small to medium; 8–11 mm.
PHENOLOGY: March through September.
FLORAL HOSTS: Specialist on *Physalis*, though also visits Fabaceae and possibly others as well.
RANGE: Southern Ontario and Maine south to Florida, and east to the Rocky Mountains.
NESTING: Ground-nesting.

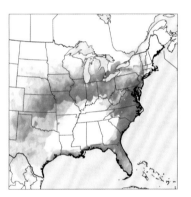

IDENTIFICATION: Medium-sized gray bee with black-and-white stripes on abdomen. HEAD: The eyes don't converge below nearly as much as in other species of *Colletes*. There is little to no malar space, with the mandible beginning just below the eye. THORAX: The punctation on the scutum is deep, with the area in between shining. LEGS: In females, T2 is square in shape, roughly the same length as its width. In both sexes, the hind basitarsus is about two times as long as broad; very wide compared with other *Colletes*. ABDOMEN: T2 has a shiny, impunctate apical margin in females. In males, the margin of S5 is concave.

Colletes latitarsus (female)

The second tergal segment has a thin impunctate band right at the end.

The hair is somewhat shorter than in other *Colletes*.

Colletes latitarsus (female)

The second tarsal segment is almost square.

Note that the hind basitarsus is very wide.

The malar space is very short.

SIMILAR SPECIES: *Colletes willistoni* females look very similar to *C. latitarsis* females, but *C. latitarsis* have a smooth and shiny margin at the apical edge of T2, while *Colletes willistoni* are punctate all the way to the apex, with no smooth and polished margin. On the hind leg, in females, the second tarsal segment of *C. willistoni* is much longer than it is wide.

Colletes latitarsus (male)

Hind basitarsus in males is longer than wide, but not by much!

— Colletes thoracicus

SIZE: Medium; 10–14 mm.
PHENOLOGY: April through July.
FLORAL HOSTS: Polylectic; commonly found on early-blooming perennial shrubs.
RANGE: From Minnesota south to Texas, east to Massachusetts and Florida.
NESTING: Ground-nesting.
IDENTIFICATION: A rusty-colored bee, as opposed to the gray or brown of other related species.
HEAD: Malar space of females short; about three times as wide as long.
THORAX: Thick brown-orange hair covers the surface, with some black hairs intermixed.
ABDOMEN: Hair bands are weaker (in older specimens, may be nonexistent) than in many other *Colletes*. Tergal segments pitted with shallow, widely spaced punctures, appearing shiny overall.

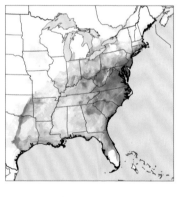

This *Colletes* has the most orange hair on the thorax, with very little black mixed in.

T1 and T2 are shiny, with very few pits.

The curve in the second recurrent vein is very evident here.

Colletes thoracicus (female)

SIMILAR SPECIES: Few *Colletes* are as rusty red or orange as this one, especially when combined with the sparse hair bands across the abdomen. Note that even in this species, hair color can be variable, so additional characteristics are needed to confirm. *C. simulans* may be slightly orange in some specimens, but the white hair bands on the thorax are usually bolder, and there is a distinct point on the front of the thorax (see *C. simulans* for more detail).

The male is slightly less orange than females.

Hind basitarsus is five times longer than it is wide.

Malar space is half as long as broad.

Colletes thoracicus (male)

— *Colletes simulans*

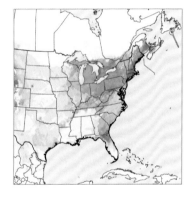

SIZE: Small to medium; 8–11 mm. **PHENOLOGY:** Late May through October; a fall bee. **FLORAL HOSTS:** A specialist on late summer and fall Asteraceae. **RANGE:** From New England and southern Canada south to Georgia, west to California. There are four subspecies, defined mostly by where they occur. **NESTING:** Ground-nesting. **IDENTIFICATION:** Moderate-sized bee with gray thorax and black-and-white abdomen. **HEAD:** The hair on the top of the head and on the back half of the thorax is light, mixed with black, though this can be variable. In males, the face has long pale hairs completely hiding the clypeus. **THORAX:** In females, the pronotum has a large protrusion, like a tooth, on each side; the size of the "tooth" is variable, but

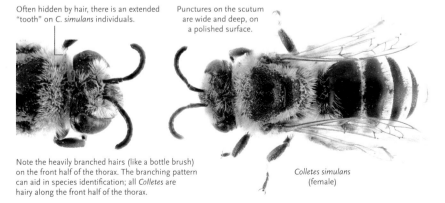

Often hidden by hair, there is an extended "tooth" on *C. simulans* individuals.

Punctures on the scutum are wide and deep, on a polished surface.

Note the heavily branched hairs (like a bottle brush) on the front half of the thorax. The branching pattern can aid in species identification; all *Colletes* are hairy along the front half of the thorax.

Colletes simulans (female)

in some specimens extends out, so that the distance between the points is wider than the back of the head. On the scutum, there are few but distinct pits on a polished surface. The hairs are heavily branched. **LEGS:** The hind basitarsi are four times as long as they are wide; five times as long as wide in males. **ABDOMEN:** The first tergal segment has fine, widely spaced pits on a shiny integument.

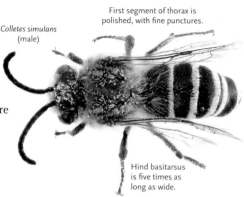

Colletes simulans (male)

First segment of thorax is polished, with fine punctures.

Hind basitarsus is five times as long as wide.

SIMILAR SPECIES: There are several subspecies of *C. simulans*. In the eastern U.S. and the Midwest is *C. simulans armatus*. In Florida and Georgia is *C. simulans miamiensis*. *Colletes hyalinus*, *C. willistoni*, and *C. nudus* all have lateral protrusions on the pronotum, as in *C. simulans*, but these protrusions are not as well developed. In all three, the forecoxae lack long spines.

HYLAEUS

— **SUBFAMILY:** Hylaeinae

OVERVIEW: Small bees, with little or no hair, and ivory markings on their face and legs. All species are twig-nesting, preferring dead stems over other materials, and all line their nests with a clear membranous material that is waterproof. Nests can also be found in nail holes, small-diameter beetle burrows, and abandoned nests of other bees. Pollen is carried to the nest, not in scopal hairs, but internally, in the crop. Nectar is also carried in the crop, resulting in a provision that is soupy. Pollen preferences are not known, as they are difficult to determine when pollen is carried internally. There is evidence that some species may prefer plants in the Rosaceae family. Seven *Hylaeus* species endemic to Hawaii are listed as endangered.
IN THE WORLD: Found worldwide, including many larger island groups (in the U.S., notably Hawaii). There are more than 700 species around the world. In mainland North America there are around 50 species, 25 of which can be found in the East.
CLEPTOPARASITES: Unknown, but a few species in Hawaii appear to be cleptoparasitic on other *Hylaeus* species.
IDENTIFYING FEATURES: Distinct bees; body is hairless with ivory markings, most prominently on face and leg joints, and more extensive in males. **HEAD:** Ivory markings are often parallel lines right next to compound eyes (though may be either more extensive or absent). Along each compound eye there is a narrow but deep groove (fovea). There is one subantennal suture. **THORAX:** The scutal surface is usually heavily pitted and roughened. **WINGS:** Two submarginal cells. The basal vein is relatively straight. **LEGS:** There are no pollen-collecting hairs.

Distinguishing between species is complicated by the significant variation in characteristics within a species. For example, most *H. mesillae* have a black pronotal collar, but some specimens have a yellow one. We have included a few common species, of the 25 found in the East, but verification with a key and a reference collection will be needed for certainty.

SIMILAR GENERA: Small Halictidae (small *Halictus, Dufourea*) may appear superficially similar to this colletid. The *Hylaeus* body shape is narrower when viewed from above, and the body is usually marked with ivory or yellow markings. Halictidae are not similarly marked, the body shape is flatter, and most have three submarginal cells.

— *Hylaeus affinis*

SIZE: Small; 5–6 mm. **PHENOLOGY:** May through late October. **FLORAL HOSTS:** Polylectic. **RANGE:** From New England and southern Canada west to Minnesota, south to Louisiana, Mississippi, and Georgia. **NESTING:** Twig-nesting, with some records in beetle burrows. Abundant in cities and other urban environments as well as grasslands.

IDENTIFICATION: Small black bee with yellow markings. **HEAD:** In females, the clypeus is usually black, with yellow extending up the sides of the face above the antennal sockets, nearly filling the entire paraocular region. In some individuals the clypeus may be yellow as well. In males, the scape on the antenna is usually marked with yellow. The fovea, running next to the compound eye, is long and linear, extending from its top halfway to the antennal sockets. **THORAX:** The pronotal collar has some yellow markings on it and is never completely black. Scutal

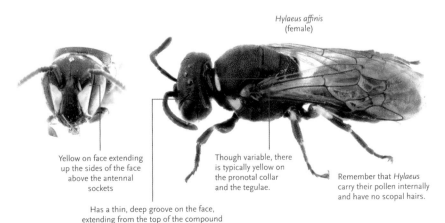

Hylaeus affinis
(female)

Yellow on face extending up the sides of the face above the antennal sockets

Though variable, there is typically yellow on the pronotal collar and the tegulae.

Remember that *Hylaeus* carry their pollen internally and have no scopal hairs.

Has a thin, deep groove on the face, extending from the top of the compound eye down toward the anntennal socket.

The antennae have yellow on the scape, as well as next to each eye. The yellow next to each eye extends beyond the antennal sockets and rounds to an end.

The tegula and pronotal collar are yellow.

Hylaeus affinis
(male)

pits are of medium size and roughened between. The tegula of males (as in females) is usually yellow. **LEGS:** The front tibiae usually have ivory to yellow markings. **SIMILAR SPECIES:** It is very difficult to differentiate females of *H. affinis* from *H. modestus* and even *H. illinoisensis;* many scientific papers do not separate these species. Several other female *Hylaeus* species are also similarly marked, including *H. hyalinatus* and *H. leptocephalus* (neither pictured in this book). In *H. hyalinatus,* there is a raised ridge running below the forewing, on the side of the body (this will distinguish males of this species as well). In *H. leptocephalus,* the markings are a lighter ivory, while in *H. affinis* they are more yellow. In males, *H. confluens, H. hyalinatus,* and *H. sparsus* have similar markings. The scape is much wider in *H. sparsus,* about half again as wide as the flagellar segments. And in *H. confluens,* the pits on the scutum are large, compared with *H. affinis.*

— *Hylaeus mesillae*

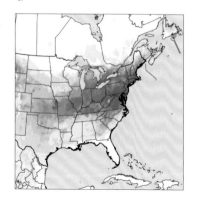

SIZE: Petite; 3–4 mm. **PHENOLOGY:** Late June through October. **FLORAL HOSTS:** Polylectic, but commonly seen visiting summer blooming Apiaceae. **RANGE:** Across the United States and Canada, from Nova Scotia to British Columbia and south to Georgia, southern Texas, and Arizona. **NESTING:** Twig-nesting but will also use nail holes and other small cavities. **IDENTIFICATION:** Extremely small but common matte-black bee. There is a gradation in coloring across the U.S., with western and southern individuals exhibiting more yellow than eastern and northern specimens. **HEAD:** In females, the clypeus is black, with maybe a small ivory mark; yellow runs up beside compound eyes, rarely extending beyond antennal sockets. In males, the antennal

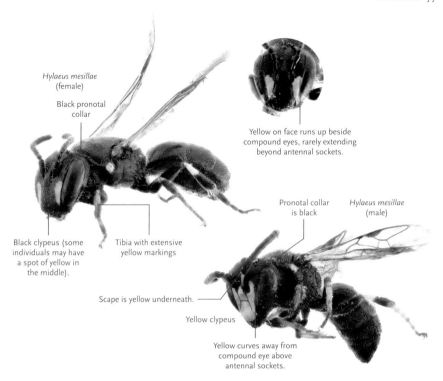

Hylaeus mesillae
(female)

Black pronotal collar

Yellow on face runs up beside compound eyes, rarely extending beyond antennal sockets.

Pronotal collar is black

Hylaeus mesillae
(male)

Black clypeus (some individuals may have a spot of yellow in the middle).

Tibia with extensive yellow markings

Scape is yellow underneath.

Yellow clypeus

Yellow curves away from compound eye above antennal sockets.

scape has some yellow, as does the clypeus, and the areas beside the compound eyes. The first flagellar segment is much shorter than the second flagellar segment. The fovea, running next to the compound eye, is long and linear, extending from its top halfway to the antennal sockets. **THORAX:** The pronotal collar of both males and females is black. On the scutum, pits are small and shallow (not very noticeable). In both sexes, tegulae are black. **LEGS:** The front tibiae usually have ivory to yellow markings. **SIMILAR SPECIES:** *Hylaeus annulatus* has only a small yellow spot on the tibia, and is larger than *H. mesillae*. In the Midwest, *Hylaeus rudbeckiae* (not shown here) overlaps and looks similar. Between the two *H. mesillae* is much more abundant. *Hylaeus rudbeckiae* is slightly larger with a wider head. The yellow markings are more extensive overall, and are usually more yellow/orange, while *H. mesillae* is more ivory-colored, and less extensively marked. *Hylaeus saniculae,* another rare *Hylaeus*, also looks similar to *H. mesillae* but lacks the extensive yellow markings on the tibia; on the face it has a yellow line across the base of the clypeus.

— *Hylaeus modestus*

SIZE: Petite to small; 4–7 mm.

PHENOLOGY: Early June through early October.

FLORAL HOSTS: Generalist. **RANGE:** Newfoundland to North Dakota, south to east Texas and Florida.

NESTING: Twig nester, usually in the upper portions of *Sumac* stems. Nest cells are separated by a clear partition made of secretions from the mother. Offspring chew around, rather than through, the partition when emerging from the nest.

IDENTIFICATION: Small black bee with yellow markings that are highly variable, making this species, and especially females, difficult to distinguish. **HEAD:** In females, face may be entirely yellow or black (as in the specimen shown here). In males, the scape on the antennae is all black. On the face, yellow runs up next to the compound eyes until the antennal socket, extending past it to a narrow point. The scape is the same width as the flagellar segments, or just slightly wider. On the labrum and mandibles, there are usually extensive yellow markings.

THORAX: Pronotal collar typically yellow, but may be all black. Tegula often black but may also have yellow markings. On the scutum, females have medium-sized, widely spaced pits. **ABDOMEN:** The first tergal segment is often without pits, or with a few widely scattered ones.

In this specimen the pronotal collar is yellow, but this character is variable for this species.

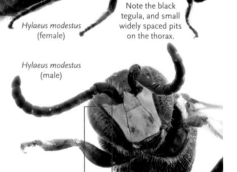

The wings tend to be smoky.

Hylaeus modestus (female)

Note the black tegula, and small widely spaced pits on the thorax.

Hylaeus modestus (male)

The scape is not yellow. The yellow next to the eyes extends only just beyond the antennal sockets, tapering to a point.

SIMILAR SPECIES: Females are slightly smaller than *H. affinis*, but females of the two species are virtually indistinguishable. Other species with females that look similar include *H. illinoisensis* (nearly indistinguishable), *H. confluens,* and *H. hyalinatus.* Most of the time *H. modestus* has dark tegula with no yellow markings, and pits that are widely separated. *Hylaeus hyalinatus* has more distinct and dense pits on T1 than does *H. modestus.* In males, *H. floridanus* and *H. hyalinatus* look similar in terms of the all-black scape, but the lack of yellow on the labrum and mandibles should distinguish. *H. confluens* is also similar, but the pits on the scutum are significantly larger than in *H. modestus.*

— *Hylaeus punctatus*

SIZE: Petite to small; 4–7 mm.
PHENOLOGY: Fall; late August through early November. **FLORAL HOSTS:** Polylectic.
RANGE: Native to Europe; recently introduced to South America and North America, where it has been found in California, Colorado, Illinois, New York, Maryland, and Ontario. First noticed in the U.S. in 1981. **NESTING:** Twig nester.
IDENTIFICATION: Small black bee seen in cities and suburbs, but not common elsewhere.
HEAD: In females, there are modest yellow markings: the clypeus is black, and the yellow beside the compound eyes does not extend above the antennal sockets. In males, the antennal scape is entirely black (though the flagellomeres are amber colored). The yellow on the face of males is restricted to below the antennal sockets and does not usually extend over the top of the clypeus. **THORAX:** The transition from the front of the bee to its side is marked by a thin raised ridge. On the scutum, punctation is large, deep, and dense, giving a very roughened appearance. The tegulae are yellow. **ABDOMEN:** Pits are sparse on T1, so that it appears shiny.
SIMILAR SPECIES: The dense, deep pits on the scutum, combined with the ridge on the side of the bee, is unique; only *H. hyalinatus* (not shown in this book) shares these characters. In *H. hyalinatus,* T1 is heavily pitted, while in *H. punctatus* it is without punctation. In males, *H. hyalinatus* has yellow markings that extend well above the antennal sockets.

The thorax has deep, rough pits densely covering it.

The first tergal segment is without pits, and shiny.

Hylaeus punctatus (female)

Hylaeus punctatus (male)

On males, the yellow on the sides of the face ends right about the top of the clypeus.

Male thorax is also covered in dense, deep pits.

Abdominal segments are polished.

Hylaeus punctatus (male)

ANDRENIDAE

The Andrenidae is a diverse family, very common in North America, that includes this continent's smallest bees and some of the biggest as well. Morphologically, the diversity of form is phenomenal, including all-yellow bees, solid black bees, some species with sky blue eyes, and very hairy bees. All are solitary, though aggregate nesting and communal nesting occurs. All species nest in the ground. Among North American species are a large proportion of specialists as well as many generalists. Interestingly, there are no cleptoparasitic bees in the Andrenidae.

The smallest bee north of Mexico (and maybe the smallest bee in the world) occurs in this family. *Perdita minima* is less than a tenth of an inch in size (2 mm). It lives in the Mojave, Chihuahuan, and Sonoran deserts, and specializes on Euphorbiaceae.

IDENTIFICATION: At the family level, Andrenidae are diverse; characters that unite the family are not immediately evident. On the face, though, all bees in the Andrenidae family have two subantennal sutures, a feature not found in any other bee family. On the legs, nearly all female Andrenidae collect pollen on the femur and even the coxa, as opposed to mostly on the tibia, as seen in other bees.

TAXONOMY: There are more than 3,000 species and 45 genera in the world; though they occur on every continent but Australia, they reach their highest richness in the Northern Hemisphere, especially North America. Here, there are more than 1,200 species in 11 genera. Andrenidae in North America occur in three subfamilies, but in the eastern U.S., one of those subfamilies is absent, and another is represented by only one genus. Characters distinguishing them are often on the genitalia or the smaller sternal segments, in males. These characters are not included in our descriptions. Of note here is the episternal groove, whose shape and presence distinguishes between tribes in the Panurginae.

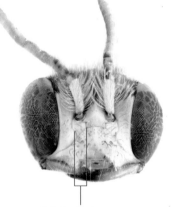

All Andrenidae have two subantennal sutures.

The episternal groove can be difficult to see in hairy species, yet its size and shape can be diagnostic of some genera in Panurginae.

— SUBFAMILY ANDRENINAE

There are three genera in this subfamily, but only one, *Andrena*, occurs in the East. All three have deep facial foveae, depressions running vertically next to each compound eye, filled with dense woolly hair.

Facial foveae

— SUBFAMILY PANURGINAE

Six genera occur in this subfamily; five are found in the eastern U.S., though some are not common. They are divided into the following three tribes. The characteristics distinguishing the tribes are not always easy, though the genera are not hard to tell apart. All Panurginae collect pollen on the tibia, and it is usually a wetter mass, rather than the dry pollen seen in other Andrenidae.

— **CALLIOPSINI:** There is only one genus in North America.

Calliopsis. On the head, there are yellow markings on the faces of both males and females, especially on the clypeus and supraclypeal area. The thorax is usually polished, but not metallic. Though hard to see, the episternal groove on the side of the thorax is short. On the wing, there are two submarginal cells.

— **PANURGINI:** All Panurgini have two submarginal cells. The episternal groove is absent or extremely reduced and curving into the scrobal groove. There are three genera, in different subtribes, in North America. Two occur in the East. *Macrotera* is found only in the West.

Panurginus. On the thorax, there is no episternal groove. In males, the legs and the clypeus are often yellow. On the abdomen, T2–T5 are usually hairy along margins.
Perdita. Minute bees with flattened appearance, especially the abdomen. On the thorax, the episternal groove is short and curves backward toward the scrobal groove. Not very hairy, but may be yellow, metallic greenish blue, or polished black. On the wing, the marginal cell is extremely truncate. Also, the veins on the wing are often ivory or white.

— **PROTANDRENINI:** Two genera. United in the subfamily by their long episternal groove, may have two or three submarginal cells, and moderately truncate marginal cell. Slender, longer bees. Males always have yellow on the face.

Protandrena and *Anthemurgus* are not covered in this book.
Pseudopanurgus. Dark, mostly hairless bees. Two submarginal cells. Females are all black, but males have yellow on face, antennae, and some leg joints. On the forecoxae of females, there is a spine near the apex (the end furthest from the body). The midtibial spur has minute, fine teeth on it.

— SUBFAMILY OXAEINAE

Not found in the East. Includes *Mesoxaea* and *Protoxaea*.

ANDRENA

— **SUBFAMILY: Andreninae**

OVERVIEW: Petite, slender bees, often delicate-looking; ubiquitous in eastern North America. Variable hair patterns ranging from rusty red to black. Ground-nesting bees, often seen in early spring, even before deciduous trees leaf out, though a suite of species also flies only in the fall. Includes many specialists, but some species are generalists.

IN THE WORLD: Found worldwide with more than 1,500 species, but absent from South America and the South Pacific. In North and Central America, they are found as far south as southern Mexico, with more than 500 species in the U.S. and Canada. There are 125 species in the East. *Andrena* have been subdivided into 47 subgenera in North America (we address several, but not all, below).

CLEPTOPARASITES: *Nomada.*

IDENTIFYING FEATURES: Identifying a bee as an *Andrena* is relatively easy with a microscope, but can be more challenging in the field. Overall, the *Andrena* bee body is flat. **HEAD:** Deep grooves run next to each compound eye, filled in with thick woolly hair. These "vertical eyebrows" are called facial foveae. Running from each antennal socket to the top of the clypeus are two sutures (subantennal sutures). The compound eyes are parallel to each other. In males, the clypeus and paraocular areas are often yellow. Mandibles of males are generally elongated, and cross in the front. Also in males, the malar space is usually much wider than it is long. **THORAX:** Many species have an elongated pronotal collar, giving the appearance of a "neck." Worth mentioning, for the student of bee taxonomy who would like to try their hand at using one of the bee keys referenced at the end of this section, is the humeral angle of the pronotum, referred to in many taxonomic keys. The pronotal collar connects the head to the thorax. If it is rounded (tubular), the humeral angle is weak; if it is sharply edged (like a long rectangle), the humeral angle is strong. This structure may be sharply angled, or rounded and indistinct. It is not always visible without a microscope and a specimen that can be turned in different directions. **LEGS:** Scopal hairs run up onto the coxa, in addition to the femur, and in some cases to the pronotum. **ABDOMEN:** Is often shiny and has a distinctive oval shape, tapering at either end.

With more than 500 species in North America, *Andrena* are notoriously difficult to identify to species, even by experts; they may be one of the most difficult groups included in this book. Many *Andrena* are specialists, limiting themselves to certain groups of flowers when collecting pollen for their offspring. Knowing the flower on which

The humeral angle of the pronotum is often used to identify different Andrena *to species, though this characteristic is not often visible without a microscope.*

an *Andrena* was seen can help narrow down which species it is. Below we provide information about some common species, but see keys listed at the end for affirming identification. Identifying the subgenus can also help, though subgenus characters are not always easy to see either.

SIMILAR GENERA: *Colletes* are probably the easiest to confuse with *Andrena* as they are the same size and share a similar body shape. The wing venation of *Colletes,* with the curved second recurrent vein, differs from the straight second recurrent vein of *Andrena*. The head of *Colletes* is heart-shaped, as the inner margins of the compound eyes converge near the bottom. The inner margins of the compound eyes in *Andrena* are parallel. Also, *Colletes* lack facial fovea.

— *Andrena (Andrena) milwaukeensis*

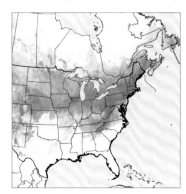

SIZE: Small to medium; 8–12 mm. **PHENOLOGY:** April through July. **FLORAL HOSTS:** Polylectic. **RANGE:** Northern states: Minnesota to New England, occasionally south through Georgia.

IDENTIFICATION: An eye-catching red-orange bee. **HEAD:** In females, the face is long, due to long malar spaces (three times as long as wide). The clypeus is elongated, though flat, with sparse punctation. Also in females, the facial foveae are wide at the top, narrowing and ending above the antennal sockets, filled with brown hair. In males, the face is not as long, with the malar space short and wide. The clypeus is flat, and the first flagellar segment is relatively long. **THORAX:** Abundantly covered in hair, and

Andrena milwaukeensis (female)

The scopal hairs are unbranched and dark.

Red-orange hair on thorax and T1 and T2 is unique in *Andrena milwaukeensis*.

Andrena milwaukeensis (male)

the pronotal humeral angle and ridge is not prominent, and the pronotal collar is not elongated. **LEGS:** Tibial scopal hairs are long and simple. **ABDOMEN:** Tergal segments are dull, with very small shallow punctation. The pygidial plate is rounded at its apex. There are two variations in hair patterns. The eastern form has long red/orange hair just on the first two terga; the western form has long red hair on T1–T4.

SIMILAR SPECIES: The eastern form of *A. milwaukeensis* is similar in appearance to *A. vicinoides*. In *A. milwaukeensis* the hair is more red than pale. Also, the clypeus on *A. milwaukeensis* females hangs down lower and is sparsely punctate. In males, the first flagellar segment is longer than in *A. vicinoides*.

— *Andrena (Cnemidandrena) hirticincta*

SIZE: Small to medium; 9–13 mm. **PHENOLOGY:** Fall; August through October. **FLORAL HOSTS:** Specialist on *Solidago*. **RANGE:** Georgia and North Carolina, north to Maine and Nova Scotia, west to Minnesota and Illinois.

IDENTIFICATION: Hairy bee, appearing blonde with a tinge of green. **HEAD:** In females, facial foveae are narrow, almost linear, and filled with dark yellow woolly hairs. They extend from the height of the middle ocellus to just below the antennal sockets. The malar space is short, but present, giving the face a round, rather than long, appearance, and the clypeus does not protrude much. In males, the malar space is significantly wider than long. **THORAX:** Straw-colored hair is abundant, over a scutum that is roughened, but not heavily pitted. In females, the humeral angle on the pronotum is somewhat developed. In males the humeral angle is strong. **LEGS:** In females, scopal hairs are black and simple. **ABDOMEN:** Tergal segments dull, with widely separated and small punctations.

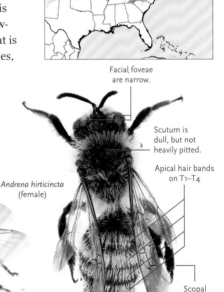

Facial foveae are narrow.

Scutum is dull, but not heavily pitted.

Apical hair bands on T1–T4

Andrena hirticincta (female)

Andrena hirticincta (male)

Malar space is small, so head looks round, not long.

Scopal hairs are simple and black.

T1–T4 have apical bands of thick straw-colored hair. The pygidial plate in females is pointed.

SIMILAR SPECIES: *Andrena colletina, A. surda,* and *A. luteihirta* look similar, and can be distinguished most convincingly by hard-to-see characters on the genitalia; however, *A. hirticincta* also appears to be slightly green, whereas the other three are bright to light yellow.

— Andrena (Holandrena) cressonii

SIZE: Small to medium; 8–11 mm. **PHENOLOGY:** March through May. **FLORAL HOSTS:** Generalist, visiting many early-blooming spring flowers. **RANGE:** Ranges across the United States and into southern Canada. Very common bee.

IDENTIFICATION: Much variability in the appearance as there are three subspecies, one of which occurs in eastern North America. Overall, larger dark bee in all three subspecies. **HEAD:** The labrum (under the clypeus) is short and ends bluntly. The face appears thick, due to a broad gena. In females, facial foveae are wide and long, extending to the antennal sockets. In males, the head is wide with yellow clypeus and yellow paraocular areas. **THORAX:** The scutum is heavily pitted. The pronotum has a strong humeral angle and the pronotal collar is pronounced. **LEGS:** In females,

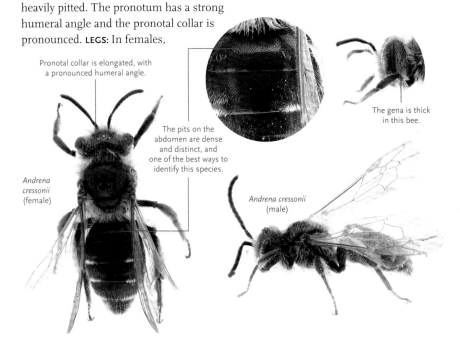

Pronotal collar is elongated, with a pronounced humeral angle.

The pits on the abdomen are dense and distinct, and one of the best ways to identify this species.

The gena is thick in this bee.

Andrena cressonii (female)

Andrena cressonii (male)

the hind tibiae are often orange and rusty red. Scopal hairs are long, simple, often pale in color. **ABDOMEN:** Thin hair bands run apically across T2–T5; these are often interrupted at the center. The terga are shiny with distinct punctures close together. In females, the base of T1 is densely punctate. In males, the apex of S6 is bent anteriorly. **SIMILAR SPECIES:** There are three subspecies, delineated by form and geography; this subspecies occurs from the eastern edge of the shortgrass prairie (eastern Montana south to eastern Texas across to Florida and Maine). *Andrena cressonii* may be confused with *Andrena (Scrapteropsis)* (6 species) or *Andrena (Trachandrena)* (10 species) subgenera due to the strong punctation of the tergites. The pronotal angle, which is strong in *A. cressonii*, will most clearly separate it from these other species, but this is most easily seen in pinned specimens under a microscope.

— Andrena (Iomelissa) violae

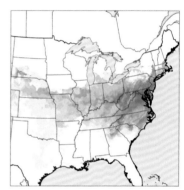

SIZE: Small to medium; 7–11 mm. **PHENOLOGY:** March through May. **FLORAL HOSTS:** Specialist on *Viola* flowers. **RANGE:** Northern Florida, west to Kansas (occasional records in Colorado), north to South Dakota, Wisconsin, and New Hampshire. **IDENTIFICATION:** Smaller dark bee; males and females look remarkably similar to each other. **HEAD:** Long face with clypeus that protrudes strongly from the face. While hard to see, the galea, glossa, and palpi are very long (likely an adaptation to specializing on *Viola*). The malar space in females is short. In males, the clypeus may be completely yellow or black, depending on the individual. **THORAX:** The pronotum has

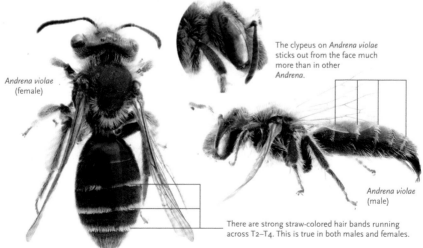

The clypeus on *Andrena violae* sticks out from the face much more than in other *Andrena*.

Andrena violae
(female)

Andrena violae
(male)

There are strong straw-colored hair bands running across T2–T4. This is true in both males and females.

weak, hard-to-see humeral angles. **ABDOMEN:** In females, T2–T4 have strong apical hair bands, usually pale in color.

SIMILAR SPECIES: *Andrena cressonii* has hair bands on the abdomen that look like those on *A. violae*, but the pronotum in *A. cressonii* has a very strong angle at the anterior end, and *A. violae* does not.

— *Andrena (Leucandrena) erythronii*

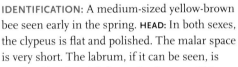

SIZE: Small to medium; 8–11 mm. **PHENOLOGY:** March through May. **FLORAL HOSTS:** Specialist on *Erythronium*. **RANGE:** Nebraska to Maine, north to Montreal, Canada, and south to Tennessee.

IDENTIFICATION: A medium-sized yellow-brown bee seen early in the spring. **HEAD:** In both sexes, the clypeus is flat and polished. The malar space is very short. The labrum, if it can be seen, is much wider than it is long. On the mandible, in females, the lower portion is extended into a thin lamella along the bottom. **THORAX:** For both males and females, humeral angles are weak and rounded, though the pronotal collar is elongated. **LEGS:** Scopal hairs are long and thin, pale in color. **ABDOMEN:** The tergal segments have pale hair bands, often weak and not well-

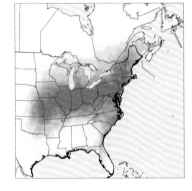

defined. The integument is not polished. In males, the sternal segments have weak bands of hair running just above the apex of each.

SIMILAR SPECIES: *Andrena barbilabris* (not shown here) is very similar and difficult to distinguish from *A. erythronii* without a key.

Andrena erythronii
(male)

Andrena erythronii
(female)

Pronotal collar is elongated, but the humeral angles are weak.

Facial foveae are wide, occupying most of the space between the compound eye and the antennae. The hair inside is brown.

— *Andrena (Larandrena) miserabilis*

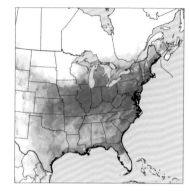

SIZE: Small to medium; 7–9 mm. **PHENOLOGY:** Very common in early spring, March through June (as early as January in Florida). **FLORAL HOSTS:** Polylectic, but often seen visiting fruit trees in the early spring (e.g., *Prunus, Malus*). **RANGE:** Georgia, north to Toronto, west to California.

IDENTIFICATION: Medium-sized, slightly long, dark bee with relatively little hair. **HEAD:** In females, the clypeus is polished in the center, lacking pits except laterally and at the base. Also in females the facial foveae are broad and long, extending from the level of the ocelli to the antennal sockets. Filled with thick white hair. Mandible black, but tip often deep red. The malar space is three times longer than it is wide. In males, the clypeus is yellow, and the underside of the flagellar segments is much lighter in color than the top. **THORAX:** The pronotal humeral angle is not strong, but the pronotal collar is slightly elongated. **LEGS:** Scopal hairs long, with a few long branched hairs. **ABDOMEN:** Tergal segments are black, and dull, with very thin white apical hair bands, usually broken in the middle. In males, T1–T3 slightly lighter in color. Pygidial plate rounded.

SIMILAR SPECIES: *Andrena erythronii* looks similar, but is overall hairier. In females, the clypeus is polished in both, but only *A. miserabilis* has a wide line that lacks pits in the center.

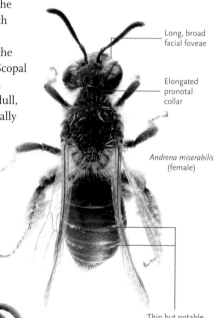

Long, broad facial foveae

Elongated pronotal collar

Andrena miserabilis (female)

Thin but notable apical hair bands run across the abdomen, which is rather dull.

Andrena miserabilis (male)

Clypeus on male is yellow, and underside of antennae is light-colored.

— *Andrena (Melandrena) carlini*

SIZE: Medium; 10–14 mm. **PHENOLOGY:** March through May. **FLORAL HOSTS:** Polylectic; often seen on early-blooming shrubs. **RANGE:** Maine south to Georgia and west to Colorado.

IDENTIFICATION: Larger *Andrena* with striking contrast between color of thorax (dense, light-colored hairs) and abdomen (dark integument, little hair). **HEAD:** In females, the clypeus has a wide area with no punctations down the middle, though the punctations to either side are thick. Clypeus of male and female hangs down below the lower margin of the face due to long malar spaces, but it does not protrude out significantly. The genal area is relatively thick, giving the bee a large head. The vertex is high, almost a point at the back of the head, with the ocelli set below it. The facial foveae are longer than in most other *Andrena*. **THORAX:** Covered in dense, pale to light brown hair, so thick that the integument is hard to see. On the sides of the thorax, the hair transitions to black. **LEGS:** In females, on the hind legs, scopal hairs are simple, and black. **ABDOMEN:** Shiny, and nearly impunctate. No notable white bands. The pygidial plate is broad.

SIMILAR SPECIES: Three species, *A. dunningi, A. vicina* (not shown), and *A. regularis* (not shown), look similar, but have sparser hair on thorax so that it isn't hidden. Hairs on the sides of the thorax of *A. vicina* are tan to light-colored. The pygidial plates of *A. dunningi* and *A. regularis* are narrower, and the clypeus of the females does not have a puncture-free line running down the middle.

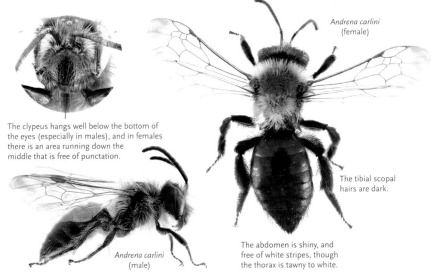

Andrena carlini
(female)

The clypeus hangs well below the bottom of the eyes (especially in males), and in females there is an area running down the middle that is free of punctation.

The tibial scopal hairs are dark.

Andrena carlini
(male)

The abdomen is shiny, and free of white stripes, though the thorax is tawny to white.

— Andrena (Melandrena) dunningi

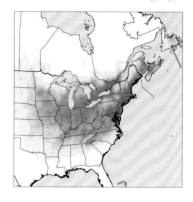

SIZE: Medium; 8–13 mm. **PHENOLOGY:** April through June. **FLORAL HOSTS:** Appears to prefer willow and hawthorn flowers, though floral records are few. **RANGE:** Toronto south to Georgia, Found west to Illinois, but more common in the northeastern portion of its range.

IDENTIFICATION: Large bee with light orange to brown hair on the thorax. **HEAD:** In females, facial foveae broad at the top, taking up two-thirds of the area between the compound eyes and the simple eyes, with light yellow/brown hair. Also in females, the clypeus is polished, lacking punctation except at the base where it meets the supraclypeal area. The malar space is long, and the clypeus extends below the bottom of the face. Orange hair covers the middle of the face. In males, the clypeus is wide and short; it projects very slightly from the face. Hairs on the face of males are tan. **THORAX:** In females, the integument is dark matte-back, with some thick red/orange hair that extends laterally to the sides of the thorax; there are no black hairs intermixed with the orange on the sides of the thorax. In males, the hairs are paler. **LEGS:** In females, the tibial scopal hairs are light-colored. **ABDOMEN:** Hair is sparse, the surface of the tergites is polished, and the pygidial plate is narrow. In females, pygidial plate is V-shaped, but blunted right at the end.

SIMILAR SPECIES: *A. pruni* (not shown) has the same general shape and coloring; in *A. dunningi* the facial foveae are broader, and *A. pruni* has dark hairs intermixed with light on the sides of the thorax. In males, *A. pruni* has long hairs on S6, which are lacking in *A. dunningi*. *A. carlini* is also similarly colored, but females lack the light color on their tibial scopal hairs.

Andrena dunningi
(female)

On the sides of the thorax, the hair is all dark yellow to orange, as on the top. In otherwise similar species, black hair is intermixed with the dark yellow. ——

Andrena dunningi
(female)

Light-colored scopal hairs on female ——

Red fringe of hairs near the apex of the abdomen ——

— *Andrena (Plastandrena) crataegi*

SIZE: Small to medium; 8–11 mm. **PHENOLOGY:** May through July. **FLORAL HOSTS:** Polylectic; may have some slight preference for rosaceous plants. **RANGE:** Northern Georgia and Alabama through Montreal, Canada. Though it is found throughout Illinois, it is largely absent from the Great Plains. Interestingly, it is abundant west of the Rocky Mountains and can be the dominant *Andrena* species in an area. **NESTING:** Communal, with many females sharing the same nest entrance or tunnels, but with separate cells inside. Nests have been found with up to four entrances. **IDENTIFICATION:** Striking black bee with minimal hair. **HEAD:** In females, facial foveae are wide and long, extending from the top of the compound eye to the antennal sockets.

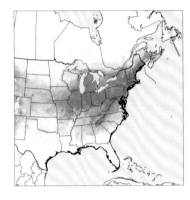

The flagellar segments are slightly rust-colored. In males and females, the clypeus is entirely black. The antennae are long, reaching almost to the propodeum when stretched back across the body. **THORAX:** Very dull due to a roughened integument, though the pits are deep and hard to miss. A line of auburn hair outlines the scutum. The pronotum has a humeral angle toward the head. Tegulae are often reddish. **LEGS:** Scopal hairs appear sparse because they are simple and unbranched. In both males and females, the hind tibial spur is strongly curved, with a flattened base and thinning to the point of being nearly see-through. Also, though hard to see, in females there is a strong ridge running along the back surface of the hind femur.

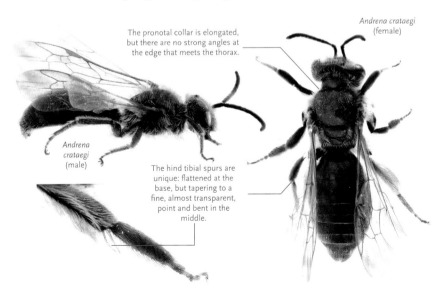

The pronotal collar is elongated, but there are no strong angles at the edge that meets the thorax.

Andrena crataegi
(female)

Andrena crataegi
(male)

The hind tibial spurs are unique: flattened at the base, but tapering to a fine, almost transparent, point and bent in the middle.

ABDOMEN: There are no hair bands, but the tip of the abdomen is lined with auburn hair, the same color as the thorax. In females, the pygidial plate is V-shaped with a rounded tip. In males, the apical margin of S6 folds back on itself, especially laterally. **SIMILAR SPECIES:** The hind femur and hind tibial characters are unique to this bee. In overall form, it looks similar to *Andrena spiraeana* (not shown), but the facial foveae on *A. spiraeana* are much narrower (almost linear), and there is more hair on the sides of the abdomen. In males, the shape of S6 on the abdomen is unique.

— *Andrena (Ptilandrena) erigeniae*

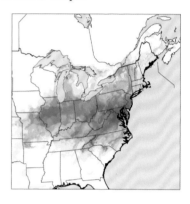

SIZE: Small; 7–9 mm. **PHENOLOGY:** March through early May. Often seen sunning on warm rocks when temperatures are cool. **FLORAL HOSTS:** Pollen specialist on *Claytonia virginica*, which blooms well before eastern deciduous trees leaf out; note that both males and females may visit other spring flowering species for nectar. **RANGE:** Minnesota to New York and south as far as Georgia. **NESTING:** Nests in the forests, or along forest edges, near patches of *Claytonia*. Often found under dry leaf litter and may nest in aggregations as dense as two dozen nest entrances per square meter. **IDENTIFICATION:** Slender black bee; females with massive scopal hairs for body size. **HEAD:** If they can be seen, the maxillary palpi are narrow and elongate, likely an adaptation to the plant on which females specialize. In females, the facial foveae are narrow and short, ending well before the antennal sockets. Malar space is very short. Clypeus with punctures deep, and large near the apex. **THORAX:** The pronotum has a distinct humeral

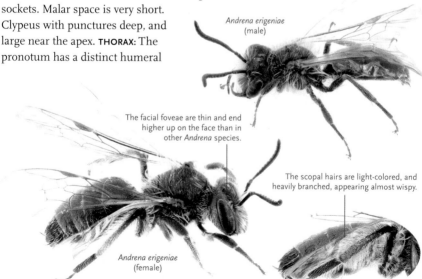

Andrena erigeniae
(male)

The facial foveae are thin and end higher up on the face than in other *Andrena* species.

The scopal hairs are light-colored, and heavily branched, appearing almost wispy.

Andrena erigeniae
(female)

angle. The scutum is not shiny but is covered in large, widely spaced punctures.
LEGS: In females, scopal hairs of the tibia, trochanter, and femur are highly branched.
ABDOMEN: In females, tergal segments appear hairless from a distance but may have some fine white hairs running apically across each segment. In males, the eighth sternal segment is forked; male specimens often die with S8 exserted, making this easy to see.
SIMILAR SPECIES: In the same subgenus, *A. distans* occurs in most areas where *A. erigeniae* is found. *Andrena distans* is more commonly associated with *Geranium* flowers, while *A. erigeniae* is most often on *Claytonia*. The vertex of *A. distans* is higher than that of *A. erigeniae*.

— *Andrena (Simandrena) nasonii*

SIZE: Small; 6–9 mm. **PHENOLOGY:** March through July. **FLORAL HOSTS:** Polylectic.
RANGE: Nova Scotia south to South Carolina, common throughout the eastern U.S., but occurring rarely as far west as Arizona and Oregon, north through North Dakota.
IDENTIFICATION: Small dark bee. **HEAD:** In females, the facial foveae are wide, and end very close to the lateral ocelli on the top of the head. In males, the antennae are long, extending back to the scutellum. In both sexes, the clypeus is dull. **THORAX:** With fine white to tan hairs.

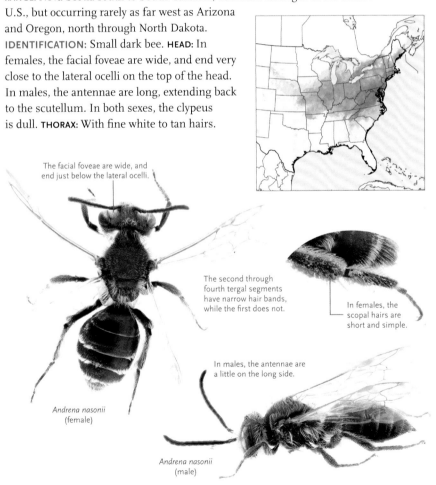

The facial foveae are wide, and end just below the lateral ocelli.

The second through fourth tergal segments have narrow hair bands, while the first does not.

In females, the scopal hairs are short and simple.

In males, the antennae are a little on the long side.

Andrena nasonii
(female)

Andrena nasonii
(male)

The pronotal humeral angle is not strongly angled, though the pronotal collar is prominent. The section of the propodeum that curves over to face the abdomen is very narrow. The most distinctive feature on *Andrena nasonii* is a "tubercle" on the underside of the thorax, between the fore- and midlegs (turn the specimen upside down to see it). This is not visible in most photos of individuals. About 10% of specimens will not have this feature, and in those cases other characters must be used. **LEGS:** In females, scopal hairs are very short and simple, and the basitarsus is broader at the apex than at the base. The scopal hairs on the trochanter are small. **ABDOMEN:** Modest apical hair bands run across the second through fourth tergal segments, but not the first. **SIMILAR SPECIES:** *Andrena wheeleri* (not shown) is similar in form. Female *A. wheeleri* have a shinier clypeus, lack apical hair bands, and have longer scopal hairs. In males, *A. wheeleri* have a longer first flagellar segment, and also lack apical hair bands.

CALLIOPSIS

— **SUBFAMILY:** Panurginae
— **TRIBE:** Calliopsini

OVERVIEW: Medium to small bees, often slightly shiny, seen from late spring through fall. Nest in the ground, usually in barren open soil, or in highly disturbed areas with hard-packed or frequently overturned soil. Usually found in nesting aggregations. Many *Calliopsis* are specialists, though some are narrow generalists.
IN THE WORLD: In all, 86 species are known. They are exclusive to the Americas, with 68 in North America. In eastern North America, 3 species occur.
CLEPTOPARASITES: *Holcopasites*.
IDENTIFYING FEATURES: Petite bees, often with yellow or ivory markings on the legs, and especially the face, and most prominently in males. **HEAD:** The face is oval-shaped, wider than long, and with a microscope the two subantennal sutures characteristic of Andrenidae are clearly visible, as there is little hair on the face. The compound eyes may appear light blue, green, or gray in living specimens. **THORAX:** Shiny, with light hair on the sides. **WINGS:** The tip of the marginal cell angles away from the edge of the wing margin. There are two submarginal cells. **ABDOMEN:** Light pale stripes of hair run across the apical edge of each tergal segment.
SIMILAR GENERA: *Halictus, Andrena, Perdita*. The wing venations of *Halictus* are distinctive and not seen in *Calliopsis*, and *Halictus* have three submarginal cells. Female *Andrena* have thick facial foveae that are not seen in *Calliopsis*; typically, *Calliopsis* have more yellow markings on the integument, especially near the leg joints, but some male *Andrena* have yellow faces. *Perdita* are rarer in the East, smaller, and the marginal cell on their wing is much more truncate.

— *Calliopsis andreniformis*

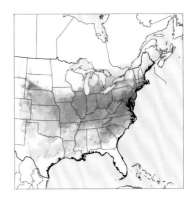

SIZE: Small; 5–8 mm. **PHENOLOGY:** April through October. **FLORAL HOSTS:** Narrowly polylectic, with a preference for small flowers in the Fabaceae, including *Trifolium* and *Melilotus*. **RANGE:** Widespread, extremely common, and often locally abundant. Maine, west to North Dakota, northern Florida west to Texas and Colorado.
IDENTIFICATION: Dainty, shiny bee, often abundant in the summer. **HEAD:** In females, yellow markings occur in three patches—one down the center of the clypeus and one next to each compound eye. In males, yellow markings are more extensive and include the antennal scape, which is completely yellow, all of the clypeus, and all areas near the antennal sockets. **THORAX:** Scutal punctation is almost absent, especially anteriorly. In males, the pronotal collar is yellow. **LEGS:** In males, legs are completely yellow. **ABDOMEN:** Short, neat hair bands extend across each segment of the abdomen.

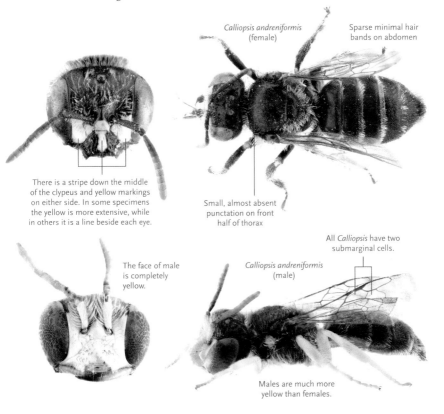

Calliopsis andreniformis (female)

Sparse minimal hair bands on abdomen

There is a stripe down the middle of the clypeus and yellow markings on either side. In some specimens the yellow is more extensive, while in others it is a line beside each eye.

Small, almost absent punctation on front half of thorax

All *Calliopsis* have two submarginal cells.

The face of male is completely yellow.

Calliopsis andreniformis (male)

Males are much more yellow than females.

SIMILAR SPECIES: *Calliopsis coloradensis* occurs throughout the Midwest, and as far east as North Carolina and Alabama. The markings on the face are more extensive in females, not occurring as three distinct vertical lines, but as an almost continuous band across the lower face. In males, the clypeus and undersurface of the antennae are a combination of yellow and black, in contrast to the all-yellow lower face of *C. andreniformis*.

Calliopsis have bluish or greenish eyes. This color fades in preserved specimens.

C. nebraskensis is less widespread, occurring mostly in northern midwestern states, east to Michigan, south to northern Arkansas, and west to Colorado. Yellow on the face of female *C. nebraskensis* is limited to beside the eyes, and a stripe across the base of the clypeus. In both sexes, *C. nebraskensis* is significantly hairier, with stronger hair bands on the abdomen. Finally, *C. nebraskensis* is a specialist on *Verbena* and most commonly seen in their vicinity.

PANURGINUS

— **SUBFAMILY: Panurginae**
— **TRIBE: Panurgini**

OVERVIEW: Small shiny black bees with a little yellow on the clypeus and legs of males. Nest in large aggregations and sometimes communally, with several solitary females sharing a nest entrance, but building their own cells inside. Nests are always in the ground. North American species include both specialists and generalists, but two of the three eastern species are polylectic.

IN THE WORLD: *Panurginus* is the only member of its tribe in the Americas. While Europe has more than 30 species, there are just 18 in North America, and 3 in eastern states and provinces.

CLEPTOPARASITES: *Holocopasites*.

IDENTIFYING FEATURES: Small inconspicuous black nearly hairless bees. **HEAD:** Slightly wider than long, flattened across the vertex, and with the inner margins of the eyes very slightly converging toward the clypeus. In females, the facial foveae (indentations beside each compound eye) are hairless. In males, the clypeus is bright yellow. **THORAX:** On the side of the body, there is no episternal groove. On the posterior end of the propodeum there are very tiny hairs on the sides. **WINGS:** There are only two submarginal cells. In *Panurginus* the first transverse cubital vein meets the second recurrent vein, making a "+" on the wing. **LEGS:** In both sexes, there are no yellow markings. **ABDOMEN:** In males, the margins of T2–T5 have at least some hair.

SIMILAR GENERA: *Pseudopanurgus* and *Panurginus* appear very similar to each other. The wing venation can be telling. In *Panurginus*, the first transverse cubital vein does not meet the first recurrent vein; it does in *Pseudopanurgus*. Darker specimens of *Perdita* look similar to *Pseudopanurgus* and both fly later in the year. The extremely truncate marginal cell in *Perdita* should distinguish the two. *Hylaeus* may also appear similar. The thorax of *Hylaeus* individuals is thinner between the tegulae, and where yellow markings occur is notably different between the two genera. Also, the face of *Hylaeus* is tapered, looking more triangular, as opposed to the wider, more rectangular face of *Panurginus*.

— *Panurginus polytrichus*

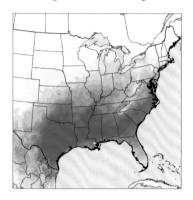

SIZE: Small; 7–8 mm. **PHENOLOGY:** Late March through May; concentrated in April over most of its range. **FLORAL HOSTS:** Generalist. **RANGE:** Common in southern states: Texas east to South Carolina and Georgia. Rarely north to Nebraska. **NESTING:** Nests in large, very dense aggregations (more than 100 nests per square meter), often in disturbed areas with sparse vegetation. Males patrol nest entrances in order to find females, and many may attempt to mate with a female at the same time, forming large mating balls.

IDENTIFICATION: Small and slender, mostly black, shiny bee with little hair. **HEAD:** The clypeus is curved gently, so that if viewed from below, the apical rim is a gentle arc. In females, the face is oval-shaped, slightly wider than it is long; the distance between the compound eyes is about as long as the length of the face. In males, the first flagellar segment is significantly longer than the second one. Males have an entirely yellow clypeus. From above, the male head appears swollen behind the compound eyes, so that the rear margin appears to curve in. **THORAX:** Light yellow hair is sparsely present. The thorax has two sizes of pits, with many fine punctures around a few deep, larger pits. The tegulae are light yellow-brown. **WINGS:** Light yellow. **LEGS:** In females, scopal hairs on the tibiae are long and sparse. In males, there is some yellow on the front tibiae and the tarsal segments. **ABDOMEN:** Tergal segments are smooth and polished, with very small punctation when viewed up close.

The face is very slightly wider than long; make sure to measure to the vertex, and not the very back of the head.

The transverse cubital vein meets the second recurrent vein in a perfect X.

Panurginus polytrichus
(female)

The clypeus is entirely yellow in this species. Barely visible here, the clypeus curves gently at its rim, rather than being strongly concave.

Behind the eyes, the gena is thick, and rounds gently to the back of the head.

The tarsal segments and the foretibia are yellow.

SIMILAR SPECIES: There are two other eastern *Panurginus* species that occur throughout most of the East. Distinguishing females can be difficult. *Panurginus atramontensis* is found more commonly in the Northeast, only slightly overlapping in range with *P. polytrichus*. *Panurginus potentillae* is also more common in the North but is a specialist on *Potentilla* and *Fragaria* (cinquefoils and strawberries). Where the three do overlap, the shape of the clypeal rim is telling: In *P. polytrichus* it is gently arced when viewed from below; in the other two it is shaped like a U, strongly bent up on the sides. In male *P. atramontensis,* the clypeus is yellow only at the

Panurginus polytrichus (male)

very base, while in *P. polytrichus* the entire clypeus is yellow. In *P. potentillae* males, the first flagellar segment is shorter than or equal to the second flagellar segment.

PERDITA

— **SUBFAMILY: Panurginae**
— **TRIBE: Panurgini**

OVERVIEW: Extremely small metallic dull green or black bees often with yellow markings on the face and abdomen, seen most commonly in the late summer and fall. Nest in the ground, occasionally in large aggregations, but nests can be hard to see because the bee is so tiny. Many species are specialists, especially on fall composites (Asteraceae). Collect pollen with a significant amount of nectar, creating a muddy pellet instead of the more typical dry pollen seen in many other bees. Generally rare in the East, but can be abundant in areas with sand and fall-blooming composites.
IN THE WORLD: More than 600 species in the world, all in the Americas. Most of them occur in North America, with close to 550 species in the western U.S. In the eastern U.S. there are 27 species of *Perdita*, but none of them are common. Eastern species are concentrated in the southeastern U.S., and minimally present in northern states and provinces.
CLEPTOPARASITES: *Hexepeolus, Neolarra* (in the West), occasionally *Sphecodes.*
IDENTIFYING FEATURES: Petite, almost flat bees. Most species have extensive yellow or ivory integumental markings on the legs, face (especially the clypeus), thorax, and abdomen. **HEAD:** On the face there are two subantennal sutures (as with all Andrenidae).

THORAX: Typically a metallic olive-green color, and not solid black (though in the West entirely yellow species also exist). An episternal groove is present and curves backward toward the scrobal groove. **WINGS:** There are two submarginal cells, often separated by milky white veins. The marginal cell ends abruptly, and sits next to a very large stigma. **LEGS:** In females, scopal hairs are sparse, and seem almost nonexistent. **ABDOMEN:** In dead specimens, the abdomen is flattened, almost paper thin. **SIMILAR GENERA:** Similar in size to some *Lasioglossum*, especially *L. (Dialictus)*. *L. (Dialictus)* do not have yellow markings on their bodies, and are not as flat as *Perdita*. If viewed up close, the three submarginal cells and tapering marginal cell of *Lasioglossum* can also distinguish the two. *Pseudopanurgus* and *Panurginus* are in the same family as *Perdita* and may superficially resemble *Perdita*. Though both can have yellow on the legs and thorax, *Perdita* often have a green-tinged integument, which does not occur in *Pseudopanurgus* or *Panurginus*. *Perdita* marginal cells are much more truncated than either *Pseudopanurgus* or *Panurginus*. Also, *Panurginus* are spring bees, and seldom overlap in flight season with *Perdita*. *Hylaeus* are also small with yellow markings; they are matte-black, however, and the markings on their faces, and their face shapes, are very different.

— *Perdita octomaculata*

SIZE: Small; 6–7 mm. **PHENOLOGY:** Late summer; September through October. **FLORAL HOSTS:** Oligolectic on Asteraceae, especially *Aster* and *Solidago*. **RANGE:** Mississippi north to Minnesota and east to southern Ontario and Prince Edward Island, northern Florida, and Georgia. **NESTING:** Nests in sandy areas—not seen in areas without significant sand nearby. **IDENTIFICATION:** For a *Perdita*, a fairly robust bee with lots of yellow markings against an

There are two submarginal cells, and the marginal cell ends very abruptly.

Perdita octomaculata
(female)

The abdomen has yellow spots on the sides, but not yellow stripes going all the way across.

On the face of females, there are usually two brown lines running down the clypeus.

There is yellow on the pronotum and also the pronotal lobes

The antennal scapes in males
have some yellow (they are all
brown in females)

Perdita octomaculata
(male)

Face is wider
than long.

otherwise matte-black integument. **HEAD:** In females, the face has yellow markings extending up either side of the clypeus that do not extend past the antennal sockets. There are generally two dark lines running down the clypeus through the yellow. Also in females, on the antennae, the scapes are dark. In males, the face is wider than its length. On the antennae, the scapes are never completely dark. **THORAX:** The pronotum and pronotal lobes are light against a dark thorax. **LEGS:** Scopal hairs are extremely simple, consisting of a few long hairs on the tibia. **WINGS:** Veins are dark brown. **ABDOMEN:** Light-colored patches, but not stripes, occur on two or more of the tergal segments. Usually there are two patches on each of T1–T4, making eight in total, hence the name *octomaculata*.

SIMILAR SPECIES: Males may look similar to *P. bequarti*, but *P. bequarti* has a yellow scape. In female specimens, *Perdita octomaculata* has very simple, very sparse scopal hairs, while *P. bequarti* has branched, wavy, more substantial scopal hairs. On the face of *P. bequarti*, the yellow markings do not usually extend up the sides of the face and are not interrupted by two thin dark lines, as in *P. octomaculata*. Male *P. bishoppi* and *P. floridensis* have dark scapes; the latter is only in Florida, where *P. octomaculata* is seldom seen. *Perdita bishoppi* overlaps in range more commonly with *P. octomaculata*, but *P. bishoppi* is generally darker and has minimal markings on the abdomen.

PSEUDOPANURGUS

— **SUBFAMILY: Panurginae**
— **TRIBE: Protandrenini**

OVERVIEW: Rare, small slender bee, usually seen in late summer or fall. Nest in the ground, often in bare open soil. Many *Pseudopanurgus* are specialists, usually on fall composites (Asteraceae).

IN THE WORLD: *Pseudopanurgus* are found only in North America, ranging from Panama to Canada. In total there are 135 species; around 70 of these are found north of Mexico, with only about 15 in the eastern parts of North America.

CLEPTOPARASITES: *Holcopasites.*

IDENTIFYING FEATURES: Small darker bee, with very little hair. **HEAD:** The eyes are relatively parallel, and the face is slightly wider than long. In males, the lower half of the face is entirely yellow. As with all Andrenidae, two subantennal sutures are evident. **THORAX:** The scutum is matte-black; there are few yellow markings in females. In males yellow is limited to yellow spots on the pronotal collar, and some yellow on the tibia. Though hard to see, in both sexes the episternal groove on the side of the thorax is long, extending below the scrobal groove that runs beside it. **WINGS:** There are two submarginal cells. The marginal cells are gently rounded, and not pointed. The first recurrent vein meets the marginal cells past the vein separating the first and second submarginal cells. **LEGS:** In females, scopal hairs are on the hind tibia and hind basitarsus. **ABDOMEN:** There are no hair bands or yellow markings. In males, T2–T5 have only very sparse hairs on the sides of each tergal segment, which may extend toward the center along the apical margin.

SIMILAR GENERA: *Hylaeus* looks remarkably similar, but female *Hylaeus* have no scopa and have longer faces, usually with white or yellow markings on the face and legs, and eyes that converge toward each other. Female *Pseudopanurgus* are black all over. *Panurginus* also look similar, but they are active only in spring while *Pseudopanurgus* are active in the summer.

Pseudopanurgus is closely related to *Protandrena,* a genus for which we do not highlight species in this book. Some taxonomists have put *Pseudopanurgus* as a subgenus of *Protandrena.* In general, *Protandrena* are less robust and less coarsely punctate. *Protandrena* may have two or three submarginal cells.

— *Pseudopanurgus andrenoides*

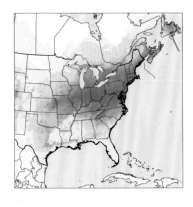

SIZE: Small; 5–8 mm. **PHENOLOGY:** August
through September. **FLORAL HOSTS:** Specialist on
late summer plants in the family Asteraceae,
often seen on *Solidago* (goldenrod). **RANGE:** Rare
and often overlooked, found from Maine to
North Carolina, west to Minnesota and Missouri.
IDENTIFICATION: Small black bee with little or
no noticeable body hair. **HEAD:** In females, the
face is entirely black, while males have a bright
yellow clypeus. The vertex is thick, with at least
the diameter of one simple eye between the
preoccipital carina and the lateral ocelli. **THORAX:** Punctation is dense, evenly spaced
in the middle, but with pits almost touching toward the edges. In males, the pronotal
lobes are yellow. **LEGS:** In males, joints in the legs are yellow. In females, on the hind
legs, there are thin, branched scopal hairs on tibia. **ABDOMEN:** The punctation on T1 is
sparse, with shiny integument in between.

SIMILAR SPECIES: All 15 *Pseudopanurgus*
species that occur in the East are very
similar looking and can be challenging
to distinguish for anyone. Differences
between species include length of the
vertex, spacing between ocelli, and
density of the pits on the thorax and
abdomen. See references for a key.

Males are yellow on
the face, the legs, and
sometimes the thorax.

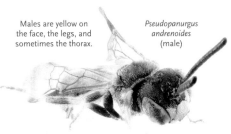

*Pseudopanurgus
andrenoides*
(male)

All Andrenidae have two subantennal
sutures, but they are really visible only in
bees without much hair on the face.

Two submarginal cells

*Pseudopanurgus
andrenoides*
(female)

MELITTIDAE

Melittidae is a small group of bees that are often overlooked. In all areas of the world where melittids occur, they are rare and usually geographically restricted. Most bees in the Melittidae family are specialists, usually narrowly so, and a few have switched to collecting oils in addition to pollens from flowering plants. All species nest in the ground and may nest in small aggregations.

Thought to be one of the oldest bee families, the group includes more than 200 species around the world. Most melittids are found in Africa, but a handful of genera have made their way to Europe, Asia, and North America. Worldwide there are 16 genera; in North America three genera can be found. In the East, none of the genera are common, and between the three there are nine species.

IDENTIFICATION: At the family level, Melittidae are difficult to unite. Overall, the body form is similar to Andrenidae or Colletidae, but the features seen on Melittidae bee specimens are a mix of things normally associated with either short- or long-tongued bees, but not both. Moreover, the characteristics that separate this group from other bee families are on the tongue and genitalia, two regions notoriously difficult to see in bees that are not pinned, and even then, they may need to be dissected. If identifying the bee family is the goal, going through the process of eliminating other families and subfamilies may be an effective strategy (scopal hairs on abdomen or not, one or two subantennal sutures, shape of important wing veins, etc.). **HEAD:** Short-tongued bees, with all labial palpi short, instead of the last ones long. The glossa is shortened and pointed.

THORAX: There is no episternal groove.

LEGS: In the field, it may be noticed that the pollen load on the leg is slightly wet, instead of dry as in many bees. Scopal hairs are typically on the hind tibia.

ABDOMEN: In *Hesperapis*, appears especially flattened in dead specimens. *Melitta* tend to be more solidly built, and *Macropis* are chunkiest, with a rounded abdomen.

TAXONOMY: In light of the relative rarity of this family, we only briefly introduce each genus, and do not provide information about any particular species. There are two *Hesperapis*, three *Melitta,* and four *Macropis* species in the eastern U.S. and Canada. They are split between two subfamilies.

All labial palpi are about the same length.

The glossa is short, and not forked or otherwise modified.

— SUBFAMILY DASYPODINAE

Only one genus appears in this group in North America: *Hesperapis*. There are two eastern species: *H. oraria* and *H. carinata*. The subfamily can be distinguished from Melittinae, the other subfamily in North America, by the bare paraglossa, and the two submarginal cells (with the second shorter than the first). The first submarginal crossvein forms a right angle with the veins demarcating the bottom of that first row, and it is close to the first recurrent vein.

— SUBFAMILY MELITTINAE

There are two genera in this group: *Macropis* and *Melitta*. The subfamily can be distinguished from Dasypodinae by the hairy paraglossa, and the two or three submarginal cells. The second submarginal cell, or the second combined with the third, are as long as, or longer than, the first. And the first submarginal crossvein is strongly angled, so that its junction is usually far away from the first recurrent vein.

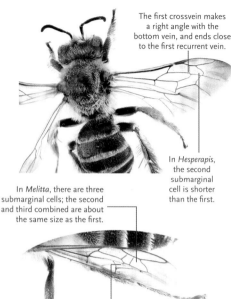

The first crossvein makes a right angle with the bottom vein, and ends close to the first recurrent vein.

In *Hesperapis*, the second submarginal cell is shorter than the first.

In *Melitta*, there are three submarginal cells; the second and third combined are about the same size as the first.

The first recurrent vein ends relatively far from the first crossvein (compare to *Hesperapis*).

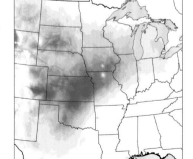

In *Macropis*, there are two equally sized submarginal cells.

HESPERAPIS

— SUBFAMILY: Dasypodinae

SIZE: Small to medium; 9–15 mm.
PHENOLOGY: Spring bees, usually active from March through May. **FLORAL HOSTS:** All *Hesperapis* are specialists, though different species specialize on different plants. Both eastern species of *Hesperapis* specialize on Asteraceae, the sunflower family.
RANGE: *Hesperapis carinata* is found primarily in the West, though it can be found as far east as the Mississippi River. *Hesperapis oraria* is found only in the coastal dunes from Mississippi to

Hesperapis carinata

Florida. **NESTING:** Both eastern species nest in sandy soil; nests can be more than 1 meter deep. **IDENTIFYING FEATURES:** Medium-sized, slight bee with relatively hairy brown or gray body. **HEAD:** Width is greater than the length, but the width is narrower than that of the thorax. **WINGS:** Two submarginal cells. **LEGS:** On the hind leg, the basitarsus is long and slender.

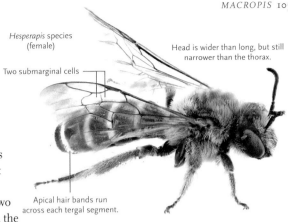

Hesperapis species (female)

Two submarginal cells

Head is wider than long, but still narrower than the thorax.

Apical hair bands run across each tergal segment.

ABDOMEN: There are contrasting light hair bands on the rim of each abdominal segment. The first through third tergal segments are highly polished, and relatively unpitted. **SIMILAR GENERA:** *Colletes, Andrena,* and *Halictus* may look superficially similar, but all three have three submarginal cells, while *Hesperapis* have only two.

MACROPIS

— **SUBFAMILY: Melittinae**

SIZE: Small to medium; 7–12 mm. **PHENOLOGY:** Summer; May through August. **FLORAL HOSTS:** Specialists on *Lysimachia.* Collect pollen and also floral oils from the plant. **RANGE:** Northeast, from Virginia through Maine, west through the northern Great Plains; occur only where *Lysimachia* plants grow. **NESTING:** Ground nesters, preferring well-drained soils, or banks with some plant cover to conceal their nest entrances. Nests are shallow, only a few centimeters deep. Often nest in large aggregations.

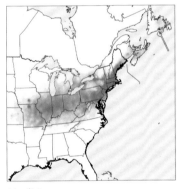

M. ciliata

IDENTIFYING FEATURES: Stout, rarely seen dark bees. There are four species in the East. **HEAD:** Wider than long. In males, clypeus is yellow. **THORAX:** Broad; scutum is smooth with only very fine but deep punctures. **LEGS:** Hind basitarsus is short and very wide with fine hairs covering it (for collecting floral oils). Scopal hairs, on the hind tibia, are entirely white. **WINGS:** Two submarginal cells. **ABDOMEN:** Very thin white bands run across each tergal segment; these can be quickly worn off.

There are four species of *Macropis* in the East. The combination of two features can distinguish them: In females, two species have pale hair on the hind basitarsus. For these two, *M. ciliata* has a smooth and polished propodeum, and *M. patellata* has a rough

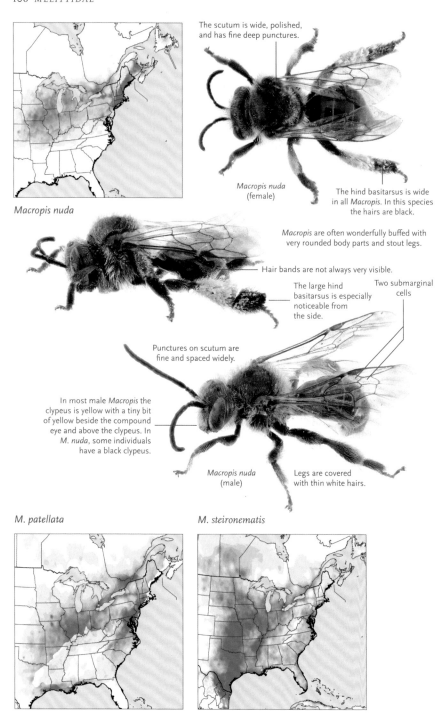

The scutum is wide, polished, and has fine deep punctures.

Macropis nuda
(female)

The hind basitarsus is wide in all *Macropis*. In this species the hairs are black.

Macropis nuda

Macropis are often wonderfully buffed with very rounded body parts and stout legs.

Hair bands are not always very visible.

The large hind basitarsus is especially noticeable from the side.

Two submarginal cells

Punctures on scutum are fine and spaced widely.

In most male *Macropis* the clypeus is yellow with a tiny bit of yellow beside the compound eye and above the clypeus. In *M. nuda*, some individuals have a black clypeus.

Macropis nuda
(male)

Legs are covered with thin white hairs.

M. patellata

M. steironematis

propodeum, dull and not at all polished. Two species have black hair on the hind basitarsus. For these two, *M. nuda* has highly polished terga, while *M. steironematis* has coarsely punctate tergal segments. Similarly in males, *M. steironematis* has close and deep pits on the unpolished abdomen; the other three species have small pits on a shiny surface. *M. patellata* and *M. steironematis* both have one small hind tibial spur. *Macropis nuda* has two hind tibial spurs. *M. ciliata* males have both hind tibial spurs reduced. **SIMILAR GENERA:** While the overall shape of *Macropis* is distinct, they look similar to some smaller members of the family Apidae. Most Apidae have three submarginal cells. Also, the close relationship of *Macropis* to loosestrife plants can aid in identification.

MELITTA

— **SUBFAMILY: Melittinae**

SIZE: Small to medium; 7–12 mm.
PHENOLOGY: Spring, March through May. **FLORAL HOSTS:** All are specialists; the three eastern species (*Melitta americana*, *M. melittoides*, and *M. eickworti*) collect pollen from Ericaceae, particularly from blueberry and cranberry flowers (*Vaccinium*). **RANGE:** *Melitta melittoides* and *M. eickworti* can be found from North Carolina through Maine and into Quebec. *Melitta americana* can be found from Louisiana through Maine, primarily in coastal areas. **NESTING:** Ground nesters, often in areas hidden by vegetation.

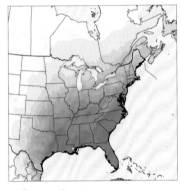

Melitta americana

IDENTIFYING FEATURES: Small dark bees with thin gray hair. Very rarely seen. **HEAD:** In males, the antennae are relatively long; the clypeus in males is not yellow. If the labrum can be seen, there is a lobe to either side of center that is not found in other bees. **THORAX:** Propodeum is wide, but not polished. **WINGS:** Three submarginal cells. The second submarginal cell is wider than long, or square shaped; it is never narrow. **LEGS:** Scopal hairs are short and thin, made of simple hairs. When full of pollen, scopal loads look incredibly large.

In *Melitta americana*, the pits on the scutum are large and densely spaced, as are the pits on T1 and T2 (so that they practically touch). In *M. eickworti*, the pits are shallow, large, and very widely spaced. On the first and second

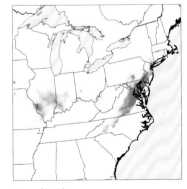

M. melittoides

tergal segments, pits are sparse and definitely not touching. The pits on T1 and T2 of *M. melittoides* are somewhere in between. Also in *M. melittoides,* the pygidial plate is lined with a distinct fringe of dense rust-colored pubescence.

SIMILAR SPECIES: *Andrena, Halictus,* and *Colletes* all share a similar body shape to *Melitta* and distinguishing them can be difficult. *Colletes* have angular faces not seen in *Melitta. Andrena* have deep facial foveae next to each compound eye (in females) not seen in *Melitta.* And *Halictus* have an arcuate basal vein that differs from the straight one seen in *Melitta.* Within the family, the three genera are somewhat similar in appearance; the three submarginal cells of North American *Melitta* will distinguish them from other melittids.

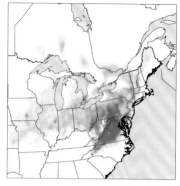

M. eickworti

There are three submarginal cells; note that the middle one is square shaped, and not very narrow.

Melitta are much fuzzier than *Macropis*; underneath the hair, the scutum isn't as polished as it is in *Macropis.*

Melitta species (female)

The basitarsus is narrower than in *Melitta,* and the scopal hairs are short and stiff.

In males, antennae are notably long.

The clypeus on *Melitta* species is not yellow in males.

Melitta species (male)

MEGACHILIDAE

Megachilidae are incredibly morphologically diverse. From yellow-and-black spotted to brilliant green, this group includes a rich array of color morphs, as well as of structural adaptations on the face and legs. Within the Megachilidae are generalists and specialists, with many preferring flowers in the mint (Lamiaceae), pea (Fabaceae), and figwort (Plantaginaceae) families. Though there are ground-nesting Megachilidae, a larger proportion of bees in this family nest in preexisting cavities: twigs, beetle burrows, snail shells, nail holes, and prefabricated bee hotels. Nests are constructed using many substrates and may include mud, sawdust, leaves, plant trichomes, petals, or small pebbles. Parasitic bees also occur in the Megachilidae, and many are very strikingly colored.

The Megachilidae bee family includes the largest bee in the world, *Megachile pluto*, which lives on an island in Indonesia. In North America, famous species include the alfalfa leaf-cutter bee and the blue orchard bee, both of which are used commercially for pollination. It also includes many introduced species, such as the widespread European wool carder bee and the giant resin bee.

IDENTIFICATION: Megachilidae are perhaps one of the easiest families to recognize without a microscope. Their bodies are robust, thick, and often cylindrical instead of the flattened or petite stature of some other bee families. Many genera have yellow-and-black markings across their bodies. All female Megachilidae that are not parasitic carry pollen on the underside of their abdomens, a characteristic not found in any other bee family. The pollen can often be seen bulging out from the sides of the abdomen, even when the abdomen is not directly visible. HEAD: Labrum (which is hinged to the clypeus) is big and hinged across its entire length, giving it a rectangular shape. Megachilidae are long-tongued bees. WINGS: Two submarginal cells, with the second being noticeably longer than the first.

TAXONOMY: In North America there are more than 600 species of Megachilidae, in 18 genera, though this is less than one-quarter of the number found worldwide (more than 4,000 bees in nearly 80 genera). Megachilidae occur on every continent and are also well represented on islands (likely a result of the tendency of many species to nest in wood). Probably for the same reason, many of the invasive species found in North America are in the Megachilidae. In the East, two subfamilies occur, one of which contains numerous tribes and the bulk of North America's genera.

— SUBFAMILY LITHURGINAE

There are two genera in this subfamily: *Lithurgus* (not included in this book—introduced from the Mediterranean; seen in the Northeast on *Centaurea* flowers) and *Lithurgopsis*. They can be distinguished from other Megachilidae by the numerous bumps and spines (tubercles) on the outer surface of the hind tibia. Males possess a pygidial plate, and in females this structure is spinelike or at least elongated.

— SUBFAMILY MEGACHILINAE

Sixteen genera occur in this subfamily; nearly all are found in the eastern U.S., though some are not common. None of these genera possess pygidial plates. A few have tubercles, as in Lithurginae, but in general, these are absent. The genera are divided into four tribes, which are relatively easy to tell apart.

— **ANTHIDIINI:** Large group of robust, often yellow-and-black bees. In addition to color patterns, the cleft tarsal claws (or at least an inner tooth) are distinctive among Megachilinae. On the wing, the stigma is usually very short. And on the hind legs, there are often numerous simple bristles covering the face. Seven genera in North America, all occur in the East. *Anthidiellum, Anthidium, Dianthidium, Paranthidium, Pseudoanthidium* (one introduced, rare species, not included in this book), *Stelis, Trachusa.*

Major characters that differ between species of Anthidiini					
	Anthidium	*Anthidiellum*	*Dianthidium*	*Paranthidium*	*Trachusa*
Number of teeth, in females	5 or more	Fewer than 5	3	Fewer than 5	Fewer than 5
Subantennal suture shape	Straight	Long and curved outward	Straight	Straight	Straight
Preoccipital ridge	Rounded	Outlined by a strong carina, overhangs scutum	Rounded	Rounded	Rounded
Pronotal lobe	Rounded, one species lamellate	Rounded	Extended as paper-thin plate toward the head	Paper-thin, but very short	Rounded
Scutellum	More or less rounded	Swollen, overhangs metanotum	More or less rounded	More or less rounded	More or less rounded
Arolium	No arolium	Arolium	Arolium	Arolium	Arolium

— **DIOXYINI:** This tribe includes just one genus in North America: *Dioxys*. It is a parasitic bee and can be recognized most evidently by the wasplike body with no scopal hairs, the slender mandibles, and the spine at the center of the metanotum. We do not feature *Dioxys* species in this book.

— **MEGACHILINI:** This tribe includes two genera in North America, *Megachile* and *Coelioxys*. Medium to large dark bees. *Coelioxys* is the parasite of *Megachile*. As a whole, the tribe can be distinguished from other Megachilidae by the dark body and the black-and-white stripes on the abdominal segments, and the lack of an arolium between the front claws. There are no yellow markings on these bees.

— **OSMIINI:** This tribe includes seven genera of small to medium-sized bees, sometimes metallic, but often matte-black. Between the tarsal claws is an arolium. *Ashmeadiella, Chelostoma, Heriades, Hoplitis,* and *Osmia,* are found in the East. *Atoposmia* and *Protosmia* are not included here as they are primarily found in the West.

Major characters that differ between species of Osmiini					
	Ashmeadiella	*Chelostoma*	*Heriades*	*Hoplitis*	*Osmia*
Parapsidal line	Long and linear	Long and linear	Long and linear	Long and linear	Shortened, dotlike
T6 in males	With 4 strong teeth	Rounded	Rounded	2 teeth, one on either side of center	Rounded
Scutum shape, tegula position	Rounded, tegula on anterior half of scutum	Very elongated, tegula midway down scutum	Rounded, tegula on anterior half of scutum	Rounded, tegula on anterior half of scutum	Rounded, tegula on anterior half of scutum
Abdomen shape	Rounded	Elongated but does not curl notably	Elongated and often curled under in males	Rounded	Rounded
Body color	Black, may have red abdomen	Black	Black	Metallic or black	Metallic or black
Anterior surface of T1	Slightly concave, no carina	Flat	Concave, with carina	Flat	Slightly concave, no carina

ASHMEADIELLA

— **SUBFAMILY:** Megachilinae
— **TRIBE:** Osmiini

OVERVIEW: Small compact black bees, typically seen in late spring and summer. Many are specialists, especially on Asteraceae, but generalists also occur. Nests are made in wood or stems, in burrows in the ground, or under rocks. These bees are occasional inhabitants of bee hotels.

IN THE WORLD: *Ashmeadiella* occur only in the Americas, and there are 57 species ranging from Costa Rica north to southern Canada. About 50 species can be found north of the Mexican border; only 2 occur east of the Mississippi River and both are uncommon.

CLEPTOPARASITES: *Stelis*.

IDENTIFYING FEATURES: Small to medium-sized bees, usually matte-black, but occasionally with red on the abdomen, and with strong punctation throughout. The body segments are rounded, not flattened, giving a stocky appearance when viewed from the side. **HEAD:** Face is longer than wide, and also thick, with a broad gena (cheek) behind the compound eyes. In males, there are four even teeth on the mandible. In females, the mandible has three teeth. **THORAX:** There is a sharp edge separating the forward and lateral faces of the side of the thorax (known as the omaulus). **WINGS:** Two submarginal cells. **LEGS:** On the foreleg there is an arolium between the tarsal claws. **ABDOMEN:** Males have four pointed teeth on T6, underneath which T7 is usually hidden. In both males and females there are thin white hair bands running across the apical margin of each tergal segment, and T1 is concave, clearly defined from the dorsal surface of T1. In females, pollen-collecting hairs are on the underside of the abdomen. In many species, the abdomen either is all red or has red segments.

SIMILAR GENERA: *Chelostoma* and *Heriades* are Osmiini with an overall similar appearance. The scutum of *Chelostoma* is significantly longer, and the abdomen of *Heriades* tends to curl under, a characteristic not seen in *Ashmeadiella*.

— *Ashmeadiella bucconis*

SIZE: Small; 6–10 mm. **PHENOLOGY:** May through August. **FLORAL HOSTS:** Specialist on Asteraceae, with a preference for *Helianthus*. **RANGE:** Mostly a western species, but is seen in the Midwest, south to Georgia. **NESTING:** Nests in small hollow twigs, in which it creates nest partitions with masticated leaf material. **IDENTIFICATION:** Completely matte-black, coarsely pitted integument, with little in the way of hair. Overall, the body appears long. **HEAD:** The gena is very pronounced, being as

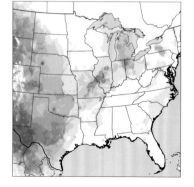

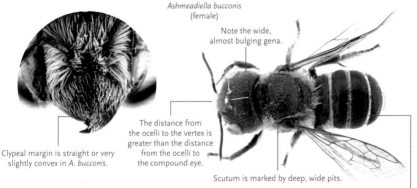

Ashmeadiella bucconis
(female)

Note the wide, almost bulging gena.

Clypeal margin is straight or very slightly convex in *A. bucconis.*

The distance from the ocelli to the vertex is greater than the distance from the ocelli to the compound eye.

Scutum is marked by deep, wide pits.

thick as, if not thicker than, the width of the compound eye. The ocelli are closer to the compound eyes than to the vertex. In males, the mandible has two teeth. In females, the clypeus is relatively short, and the lower margin is a straight, to very slightly convex, line. **THORAX:** Scutum is covered in wide, deep punctation. **ABDOMEN:** T6 in males has two small rounded teeth on either side of the center. See characteristics of the genus for more.

Ashmeadiella bucconis
(female)

Narrow hair bands run across the apical margin of each tergal segment.

In *Ashmeadiella*, the change between the lateral and forward faces of the side of the thorax are marked by a sharp edge, especially ventrally.

Each segment has a thin but complete band of white hair.

Between the front claws of *Ashmeadiella* is an arolium.

Ashmeadiella bucconis
(male)

All male *Ashmeadiella* have teeth on T6, those of *A. bucconis* are particularly small.

SIMILAR SPECIES: *Ashmeadiella bucconis* is the most widespread of the two species in the East, but overlaps in North Carolina and Georgia. In females of *A. floridana* the clypeus is gently concave, as opposed to the straight rim seen in *A. bucconis.* Also in *A. floridana,* the head is not as thick, with the width of the gena less than the width of the compound eye. Finally, *A. bucconis* is much rarer than *A. floridana* in the lower Atlantic states, while *A. bucconis* is more common to the north.

CHELOSTOMA

— **SUBFAMILY:** Megachilinae
— **TRIBE:** Osmiini

OVERVIEW: Long-bodied bees, petite with cylindrical bodies. Bees are small, spring to summer fliers. Most appear to be specialists, but pollen preferences are unknown for many species. *Chelostoma* nest in cavities, usually small beetle burrows in trees, but may also nest in hollow twigs, nail holes, or other preexisting holes.
CLEPTOPARASITES: *Stelis.*
IN THE WORLD: *Chelostoma* occur widely throughout the Northern Hemisphere, with more than 50 species. In North America there are 11 species, 3 of which are found in eastern North America and Canada. Two are native to Europe and are relatively recent introductions to North America.
IDENTIFYING FEATURES: Small slender bee, matte-black with only minimal white hair.
HEAD: In females, the mandible can have two, three, or four teeth (eastern species have three). **THORAX:** The distance between the tegulae is less than the length of the thorax; a line drawn between the anterior margins of the tegulae is in the posterior half of the scutum. A long parapsidal line is visible. The propodeum is normally pitted, with no row of strong pits running across the posterior end. The sides of the thorax run smoothly from the forward face to the sides. **WINGS:** Two submarginal cells. **LEGS:** There is an arolium between the tarsal claws. **ABDOMEN:** T1 does not have a carina separating the anterior and dorsal faces. In males, T6 does not have four distinct teeth along the apical margin, though there may be teeth on T7. In females, pollen-collecting hairs are on the underside of the abdomen.
SIMILAR GENERA: *Hylaeus* individuals are a similar color and size and also have long bodies, but *Chelostoma* lack the yellow markings so prevalent in *Hylaeus. Ashmeadiella, Heriades,* and *Hoplitis* are in the same tribe (Osmiini), so share a similar overall body shape. Of the four, *Chelostoma* exhibit the longest, narrowest thorax. *Heriades* and *Hoplitis* often have light hair bands on the abdomen, which are less common in North American *Chelostoma.* The abdomens of *Heriades* tend to curl under, while *Chelostoma* do not. *Ashmeadiella* males have teeth on T6 that characterize them, and both male and female *Ashmeadiella* have a strong carina separating fore and lateral faces of the side of the thorax.

— *Chelostoma philadelphi*

SIZE: Small; 6–8 mm. **PHENOLOGY:** March through July. **FLORAL HOSTS:** Specialist on mock orange (*Philadelphus*). **RANGE:** Southern Ontario south to Georgia, and including all of the Eastern Seaboard. West as far as Kansas. **NESTING:** Nests in small holes in wood, usually old beetle burrows.
IDENTIFICATION: Small lightly polished black bees with a long face and slightly converging eyes. **HEAD:** In females, the clypeus is broad with mandibles that have three teeth. The mandible is very long, more than three-quarters the length of the compound eye. The antennal sockets are very close together. In males, mandibles have

two teeth. **THORAX:** Pits are small but distinctive. At the posterior end of the thorax, the face that drops to connect with the abdomen (the propodeal triangle) is dull, not shiny at all. The legs are black, with slender tarsus, and covered in short, thin, white hairs. **ABDOMEN:** Very thin and sparse hair bands may run apically across each segment; these are often absent or present only on the sides so that the abdomen appears black. In males T7 has a series of teeth; the middle two are fairly pointed, and the outermost teeth are shorter and rounded. Also in males, S2 appears swollen.

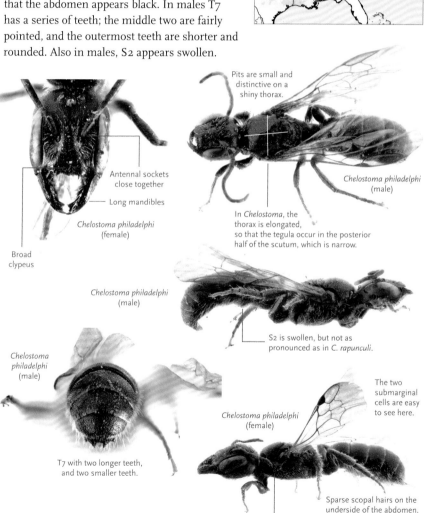

Pits are small and distinctive on a shiny thorax.

Antennal sockets close together

Long mandibles

Chelostoma philadelphi
(female)

Broad clypeus

Chelostoma philadelphi
(male)

Chelostoma philadelphi
(male)

In *Chelostoma*, the thorax is elongated, so that the tegula occur in the posterior half of the scutum, which is narrow.

S2 is swollen, but not as pronounced as in *C. rapunculi*.

Chelostoma philadelphi
(male)

The two submarginal cells are easy to see here.

Chelostoma philadelphi
(female)

T7 with two longer teeth, and two smaller teeth.

Sparse scopal hairs on the underside of the abdomen.

No strong carina separating the fore and lateral faces of the thorax.

SIMILAR SPECIES: Two other species of *Chelostoma* occur in the East. Both are introduced species from Europe. The host plant may help: both invasive species are specialists on *Campanula*. Morphologically, *C. rapunculi* is the easiest to distinguish from *C. philadelphi*: Females have thick white hair bands running across the first four tergal segments; these may become worn in the center, but are usually visible on the sides. On the head, the antennal sockets are widely spaced. The back of the head turns down abruptly, creating a strong ridge along the back edge. And the mandible is shorter. Finally, the propodeal triangle, at the back of the thorax, is very shiny. In males T7 does not have four teeth, but is flattened into three broad sections. Ventrally, S2 has a large protuberance that stands out notably, rather than the subtle bump seen in *C. philadelphi*. *Chelostoma campanularum* is more similar to *C. philadelphi*. In females, the mandible is short, less than three-quarters the length of the compound eye. On the thorax, the propodeal triangle is shiny. In males, T7 has just two long teeth, one on either side of the center of the segment.

HERIADES

— **SUBFAMILY:** Megachilinae
— **TRIBE:** Osmiini

OVERVIEW: Petite, cigar-shaped black bees, easily overlooked as they visit flowers in the summer. Includes both generalist and specialist species. Nest in very small preexisting cavities, usually in wood (one western species reported in pine cones). Nest cells are usually separated from each other by resin.

IN THE WORLD: Worldwide there are around 140 species, found in North America, Europe, Asia, and Africa. Eleven species occur in North America. In the East, just 2 species are common, though 2 others occur occasionally; among the rare ones is an introduced species from Europe.

CLEPTOPARASITES: *Stelis, Coelioxys*.

IDENTIFYING FEATURES: Small, rather long dark bee with thin white stripes of hair on the abdomen.

HEAD: Appears slightly longer than wide and is often thick. **THORAX:** The pits are large and deep, giving the bee a roughened appearance. There is a distinct row of square pits that makes up the dorsal surface of the propodeum.

WINGS: Two submarginal cells.

LEGS: There is an arolium.

ABDOMEN: First tergal segment is concave, forming a deep cavity that is lined by a strong ridge. From above, each section of the abdomen appears to constrict at the apical end, giving the sides of the abdomen a wavy look. In females, pollen-collecting

Heriades have a strong carina that runs around the anterior face of T1.

hairs are on the abdomen. Most distinctive, the abdomen curls under, forming a comma shape; this is especially evident in dead male specimens.

SIMILAR GENERA: Some of the other small Osmiini look similar. *Heriades* has a concave face to the front of T1 that is missing from other Osmiini. Also, while *Chelostoma* has a long body like *Heriades,* the abdomen differs significantly between the two. The abdomen of *Heriades* constricts after each segment, while that of *Chelostoma* does not. The abdomen of *Chelostoma* also doesn't curl under, nor does it have white stripes as predominantly across the abdomen. *Hoplitis* tends to be shinier and more polished and lacks the concave section on T1. Small *Megachile* may look similar, but the waviness on the sides of the abdomen in *Heriades* should separate it. Also, *Megachile* lack an arolium, which is found in *Heriades* individuals.

— *Heriades carinata*

SIZE: Small; 7–9 mm. **PHENOLOGY:** May through August. **FLORAL HOSTS:** Polylectic, visiting a wide array of flowering plants. **RANGE:** Georgia north to southern Quebec and Maine, west to Washington and Arizona. **NESTING:** Solitary cavity nester, usually in twigs, especially sumac (*Rhus*), but also small holes or cracks in wood logs. **IDENTIFICATION:** Small black bee with very light white stripes running across the abdomen. **HEAD:** Relatively thick; when viewed from the top the distance from the lateral ocelli to the back of the head is greater than the distance between the ocelli. In females, on the head, the clypeus has small projections (tubercles) at the sides. These are swollen to about half the size of the ocelli. The mandible is very square, with only one large

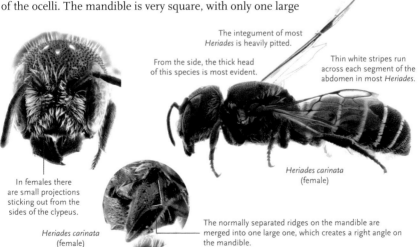

The integument of most *Heriades* is heavily pitted.

From the side, the thick head of this species is most evident.

Thin white stripes run across each segment of the abdomen in most *Heriades.*

Heriades carinata
(female)

In females there are small projections sticking out from the sides of the clypeus.

Heriades carinata
(female)

The normally separated ridges on the mandible are merged into one large one, which creates a right angle on the mandible.

This species has an especially thick head, as evidenced by the distance from the ocelli to the back of the head.

Male *Heriades* abdomens curl under very distinctively.

ridge running its length. **ABDOMEN:** In males the underside of the abdomen has a strong projection on the first sternal segment.

SIMILAR SPECIES: There are two other native eastern *Heriades* that may occasionally be seen, though *H. carinatus* is the most widespread. In males, *Heriades leavitti* and *H. variolosa* lack the projection on T1, having instead a low small bump. In females, the mandible shape is distinctive in *H. carinatus* because the normally separate ridges merge into one large one. Also, no other eastern *Heriades* have swollen projections on the sides of the clypeus as *H. carinatus* does. *Heriades truncorum* is a non-native European species that has apparently been seen only a few times in the East.

The mandible of *H. variolosa* is not nearly as dramatically angled as that of *H. carinata*.

HOPLITIS

— **SUBFAMILY: Megachilinae**
— **TRIBE: Osmiini**

OVERVIEW: Black, medium-sized bees, often with a fuzzy thorax, seen in the spring. Typically found at higher elevations where other bees drop out, but plenty of low elevation species occur too. Include generalists and specialists. *Hoplitis* nesting habits are diverse, with species nesting in preexisting cavities in wood, in twigs, in the ground, or even in external nests made of pebbles and mortar stuck to the surface of larger rocks. May nest in aggregations.

IN THE WORLD: There are around 360 species around the world, occurring in Africa, Europe, Asia, and even Malaysia, but not in Australia or South America. In North America there are around 60 species, with 10 in the East. One North American species is introduced (*Hoplitis anthocopoides*).

CLEPTOPARASITES: *Stelis, Dioxys* (not in this book).

IDENTIFYING FEATURES: Medium-sized shinier black bee (green species in the West) with modest white hairs on abdomen and thorax. **HEAD:** In males, the final segment of the antennae is hooked, or tapers to a very thin point. **THORAX:** Parapsidal lines are long lines, instead of small points. The scutum is wide, with the distance between the tegulae greater than the scutal length. **WINGS:** Two submarginal cells. Stigma longer than it is wide. **LEGS:** There is an arolia between the tarsal claws. **ABDOMEN:** T1 is flat, without a notable concavity. Short white hairs line each tergal segment. Pits on the abdomen are small and widely spaced. At the end, the abdomen tapers gently to a point rather than abruptly ending. In females, pollen-collecting hairs are on the underside of the abdomen. In males, S6 has a pair of translucent, thin, hairless flaps that emerge from the base. These are unique to *Hoplitis*. Also in males, T6 usually has a tooth at either side. Though these characters are hard to see in individuals on flowers, they are very distinctive.

SIMILAR GENERA: *Hoplitis* look most similar to *Osmia,* and the most distinguishing feature is the parapsidal line, which is only a small dot in *Osmia* but a long line (more typical in bees) in *Hoplitis*. *Heriades* are similar in coloring and size to eastern *Hoplitis*, but the front of the abdomen is not concave in *Hoplitis* as it is in *Heriades,* and there are no strong punctations associated with the posterior edge of the propodeum in *Hoplitis*. *Heriades* are more common in the summer, while *Hoplitis* are earlier in the year.

In general, *Hoplitis* can be difficult to distinguish from each other. We have included three species here that are commonly seen, but there are seven other species in the East, and the differences between them are variable, and minute.

— *Hoplitis pilosifrons*

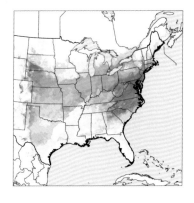

SIZE: Small; 6–8 mm. **PHENOLOGY:** Early April through July. **FLORAL HOSTS:** Polylectic, visiting a wide array of flowering plants. **RANGE:** Widespread east of the Rocky Mountains, north to Nova Scotia, southern Manitoba, and central Saskatchewan provinces. **NESTING:** Solitary, nests in hollow stems, including *Helianthus* (sunflowers); nest cells are partitioned using masticated leaf material. **IDENTIFICATION:** All-black small-sized bee, with white hair bands. **HEAD:** In females, the head is long. The clypeus has a distinct rim that flips out from the plane of the clypeus. At its center, the clypeus is notched. In males, the antennae end in a very fine point. **THORAX:** The tegulae are shiny. Pits on the scutum are fine, shallow, and not well defined. Fine, short, white hair lines the scutum and other segments of the thorax. **ABDOMEN:** In females, white hair bands fade in the middle of T1 and T2, but are more complete on T3 and T4. In males, there is a large rounded projection on the second sternal segment. Additionally, the apex of S3 is hard to see, as it is covered by a thick

Hair bands on T1 and T2 are interrupted in the middle, but T3 is complete.

Hoplitis pilosifrons
(female)

Small projections occur at the lateral edge of the clypeus.

The clypeus is notched at the center in females.

The tip of the antenna is drawn to a narrow point.

There are tiny teeth on the sides of T6 in all *Hoplitis*.

Projection on S2 is rounded.

Hoplitis pilosifrons
(female)

The 7th tergal segment is long and draws to a point in this species. The sides are parallel.

fringe of hair, which gets thicker in the center. Finally, T7 has a large fingerlike projection in the center that is parallel-sided.

SIMILAR SPECIES: *Hoplitis pilosifrons* and *H. producta* look very similar to each other. Females can be almost impossible to distinguish. In males, the shape of the bulge on S2 differs between the two species. In *H. pilosifrons* it is less pronounced. In addition, the shape of the projection on T7 differs. In *H. pilosifrons* the projection has long parallel sides, as opposed to the triangle shape seen in *H. producta*.

— *Hoplitis producta*

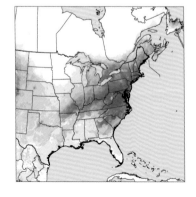

SIZE: Small; 6–8 mm. **PHENOLOGY:** Mid-April through July. **FLORAL HOSTS:** Polylectic, visiting a wide array of flowering plants.
RANGE: Widespread east of the Rocky Mountains; absent from Florida and Gulf regions. North to central Quebec and southern Manitoba.
NESTING: Solitary, nests in hollow stems, including elder, sumac, and rose.
IDENTIFICATION: All-black small-sized bee, with white hair bands. **HEAD:** In females, the head is

The hair bands on T1–T3 are all interrupted.

In females, the clypeus is gently curving, but not notched.

Hoplitis producta (female)

Hoplitis producta (male)

S2 has a strong, sharp projection on it.

The tips of the male antennae are flattened and very slightly curled.

The tip of T7 is a triangular point.

Projections to either side of T6

as long as wide. The clypeus has a distinct rim that flips out. At its center, the clypeus is gently concave, but not notched. In males, the antennae taper to a fine point that hooks slightly. **THORAX:** Pits are deep, and distinct, but the space in between is shiny. **ABDOMEN:** Thick white hair bands run across all of the tergal segments, though they are interrupted on T1–T3. Seventh tergal segment has a large projection in the center, shaped like a very narrow isosceles triangle. On S2, there is a large pointed projection, steeply angled on both sides.

SIMILAR SPECIES: See *Hoplitis pilosifrons*.

— *Hoplitis truncata*

SIZE: Small to medium; 8–10 mm.
PHENOLOGY: April through early July
(March in Florida). **FLORAL HOSTS:** Polylectic,
visiting a wide array of spring flowering plants.
RANGE: Kansas and North Dakota east to Maine
and south to Florida. Some records in southern
Ontario. **NESTING:** Solitary, nests in hollow stems.
IDENTIFICATION: Medium-sized black bee with
white stripes running across the abdomen, and
short white hair throughout. Not shiny, with heavy
punctation on the head, thorax, and abdomen.

HEAD: In females, the clypeus is heavily pitted, but the pits are distinct from each other. In the center there is usually a line that is without punctation. The mandibles have three distinct teeth. In males, the final flagellomere is strongly hooked. **THORAX:** The scutum has two sizes of pits: Large ones, and smaller ones that are about four-fifths the size of the larger. **ABDOMEN:** In females, scopal hairs are white. In males, on the abdomen, T7 is squared off, and not at all pointy. T6 is clearly visible, not obscured by hairs.

SIMILAR SPECIES: *Hoplitis truncata* looks similar to *H. simplex;* between the two, *H. truncata* is slightly bigger. *Hoplitis simplex* lacks the impunctate line running down the center of the clypeus in females, and all punctation on the thorax and abdomen is of one size.

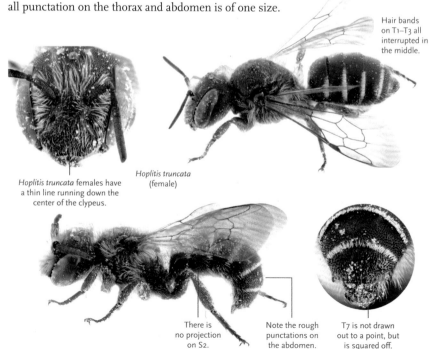

Hair bands on T1–T3 all interrupted in the middle.

Hoplitis truncata females have a thin line running down the center of the clypeus.

Hoplitis truncata (female)

There is no projection on S2.

Note the rough punctations on the abdomen.

T7 is not drawn out to a point, but is squared off.

OSMIA

— **SUBFAMILY:** Megachilinae
— **TRIBE:** Osmiini

OVERVIEW: Often boldly metallic-colored, easy-to-see bees that fly mostly in the early spring (many overwinter as adults, needing little time to complete development when temperatures warm in the spring). Range from solid black to shining metallic green or blue, but usually with long hairs on the thorax that may be white or black. Appearance is generally of rounded body parts. Many are generalists, but also include specialists with hosts in a diverse array of plant families. Because they fly early, many generalist species are managed as pollinators of fruit trees, including apples, cherries, and almonds. They have also been used in pollinating blueberries. As a result of their effectiveness as commercial pollinators, there are several non-native species in the U.S., imported from Asia. Nesting biology is not known for all species, but it is known that some species nest in the ground, while others nest in plant stems, or holes in wood. Nests are often sealed with a pat of mud or masticated leaf material. All species are solitary, but they may nest gregariously.

IN THE WORLD: More than 350 species can be found worldwide; around 145 species occur in North America, with 32 species occurring in the East. Three of these are not native (one of which is not covered here: *O. caerulescens*).

CLEPTOPARASITES: *Stelis.*

IDENTIFYING FEATURES: Medium-sized, often metallic bees, with rounded thorax and rounded abdomen. May be black or metallic green or blue, but are never red or yellow. Females are slightly bigger than males, and males have long, skinny antennae. **HEAD:** Mandibles are usually robust, especially in females, and may have extra protrusions or modified structures presumed to be used in nest construction. The face may also have small "horns" or other projections; note there are other bee genera that may have facial modifications as well. **THORAX:** In the place of parapsidal lines seen in most bees, and certainly North American Osmiini, are small indentations; there is no long groove. **WINGS:** Two submarginal cells. **ABDOMEN:** No pygidial plate. Scopal hairs are on the underside of the abdomen in females. In males, the apical margin of T6 is usually smooth, with no teeth, notches, or lobes.

SIMILAR GENERA: *Hoplitis* are the most similar-looking bees to *Osmia* in North America, and several subgenera have been moved between the two genera over the last 100 years. In general, *Osmia* have shorter bodies. The parapsidal line on the thorax is long and linear in *Hoplitis,* while short, almost dotlike in *Osmia. Hoplitis* males tend to have more interesting tips on their antennae: clubs, points, hooks, etc. And S6 in *Hoplitis* has basal, hairless flaps that are not seen in *Osmia.*

Identifying male *Osmia* to species is very difficult, relying on subjective characters that are best assessed when looking at multiple specimens at once, for comparison. Many of the characters are associated with the size, density, and general character of the punctation, while others are associated with the shape of the propodeal pit (between the abdomen and thorax). Females are in general easier, but many characters are nuanced. The shape and presence of ridges on the underside of the head are diagnostic. We include five commonly seen *Osmia* species here, but there are many others that should be considered as candidates when a positive identification is required.

— Osmia bucephala

SIZE: Medium to large; 13–16 mm.
PHENOLOGY: Early April through May. **FLORAL HOSTS:** Visits numerous flowering plants, but may have a preference for Asteraceae. **RANGE:** Widespread throughout North America, occurring as far north as the Northwest Territories and Alaska. Not found in Florida or Gulf states. **NESTING:** Nests in cavities in wood. Caps nest with a conglomerate of "sawdust" and leaf material.

IDENTIFICATION: Larger species, with very light metallic-blue shine to a dark body and a large, thick head. **HEAD:** The clypeus bulges out along its apex, appearing swollen. The head is twice as thick as the width of the eyes. On the mandible, just before it meets the malar space, there is a deep groove. **THORAX:** Punctation is fine and dense. Females have straw-colored hair covering the thorax, while males have white to straw-colored hair. **LEGS:** In males, the midtarsal segments are flattened and greatly expanded and the inner hind tibial spurs are much enlarged. **ABDOMEN:** In males, the sides of the apex of T5 and T6 flare out. In females, scopal hairs are black.

Osmia bucephala (female)

Notice how thick the gena is, thicker than the width of the compound eye.

Fine, dense punctation

O. bucephala is very lightly metallic blue.

Inner hind tibial spur is very large.

Hair on the male is white, while on the female it is yellower.

Osmia bucephala (male)

The tarsal segments on the male are flattened and very wide.

There is a thin margin that is impunctate at the apex of each tergal segment.

The light blue highlights are evident on the face here.

There is a deep groove on the mandible just before it meets the malar space.

Osmia bucephala (female)

SIMILAR SPECIES: Similar in color and general vestiture to *Osmia nigriventris*, which is less common, but overlaps the range of *O. bucephala*. *Osmia nigriventris* is completely black, without the slight metallic sheen seen in *O. bucephala*. While both species have thick heads, *O. bucephala* is slightly thicker. *Osmia bucephala* also has more malar space between the bottom of the eye and the beginning of the mandible than does *O. nigriventris*.

— Osmia cornifrons

SIZE: Small to medium; 8–11 mm.
PHENOLOGY: March through June.
FLORAL HOSTS: Generalist, but common on Rosaceae (*Malus, Prunus,* and *Rubus*), but also seen on Ericaceae. **RANGE:** Native to Asia. Introduced to North America in order to pollinate early-blooming fruit trees. Now occurs from Maine south to Georgia and east to Iowa, with isolated populations on the West Coast.
NESTING: Nests in open cavities, especially dead wood, and common inhabitant of "bee hotels."

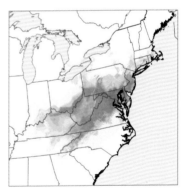

IDENTIFICATION: Smaller *Osmia* with dark integument and a very slight coppery sheen under thin honey-colored hair on thorax and abdomen. **HEAD:** In females, two large spinelike projections are obvious, protruding from the sides of the clypeus; between them, on the apical rim of the clypeus is a small pointy projection. Also in females the clypeus is smooth, lacking punctation on its lower half, but densely punctate on the upper half. The face is hairy, with hair descending as far as the tops of the horns. Female mandibles have four teeth, none of which are very pronounced, and the innermost one is curved in so it is not easily seen. Males have no "horns" on the face. The clypeus has irregular notches in the middle. In males, the first flagellar segment is shorter than the second. **THORAX:** Punctation is dense and fine. In males, the propodeal pit is shaped like a long rectangle, with parallel sides, and some width (not a narrow line). **ABDOMEN:** In females, the scopae are light yellow or orange to tan (not

Males have light straw-colored to white hair.

Osmia cornifrons (male)

The puncture marks extend across the entire length of each tergal segment — there is no polished rim. This is especially evident on T2.

Even from above, the "horns" on the face are visible.

Osmia cornifrons (female)

The four teeth are visible here; note that none of them sticks out very far. The fourth one curves in and is harder to see.

Light straw-colored hair covers the body of *O. cornifrons*.

white or off-white). Each tergal segment is covered in long hairs in females, light yellow on T1–T3, dark brown on T4–T6. In males, the apical margin shows a thin band of white hair, and on T2 pits extend all the way to the apical margin of the segment.

SIMILAR SPECIES: *Osmia cornifrons* and *O. taurus* are the only *Osmia* species found in the East with large projections extruding from the clypeus. They can be difficult to distinguish (so much so that it led to the accidental introduction of *O. taurus* to the U.S.). Females of *O. taurus* do not have dense punctations on the upper (basal) half of the clypeus. Females of *O. taurus* lack the thick hair running across each tergal segment. There may be a small amount of hair; it does not obscure the body below. In males, *O. taurus* is redder on the abdomen than *O. cornifrons*. In dead older specimens, this character fades.

— *Osmia lignaria*

SIZE: Small to medium; 9–11 mm.
PHENOLOGY: March through June.
FLORAL HOSTS: Generalist, visiting a wide array of plants for pollen. **RANGE:** Widespread across North America. **NESTING:** Nests in preexisting cavities in wood or pithy plant stems; has also been seen nesting in old *Xylocopa* nests, narrow crevices, and abandoned nests of mud or paper wasps. Individual nest cells are partitioned using mud dividers and completed nests are capped with mud. In many areas, these are common inhabitants of "bee hotels."
IDENTIFICATION: Deep metallic blue-green species, with mostly light-colored hair on thorax and first one or two segments of the abdomen.
HEAD: In females, the clypeus has a deep and wide notch right in the middle, and the malar space is swollen into a projection. The clypeus has some punctation, wide pits that do not touch

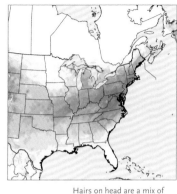

Hairs on head are a mix of white and some black.

Osmia lignaria (female)

Hair on the thorax and abdomen is mostly white, with some black interspersed.

Deep blue-green color

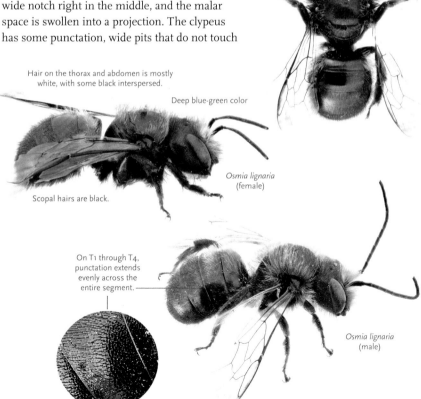

Scopal hairs are black.

Osmia lignaria (female)

On T1 through T4, punctation extends evenly across the entire segment.

Osmia lignaria (male)

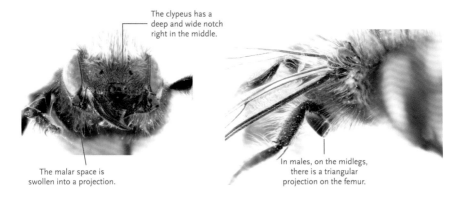

The clypeus has a deep and wide notch right in the middle.

The malar space is swollen into a projection.

In males, on the midlegs, there is a triangular projection on the femur.

each other. The head is slightly thickened, with the gena almost twice as wide as the eye. On the face is a mix of white and black hair, with more dark hair near the vertex. **THORAX:** Deep wide pits occur. **LEGS:** In males, on the midlegs, there is a triangular projection on the femur. Also in males, the hind basitarsus has a tooth. **ABDOMEN:** In both sexes, there are no apical hair bands. In females, scopal hairs are black. **SIMILAR SPECIES:** The blue-green color and the malar space projections are unique to *O. lignaria,* and make females easy to identify. In males the unique triangular projection on the midfemur is also helpful. There are two subspecies of *O. lignaria. Osmia lignaria lignaria* has tridentate mandibles, and short horns to either side of the clypeus (in addition to the projections on the malar space). *Osmia lignaria propinqua* has four teeth, though these are difficult to see. Males are difficult to distinguish.

— *Osmia pumila*

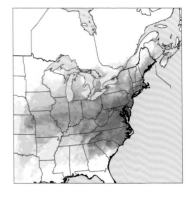

SIZE: Small; 7–8 mm. **PHENOLOGY:** March through June. **FLORAL HOSTS:** Generalist, but preference for Rosaceae and Fabaceae. **RANGE:** Texas north through Nebraska to Manitoba, east to the Atlantic coast, absent from Florida and the Gulf Coast. **NESTING:** Holes in wood or hollow plant stems. Holes are plugged with leaf material.

IDENTIFICATION: Small metallic aquamarine bee with sparse white hairs on thorax and abdomen. One of the smallest *Osmia* in the East. **HEAD:** In females, the apical margin of the clypeus is very slightly concave or may even be entirely straight. There are no teeth or other projections on the face. On the mandible, the distance between the first two teeth is greater than the distance between the second two. **THORAX:** Hair is yellow to white, long, but not hiding the surface. **ABDOMEN:** Each of the tergal segments has pits that extend all the way to the posterior edge of the segment. The anterior face of T1 (facing the thorax) is roughened and dull, with tiny lines. There are no distinct hair bands on any of the tergal segments.

No shiny impunctate bands on the ends of the tergal segments

This surface is roughened and dull on *Osmia pumila*.

White scopal hairs

Osmia pumila (female)

This is probably the smallest *Osmia* in eastern North America.

The abdomen is heavily pitted.

Osmia pumila (male)

Osmia pumila (female)

In females, scopal hairs are white, with some dark hair on the fifth sternal segment. In males, there is a small notch at the center of T6.

SIMILAR SPECIES: Can be very difficult to distinguish *O. albiventris* females from *O. pumila* females. *Osmia pumila* is slightly smaller than *O. albiventris*. On T3, the punctations at the center fade and become sparse in *O. albiventris*, while there is no change in the punctation across the surface of T3 in *O. pumila*.

— *Osmia taurus*

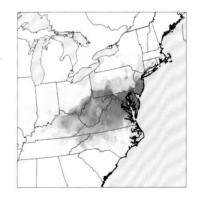

SIZE: Small to medium; 9–12 mm.
PHENOLOGY: March through May.
FLORAL HOSTS: Generalists, with some preference for Rosaceae, but also visit Fabaceae, Brassicaceae, and others. **RANGE:** Southeastern Canada (Ontario, Quebec) south through Georgia, west to Illinois. **NESTING:** Cavity nesting in wood or hollow twigs.
IDENTIFICATION: Small to medium bee with abundant blonde or auburn hair. Integument is dark, but may have a slight green hue. **HEAD:** In females, there are two protrusions from either side; the center is arced upward, and the base is smooth with few punctations. Face is hairy. Mandibles are large with four teeth; the innermost is truncate and hard to see. **THORAX:** Hair is a light orange and is

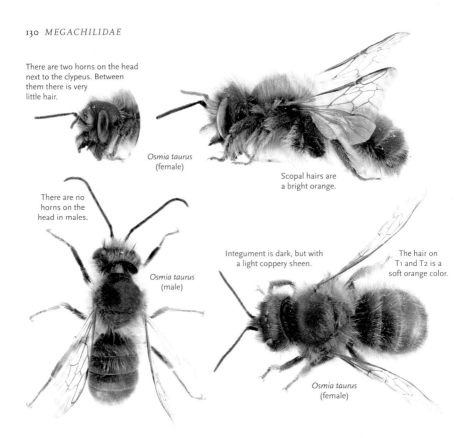

There are two horns on the head next to the clypeus. Between them there is very little hair.

Osmia taurus (female)

Scopal hairs are a bright orange.

There are no horns on the head in males.

Osmia taurus (male)

Integument is dark, but with a light coppery sheen.

The hair on T1 and T2 is a soft orange color.

Osmia taurus (female)

thick, extending to the first several sections of the abdomen. **LEGS:** On the tibia and femur light reddish hair is also visible. **ABDOMEN:** Punctation covers each tergal segment, extending from base to apex of each. In females, scopal hairs are yellow-orange. **SIMILAR SPECIES:** For females, only *Osmia cornifrons* and *O. taurus* have large horn-like projections extruding from the head. For these two, *O. cornifrons* has more punctation on the basal half of the clypeus. Overall, *O. taurus* is redder than *O. cornifrons,* for both males and females. In general, males of the two can be hard to distinguish.

COELIOXYS

— **SUBFAMILY:** Megachilinae
— **TRIBE:** Megachilini

OVERVIEW: *Coelioxys* are not common, but striking when seen, because of their black-and-white markings and distinctive body shape, which features a very pointed abdomen. *Coelioxys* are cleptoparasites of *Megachile* and are mostly associated with wood- or twig-nesting species. In most cases, a female visits a nest while the host bee is away. She uses her pointed abdomen to make an incision in the leaf-lining of a completed nest cell, and then inserts an egg through the opening.

IN THE WORLD: Worldwide there are 500 species, found on every continent. In the U.S. and Canada there are 46 species, with around 25 occurring east of the Mississippi River. Distinguishing between species of *Coelioxys* is difficult, involving minute characters that grade into each other. We highlight one common, easily identified species here.

PARASITIZES: *Megachile.*

IDENTIFYING FEATURES: Stout bees with a thickened exoskeleton and hair only in thick white patches that stand out starkly on the matte-black thorax and abdomen. **HEAD:** The compound eyes are covered with minute hairs. **THORAX:** The lateral plates behind the scutum (axilla) are extended into points that hang out over the scutellum, and perhaps to the propodeum. **WINGS:** Often a dusky gray. Two submarginal cells. **ABDOMEN:** Extremely pointed abdomen, in which the sixth sternal segment is elongated, almost beyond the length of the final visible tergal segments; in males, there may also be four to eight teeth or spines. First tergal segment has a sharp concavity on the side that faces the thorax, delineated by a sharp ridge. A few species are red on the first few segments of the abdomen, and some have red legs.

SIMILAR GENERA: Few genera resemble *Coelioxys*; the pointed abdomen is very distinct, as are the acute axilla. *Dioxys* (not covered in this book) may appear somewhat similar in the matted hair and red legs. The abdomen on *Dioxys* does not taper as notably, and the axilla are not pointed.

— *Coelioxys sayi*

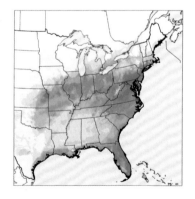

SIZE: Medium; 10–12 mm.
PHENOLOGY: Late May through October. **FLORAL HOSTS:** As cleptoparasites, they do not visit flowers for pollen. They can be found collecting nectar from a wide array of flowering species. **RANGE:** Florida north to southern Quebec and Ontario, west to California. **NESTING:** Parasitizes *Megachile.*
IDENTIFICATION: Moderately sized black bee with tarsi and tibiae that are often reddish (though may be brown or black). **HEAD:** In females, the clypeus is thickened at the apical margin, which is not flat, but arcs inward at the center, creating two modest lobes on either side. The mandibles are covered with short dense hair for more than half the base. **THORAX:** The axillae, which are long in some species, are shortened here, barely exceeding the margin of the scutellum. **ABDOMEN:** Thick white bands of hair cover the apical margin of each tergal segment. In males, on the abdomen, T5 has well-separated pits that do not touch. T3 has a groove running across the middle that becomes shallow and disappears toward the middle. **SIMILAR SPECIES:** *Coelioxys sayi* individuals can be very difficult to distinguish from *C. octodentatus.* In males, the groove running across T3 is complete, and deep for its entire length in *C. octodentatus*, but not in *C. sayi.* In general *C. octodentatus* has more

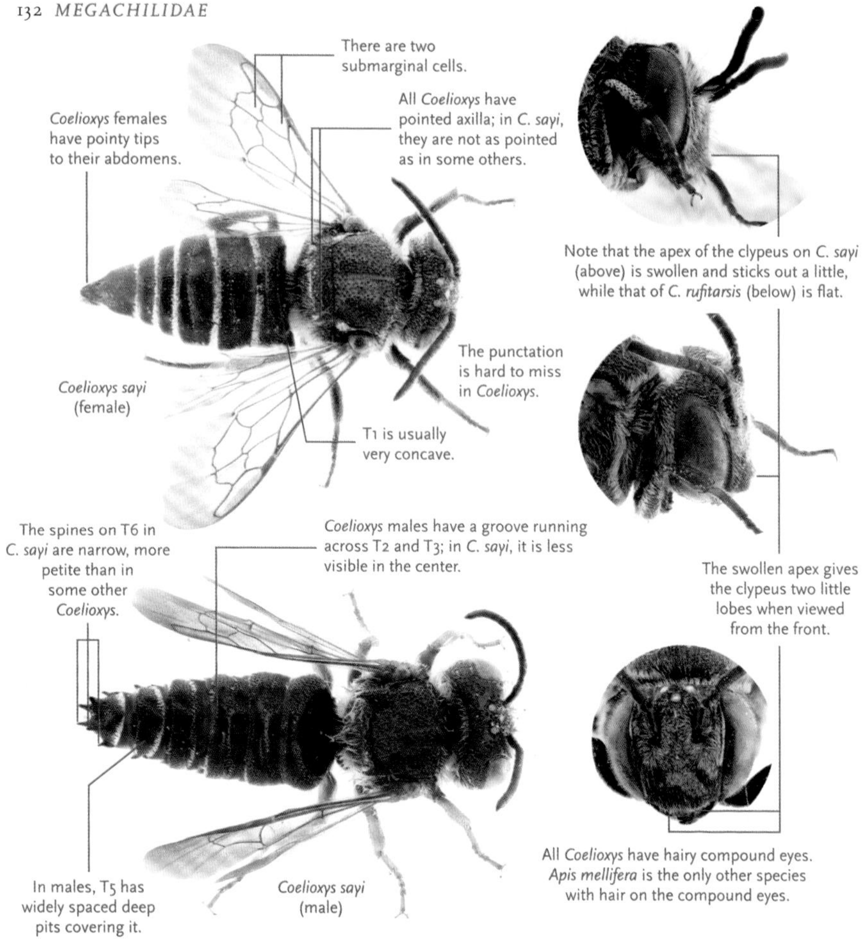

There are two submarginal cells.

Coelioxys females have pointy tips to their abdomens.

All *Coelioxys* have pointed axilla; in *C. sayi*, they are not as pointed as in some others.

Note that the apex of the clypeus on *C. sayi* (above) is swollen and sticks out a little, while that of *C. rufitarsis* (below) is flat.

Coelioxys sayi (female)

The punctation is hard to miss in *Coelioxys*.

T1 is usually very concave.

The spines on T6 in *C. sayi* are narrow, more petite than in some other *Coelioxys*.

Coelioxys males have a groove running across T2 and T3; in *C. sayi*, it is less visible in the center.

The swollen apex gives the clypeus two little lobes when viewed from the front.

In males, T5 has widely spaced deep pits covering it.

Coelioxys sayi (male)

All *Coelioxys* have hairy compound eyes. *Apis mellifera* is the only other species with hair on the compound eyes.

orange on the femur. In females, the clypeus of *C. sayi* appears swollen on the sides and covered in short thick hair, which is not the case for *C. octodentatus*. *Coelioxys rufitarsis* females are similar to *C. sayi*. The distinctive clypeal rim of *C. sayi* can be useful—the clypeal margin of *C. rufitarsis* is straight. *Coelioxys rufitarsis* males are significantly more robust, and have more hair running across T2.

MEGACHILE

— **SUBFAMILY:** Megachilinae
— **TRIBE:** Megachilini

OVERVIEW: Gray to matte-black bees, small to medium-sized, often with a fuzzy thorax, and stripes across the abdomen. Incredible diversity in form and body shape. Usually seen in the summer. Includes specialists and generalists. Nesting can be in the ground or in preexisting cavities, including man-made cavities. Most species use pieces of leaf to line nest cells and protect eggs and pollen provisions; a few use resin. Some species are used commercially for the pollination of crops, including alfalfa. Though nesting is solitary, nests may be gregarious, with many females nesting in close proximity to each other (especially in "bee hotels").

IN THE WORLD: More than 1,520 species can be found around the world. They occur on every continent as well as most islands. In North America there are more than 140 species, most occurring in the western U.S. Forty species occur in the East.

CLEPTOPARASITES: *Coelioxys.*

IDENTIFYING FEATURES: Chunky dark bees, never metallic, with white hair bands across the abdomen. **HEAD:** The mandibles have three to five teeth. **THORAX:** Generally wide, and the transition from the dorsal face of the propodeum to the anterior face is abrupt. **LEGS:** No arolium. In males, the front coxae usually have small spines, and the front tarsal segments are often modified. **WINGS:** Two submarginal cells. **ABDOMEN:** The first tergal segment is gently concave, but there is no ridge around it, with the transition to the dorsal face being smooth. Females have copious scopa on the underside of their abdomens. In males, the sixth tergal segment turns down abruptly, forming a noticeable rim.

SIMILAR GENERA: *Lithurgopsis,* which is slightly longer, has arolia, and also large projections (almost like horns) on the front of the face. No *Megachile* fit this combination of characters. *Ashmeadiella, Heriades, Chelostoma,* and other small dark Osmiini may appear similar to small *Megachile.* Osmiini have an arolium between the front claws. *Megachile* do not. Finally, larger darker *Megachile* may appear similar to *Xylocopa. Xylocopa* have three submarginal cells, while *Megachile* have two.

Distinguishing between species of *Megachile* can be difficult, especially with males; characters are often on the sternal segments and can be difficult to see in photos or on less than pristine specimens. There are a few species that stand out. We highlight easily discernible members of the genus, as well as several of the most commonly seen, but for most accurate identifications, it is best to use a key that includes all species.

— *Megachile brevis*

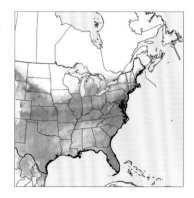

SIZE: Small to medium; 7–12 mm (males are much smaller than females). **PHENOLOGY:** July through mid-October. **FLORAL HOSTS:** Polylectic, but with preference for Asteraceae. **RANGE:** Widespread throughout eastern North America. **NESTING:** Any hollow tunnel, including grass stems, cornstalks, *Helianthus, Erigeron, Vernonia, Cirsium, Ambrosia* stems, termite holes in wood, in mats of grass, under dry cow patties, or in holes in the ground. Nests are lined with leaf material, especially from *Rosa,* or petal pieces.

Some gray/white hair on the thorax and head of *M. brevis*

Megachile brevis (female)

Scopal hairs are white to off-white.

T6 in females is notched, rather than evenly tapering.

The hair on T2 is black, before the apical hair band.

The hair on males is slightly tanner than on females of the same species.

Megachile brevis (male)

Tarsal segments are brown.

T6 of male *M. brevis* has a patch of thick white hair, and a notch in the center.

IDENTIFICATION: Medium-sized black bee, with some rust-colored and some yellow hair on the head and thorax, and strong white bands of hair on the abdomen. **HEAD:** In females, there are four teeth on the mandible. In males, the mandible has three teeth and the face has thick white or ivory-colored hair. **THORAX:** There is white hair near the posterior end, though the scutum has black hairs. **LEGS:** In males, forecoxae have spines; the tarsi are brown. **ABDOMEN:** In females, the scopal hairs are usually light yellow or white. Also in females, T2 has black hair before the white apical hair band, and T6 is notched when viewed in profile, rather than tapering gently. In males, T6 has flattened white woolly hairs near its tip. Underneath, S6 has some black flattened hairs.

SIMILAR SPECIES: *Megachile brevis* looks similar to *M. onobrychidis*, *M. pseudobrevis*, and *M. coquilletti* (not included in this book). Females of *M. coquilletti* and *M. onobrychidis* have completely black hair on S6. None of these species have flat thick white hairs on T6 in males. *Megachile coquilletti* has yellow tarsi, instead of brown, in males.

— *Megachile mendica*

SIZE: Small to medium; 8–13 mm (males are much smaller than females). **PHENOLOGY:** July through mid-October. **FLORAL HOSTS:** Polylectic, but with preference for Asteraceae. **RANGE:** Widespread throughout eastern North America.

NESTING: Flexible nester; nests have been found in the ground, especially in sandy soils, as well as in preexisting holes in wood. Nest cells are lined with leaf pieces. Pollen is coated with an odoriferous secretion that may play a role in preventing bacterial and fungal growth.

IDENTIFICATION: Medium-sized black and gray bee with narrow hair bands on the abdomen. **HEAD:** In females, the mandible has four teeth. In males, there are three teeth on the mandible. The angle between the third and fourth tooth is abrupt. **LEGS:** Tarsal segments are dark. In males, the forecoxae have a small (hard-to-see) spine. **ABDOMEN:** In females, T6 is not concave, but straight when viewed in profile, and S6 has thin

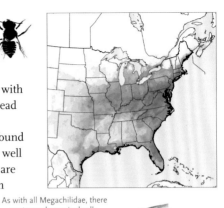

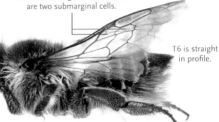

As with all Megachilidae, there are two submarginal cells.

T6 is straight in profile.

Megachile mendica
(female)

Most of the scopal hairs are yellow, though there is very little on S6, and what is there is black.

Narrow hair bands on the abdomen

Megachile mendica
(female)

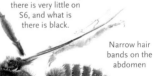

Megachile mendica
(male)

There is a notch in the center of T6, with a light patch of white hair around it.

Tarsal segments are dark brown/black.

black scopal hairs, while the other sternal segments have yellow scopae. In males, the pits on T4 and T5 are widely separated and distinct; there are no white hairs running along T5, and T6 has a deep notch in the center.

SIMILAR SPECIES: *Megachile gentilis* look similar to *M. mendica.*

Punctation on T4 and T5 is widely spaced and deep.

Tarsal claws are dark.

In females, they differ in the shape of T6, which is concave in *M. gentilis*, but flat in *M. mendica*. In males, they differ in the punctation on T4 and T5; on *M. gentilis* the pits are very close together.

— *Megachile rotundata*

SIZE: Small; 7–9 mm. **PHENOLOGY:** June through October. **FLORAL HOSTS:** Polylectic, but widely used in the Northeast and Canada to pollinate lowbush blueberry. **RANGE:** Introduced from Europe in the 1940s; widespread throughout North America. **NESTING:** Cavity nester, often gregariously, takes readily to human-made holes in wood, or paper straws. **IDENTIFICATION:** Slightly smaller species than other common *Megachile*. **HEAD:** In females, the mandible has four teeth. The clypeus rim is slightly thickened, but straight (not concave) in the center. **THORAX:** Punctation is very dense, and especially coarse in the center. **ABDOMEN:** Thin white hair bands run across each tergal segment. T2 has thick patches of very short hair covering the surface on either side of center (often most visible when viewed at a slight angle). In females, the scopa is white to golden orange; underneath the scopal hairs there are white hair bands. T3 and T4 have thick black hairs laterally. The sixth tergal segment is flat, or slightly concave, but not notched; there are short black bristles on this segment. In males, T6 is jagged to round, but not deeply notched.

SIMILAR SPECIES: *Megachile apicalis* shares many similar features, but on the whole is slightly larger. In females, the clypeus is concave in the middle. In both males and females, the second and third tergal segments have oblong patches of thick white hair laterally. In *M. rotundata,* the white hair patches are only on the second tergal segment. *Megachile mendica* also looks similar; in males the sixth tergal segment has a deep notch in the center, unlike *M. rotundata. Megachile texana* may also look similar, but the scopal hairs are bright white and puff out to either side in *M. texana.*

Megachile rotundata
(female)

Megachile rotundata
(male)

Megachile rotundata
(female)

White hair bands
run across each
tergal segment.

The sixth tergal segment
is slightly concave.

Underneath the scopal hairs
there are thin white hair bands.

The sixth sternal
segment has all
black hairs.

Megachile rotundata
(male)

The sixth tergal segment ends
in a jagged line without
a deep notch in it.

— Megachile sculpturalis

SIZE: Large; 19–25 mm. **PHENOLOGY:** July through September. **FLORAL HOSTS:** Appears to prefer oriental cultivars, including *Saphora, Ligustrum, Lythrum, Vitex, Buddleja,* and *Koelreuteria.* It also forages on native flowers, including *Catalpa* and *Asclepias.* The presence of this bee can be discerned by the marks it leaves on the petals of pea flowers. When it lands on the keel and wing petals, it bites the base of the banner petal, leaving a wound that discolors over time. **RANGE:** Invasive species, native to Asia. In the U.S., it has been seen from New York through Georgia, west to Alabama, Ohio, and Illinois. **NESTING:** Cavities in wood, with nest cells separated by barriers made of plant resin.

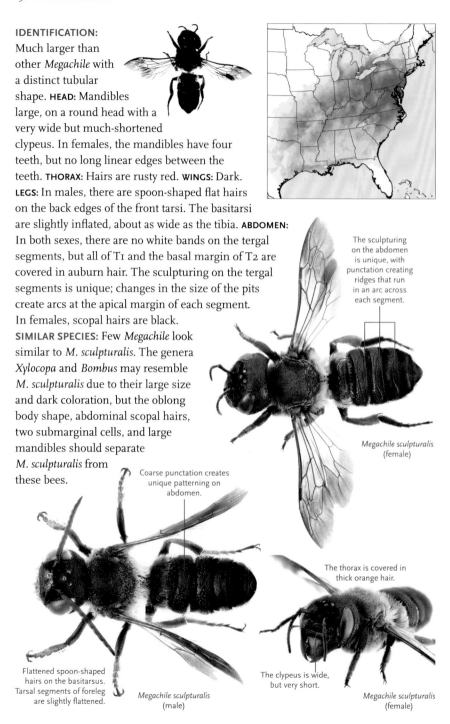

IDENTIFICATION: Much larger than other *Megachile* with a distinct tubular shape. **HEAD:** Mandibles large, on a round head with a very wide but much-shortened clypeus. In females, the mandibles have four teeth, but no long linear edges between the teeth. **THORAX:** Hairs are rusty red. **WINGS:** Dark. **LEGS:** In males, there are spoon-shaped flat hairs on the back edges of the front tarsi. The basitarsi are slightly inflated, about as wide as the tibia. **ABDOMEN:** In both sexes, there are no white bands on the tergal segments, but all of T1 and the basal margin of T2 are covered in auburn hair. The sculpturing on the tergal segments is unique; changes in the size of the pits create arcs at the apical margin of each segment. In females, scopal hairs are black.

SIMILAR SPECIES: Few *Megachile* look similar to *M. sculpturalis*. The genera *Xylocopa* and *Bombus* may resemble *M. sculpturalis* due to their large size and dark coloration, but the oblong body shape, abdominal scopal hairs, two submarginal cells, and large mandibles should separate *M. sculpturalis* from these bees.

The sculpturing on the abdomen is unique, with punctation creating ridges that run in an arc across each segment.

Megachile sculpturalis
(female)

Coarse punctation creates unique patterning on abdomen.

The thorax is covered in thick orange hair.

Flattened spoon-shaped hairs on the basitarsus. Tarsal segments of foreleg are slightly flattened.

Megachile sculpturalis
(male)

The clypeus is wide, but very short.

Megachile sculpturalis
(female)

— *Megachile xylocopoides*

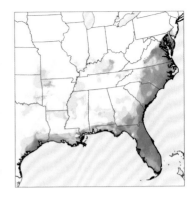

SIZE: Medium; 10–15 mm.
PHENOLOGY: June through October.
FLORAL HOSTS: Visits numerous
flowering plants, but may have a preference
for Asteraceae. **RANGE:** Texas west to Florida,
north to New Jersey and west through Missouri.
NESTING: Nests in large holes in wood.
IDENTIFICATION: Large black bee—no other
Megachile in the East exhibits such a dark profile,
especially in females. **HEAD:** In females, the
mandible has five teeth and a long straight edge
between the second and third. In males, mandible with four teeth. The face has sparse
light hairs between the eyes. At the end of the gena, near the lower margin of the eye,
long thick hairs sprout very suddenly from the face. **THORAX:** Tegulae black. In males,
the end of the thorax often sports long light-colored hairs. **WINGS:** Smoky. **LEGS:** Black.
In males, front legs are yellow but mid- and hind legs are dark. The front basitarsal
segments are inflated, so that they are much wider than the tibia. **ABDOMEN:** In males,
the first and second tergal segments are often covered with light-colored hairs;
on the second tergal segment these yellow hairs are intermixed with
black hairs. In females, scopal hairs are completely black.

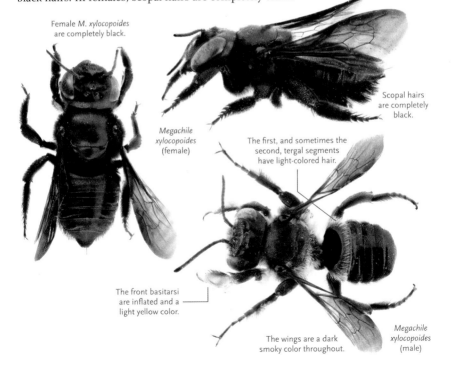

Female *M. xylocopoides*
are completely black.

Scopal hairs
are completely
black.

*Megachile
xylocopoides*
(female)

The first, and sometimes the
second, tergal segments
have light-colored hair.

The front basitarsi
are inflated and a
light yellow color.

The wings are a dark
smoky color throughout.

*Megachile
xylocopoides*
(male)

SIMILAR SPECIES: Few *Megachile* females can be confused with *M. xylocopoides* due to the striking nature of the black hair and black integument. *M. mucida* and *M. pruina* males share similar features to males of *M. xylocopoides* (inflated forebasitarsi, yellow forelegs, long hairs on cheek, etc.); *M. pruina* has distinct hair bands on T2–T5, which is not the case for the other two. In *M. mucida*, the wings are dark only along the edges, and T2 is largely covered with pale yellow hair with very little black hair.

ANTHIDIELLUM

— **SUBFAMILY:** Megachilinae
— **TRIBE:** Anthidiini

OVERVIEW: *Anthidiellum* are tiny but robust black and yellow or red bees, known for hovering conspicuously near plants before landing. They are abundant in the summer, but are generalists and will visit many different kinds of flowering plants. Nests are external structures attached to rocks, branches, or leaves. Nest is made of resinous material and is shiny, fairly smooth, and not always large, containing only one or two cells.

Males are hard to miss, as they establish territories and patrol constantly, flying in a straight line for several meters and then hovering in place for a period, before flying in another direction to a new spot to hover. If an insect or other "intruder" is spotted, males will bowl into them. Patrolling is broken up by periods of time resting within his territory, or taking nectar from flowers.

IN THE WORLD: Around 70 species can be found around the world, ranging from northern Mongolia and Finland to South Africa and Australia. Five species occur in the Americas, with four of them in North America. East of the Mississippi River there are two species; only one, *A. notatum*, occurs as far north as Canada.

CLEPTOPARASITES: *Stelis*.

IDENTIFYING FEATURES: Small robust bees with notable yellow and black stripes. In flight, *Anthidiellum* appear smaller and more compact than other insects as they tuck their appendages in very tightly. **HEAD:** Has a shelf-like ridge behind the ocelli, hanging out so far as to almost cover the beginning of the thorax in some species. The subantennal suture is unique among Anthidiini in being strongly outwardly curved. In females, the mandible has four teeth, and males have three. **THORAX:** Scutellum is swollen, extending out over the

Anthidiellum species have a shelf at the back of their head; sometimes it is thick, but in other species it is paper thin.

In *Anthidiellum* the scutellum is also elongated, extending over the propodeum and hiding the end of the thorax and the beginning of the abdomen.

propodeum. **WINGS:** Long, extending past the end of the body. **LEGS:** Arolia between front tarsal claws. In males, on the hind coxa, there is no spine. **ABDOMEN:** Scopal hairs on sternal segments.

SIMILAR GENERA: *Dianthidium* are similar in size and coloring, but *Anthidiellum* lack the pronotal lobe modifications seen in *Dianthidium*. In addition, the hind coxa in males on *Dianthidium* has a notable spur, which isn't present in *Anthidiellum*. *Anthidium*, though similar in coloration, are generally larger, have more teeth in their mandibles (five or more) and lack an arolium. *Paranthidium* has a rounded preoccipital ridge, and is not shelf-like, as in *Anthidiellum*.

— *Anthidiellum notatum*

SIZE: Small; 8 mm. **PHENOLOGY:** April through mid-September. **FLORAL HOSTS:** Polylectic, visiting a wide variety of plants for pollen and nectar. **RANGE:** Widespread; New Hampshire to Florida, west to California. **IDENTIFICATION:** Small compact bee with yellow markings on thorax, head, legs, and abdomen. **HEAD:** In females, the yellow markings on the face that occur behind the ocelli end about where the head rounds to the sides. In both sexes, the area between the ocelli is polished and swollen, appearing as a

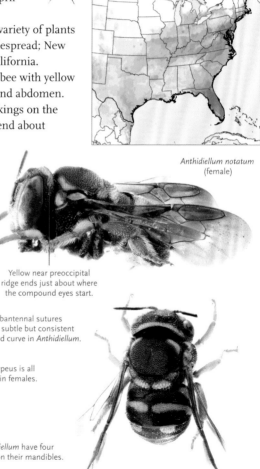

Anthidiellum notatum
(female)

The area between the three ocelli is slighly swollen and shiny.

Yellow near preoccipital ridge ends just about where the compound eyes start.

The subantennal sutures form a subtle but consistent outward curve in *Anthidiellum*.

The clypeus is all yellow in females.

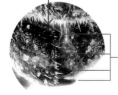

Anthidiellum have four teeth on their mandibles.

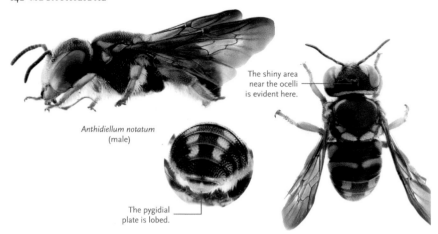

The shiny area near the ocelli is evident here.

Anthidiellum notatum
(male)

The pygidial plate is lobed.

modest bump on the top of the head. The clypeus is also usually very yellow.
THORAX: Scutal punctures are rough throughout. **LEGS:** Almost entirely yellow.
ABDOMEN: In males, the pygidial plate is lobed.
SIMILAR SPECIES: There are four subspecies of *A. notatum* found across North
America. In the East, *A. notatum notatum* is the most widespread. It is yellower
than some of the other subspecies that are also found in the East but have more
limited distributions. *Anthidium perplexum* looks similar to *A. notatum*, but can be
distinguished by the differences in the shape of the pygidial plate and the location of
the yellow markings on the face in females (see *A. perplexum* for specifics).

— *Anthidiellum perplexum*

SIZE: Small; 8–9 mm. **PHENOLOGY:** April
through October, later and earlier in
Florida. **FLORAL HOSTS:** Polylectic, though may
focus on one plant if it is locally abundant.
RANGE: South Atlantic states.
IDENTIFICATION: Small compact rust-red
or yellow bee with black stripes across the
abdomen and thorax. **HEAD:** In females, yellow
to red markings on the face extend down the
sides of the face, past where the compound
eyes start. The area between the ocelli is not
polished or raised, and appears the same as the rest of the head. The clypeus is
black. **THORAX:** Punctation is fine, and evenly spaced. **LEGS:** Mostly red or red-orange.
ABDOMEN: In males, the pygidial plate is not lobed.
SIMILAR SPECIES: Males can be distinguished from the similar *A. notatum* by the
straight margin of the pygidial plate. In females, the difference in markings on the
face, especially the clypeus and the area behind the eyes, is most telling. In general, *A.
perplexum* appears slightly redder.

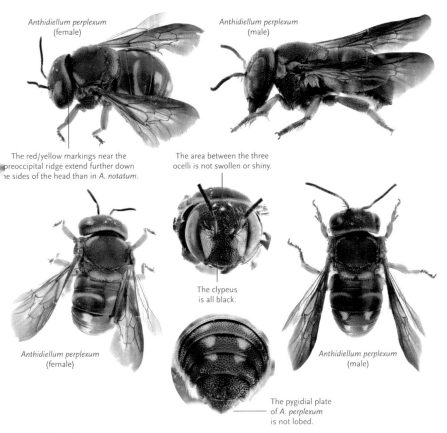

Anthidiellum perplexum
(female)

Anthidiellum perplexum
(male)

The red/yellow markings near the preoccipital ridge extend further down the sides of the head than in A. notatum.

The area between the three ocelli is not swollen or shiny.

The clypeus is all black.

Anthidiellum perplexum
(female)

Anthidiellum perplexum
(male)

The pygidial plate of A. perplexum is not lobed.

ANTHIDIUM

— **SUBFAMILY:** Megachilinae
— **TRIBE:** Anthidiini

OVERVIEW: Known as wool carder bees, *Anthidium* are distinctive, noisy, yellow and black bees seen abundantly in summer months. Most are generalists, but a handful of specialists are also known among western species. The majority are ground nesters, but a few nest in holes in wood, or other types of cavities. In the East, the native species nest in the ground, while the two invasive species are both cavity nesters. All of them use plant hairs (trichomes) that they "shave" from woolly plants to pad nest cells.

IN THE WORLD: *Anthidium* are most abundant in the Northern Hemisphere (Europe, northern Asia, and North America). They can be found in northern African countries, South America, and India, but are absent from Australia, Indonesia, and the tropics of southeastern Asia. More than 160 species occur in the world. There are 92 species in North, Central, and South America, but only 4 in eastern North America; of those, 2 are not native, having arrived in North America in the last 30 to 40 years.

CLEPTOPARASITES: *Stelis, Dioxys* (not covered in this book).

IDENTIFYING FEATURES: Yellow and black medium-sized bees with pollen-collecting hairs on the underside of the abdomen of females. Body segments are round to cuboid, giving them a robust appearance. **HEAD:** Mandibles of females have between five and seven small teeth. In both males and females, the subantennal suture is very straight. The back of the head rounds gently, with no strong carinae or ridges. **THORAX:** Pronotal lobe is rounded, with no paper-thin ridges. Scutellum is not overly inflated or shelf-like. **WINGS:** Two submarginal cells (as in all Megachilidae). **LEGS:** No arolium. **ABDOMEN:** In males, teeth occur laterally on T5 and T6.

SIMILAR GENERA: *Anthidiellum* may be similar in terms of the yellow and black striping. *Anthidiellum* is generally smaller and has an enlarged scutellum and shelf-like back of its head. Those characters, plus the presence of arolia and the fewer teeth on the mandible, should distinguish *Anthidiellum* from *Anthidium*. They can be confused with *Trachusa*, because both genera are larger bees, but *Anthidium* have five or more teeth, while *Trachusa* have fewer than five teeth.

— *Anthidium maculifrons*

SIZE: Small to medium; 9–12 (but up to 16) mm. **PHENOLOGY:** March through April in the South; May through July in the North. **FLORAL HOSTS:** Generalist, with some preference for Fabaceae. **RANGE:** Great Plains, Texas, and south-central U.S., but ranges as far east as Florida and West Virginia, where it is rare. Absent from the Northeast. **NESTING:** Solitary ground nester. **IDENTIFICATION:** Medium-sized fast-flying bee marked with yellow on a predominantly black integument. **HEAD:** In females, the clypeus is rounded outward and clearly visible in profile. On the mandible, there are six or seven teeth, all about the same size. Often the clypeus has yellow spots instead of being solid yellow across the lower half, though this can vary between individuals. In males, antennae appear white or light yellow, the clypeus is entirely yellow, and there is yellow beside the eyes, but it ends about where the antennal sockets begin. **THORAX:** The posterior margin of the scutellum is smooth, lacking any small teeth where it drops over to the propodeum. **LEGS:** In males, the hind coxa and trochanter have a small spine, visible from underneath. In females, the hind tibia has a carina on the anterior face. **ABDOMEN:** In females, T6 is completely smooth across the apical end. On T6 of males, the lateral spine is very curved, and quite long. T7 has a fingerlike projection laterally, with one narrow spine centrally.

SIMILAR SPECIES: *Anthidium psoralea* occurs in much the same habitat as *A. maculifrons*. In females, the clypeus of *A. psoralea* is usually entirely black, lacking any yellow as is seen in *A. maculifrons*. On the abdomen, there is a median projection on T6 of females in *A. psoralea* that is bidentate. T6 in males is smooth apically. In males, the scape has a yellow stripe in *A. maculifrons*, and is solid black in *A. psoralea*.

Anthidium have rounded pronotal lobes, with no paper-thin projections.

Overall, *Anthidium maculifrons* is a dark bee, without much yellow.

Anthidium maculifrons (female)

T6 is smooth, with no projections in females.

Anthidium maculifrons (male)

The clypeus is entirely yellow, as is the area beside the compound eye, though it ends at the antennal sockets. The undersides of the antennae are also yellow.

Anthidium maculifrons (male)

In males, the lateral spines on T6 are long and curved

— *Anthidium manicatum*

SIZE: Medium to large; 9–18 mm.
PHENOLOGY: May through October; multivoltine. **FLORAL HOSTS:** Generalist; some preference for flowers with long corollas and blue petals.
RANGE: Not native to North America; found naturally in Europe. Now occurring from coast to coast in the U.S. and Canada. Most common in urban areas. For eastern states: seldom seen in the Great Plains, or in the Southeast, but common from Minnesota to Nova Scotia and Virginia and all northern points in between. Occasional observations south as far as North Carolina. **NESTING:** Cavity nester, usually high above the ground.

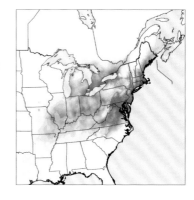

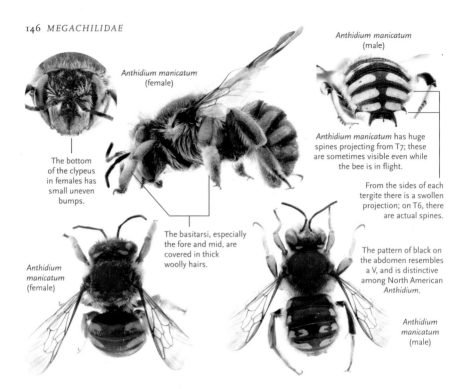

Anthidium manicatum
(male)

Anthidium manicatum
(female)

The bottom
of the clypeus
in females has
small uneven
bumps.

Anthidium manicatum has huge
spines projecting from T7; these
are sometimes visible even while
the bee is in flight.

From the sides of each
tergite there is a swollen
projection; on T6, there
are actual spines.

The basitarsi, especially
the fore and mid, are
covered in thick
woolly hairs.

*Anthidium
manicatum*
(female)

The pattern of black on
the abdomen resembles
a V, and is distinctive
among North American
Anthidium.

*Anthidium
manicatum*
(male)

Anthidium manicatum is invasive in the Western Hemisphere (see also *A. oblongatum*). It arrived in the United States in the early 1960s, but it has made its way to the West Coast in the last 50 years and is now widespread throughout North America. This bee (primarily the male) is extremely aggressive toward other insects when defending its territory, and will attack and kill offenders. There are five spines on the lower tergal segments that it uses to pierce the exoskeleton of other insects, and it can damage other bees so severely that they can't fly. There is some concern that it diminishes both floral resource availability for other pollinators in the area where males have established territories, as well as diminishing seed set of those same floral resources. **IDENTIFICATION:** Strong black and yellow species with males much larger than females. Most notable, the yellow stripes running across each tergal segment of the abdomen are broken up in the middle, and form the overall impression of a black "V" down the middle of the abdomen. **HEAD:** In females, the apical margin of the clypeus has numerous small uneven bumps across its length. **LEGS:** The basitarsi are covered in dense white fuzz, and on the hind tibia, there is a notable strong ridge running its length. **ABDOMEN:** In males, T2–T5 bulge at the sides, and T7 has strongly curved spinelike projections. In addition, male tergal segments have copious curved hairs sprouting from the sides. **SIMILAR SPECIES:** This is the biggest of the *Anthidium*, and the most insufferable, seen very commonly in urban areas of eastern North America. Despite its attitude, it is possible to mistake it for other species of *Anthidium*. The most notable features are the large spines at the end of the abdomen in males. The spines are not as prominent in most other *Anthidium*; they do occur in *A. maculifrons*, but are more modest. In both males and females the color pattern on the abdomen, with a distinctive black *wide* "V" down the middle, should aid in identification. Other species, especially *A. oblongatum*, may have interrupted yellow stripes, but the width of the black interruption is much greater in *A. manicatum*.

— *Anthidium oblongatum*

SIZE: Small to medium; 8–12 mm.
PHENOLOGY: May through October.
FLORAL HOSTS: Generalist. **RANGE:** Not native to North America, having arrived from Europe. In North America, it is currently found from New Hampshire and Ontario south to Virginia and west to Illinois. **NESTING:** Nests in dry warm areas, and often near disturbed sites with rocky ground and uneven terrain. Nests are in hollows in bricks, mortar, rock outcrops, or conglomerate rock piles, plant stems, or even pre-made holes in the earth.

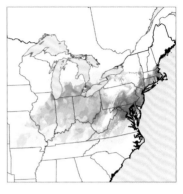

IDENTIFICATION: Smallish black and yellow bee often seen hovering in front of flowers. **HEAD:** In females, the margin of the clypeus is straight or slightly arced. On the mandibles, the teeth are not uniform: The lower teeth are longer than the top teeth; as a result the mandible does not look as blocky as it does in other *Anthidium*. This is the only member of the *Proanthidium* subgenus found in North America; like *A. manicatum* it is invasive, having arrived in North America sometime in the early 1990s.

Anthidium oblongatum
(male)

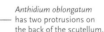

Anthidium oblongatum has two protrusions on the back of the scutellum.

Anthidium oblongatum
(male)

Anthidium oblongatum has a notch in the middle of the seventh tergal segment, and a spine in the middle of the sixth.

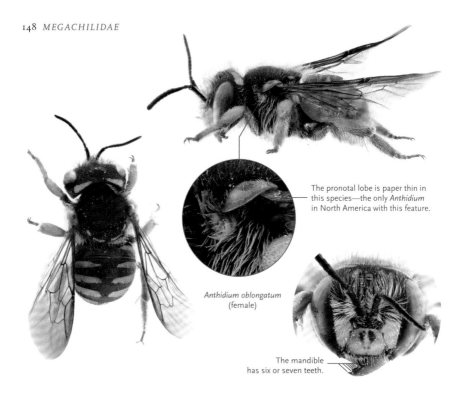

The pronotal lobe is paper thin in this species—the only *Anthidium* in North America with this feature.

Anthidium oblongatum (female)

The mandible has six or seven teeth.

THORAX: The pronotal lobe is extended anteriorly as a thin, see-through plate. The scutellum has two small teeth laterally. **ABDOMEN:** In females, the posterior margin of T6 is smooth. In males, T6 has a small, blunt spine in the middle. T7, which is strongly spined in other species, lacks any spines, and instead has a broad notch in the center. **SIMILAR SPECIES:** The size of this bee should aid in distinguishing it from *A. manicatum,* which is significantly larger. *A. oblongatum* is the only North American *Anthidium* with short spines on the posterior edge of the scutellum. In addition, the thin pronotal lobe is distinctive. Finally, the uneven teeth on the mandible differ from those of other *Anthidium* of similar size, in which all teeth are more or less the same size and shape.

DIANTHIDIUM

— **SUBFAMILY: Megachilinae**
— **TRIBE: Anthidiini**

OVERVIEW: Small-sized black and yellow bees commonly seen hovering in front of flowers, especially Asteraceae. Most common in the summer. The genus includes both generalist and specialist species. Most species construct nests out of gravel or pebbles stuck together with mud and resin, and placed on branches or twigs, but a few ground-nesting species also occur. May also nest in beetle burrows or preexisting holes in the ground.

IN THE WORLD: Approximately 30 species in the world, found throughout North and Central America (many Mexican species). In the U.S. and Canada there are 23 species, with 2 occurring east of the Mississippi River and 4 other species occurring across the plains.

CLEPTOPARASITES: Unknown, maybe *Stelis.*

IDENTIFYING FEATURES: Small, black and yellow bees. **HEAD:** The back edge of the head is a carina. In females, the mandible has three teeth. The subantennal suture runs straight between the antennal socket and the epistomal suture. **THORAX:** Posterior end of the metanotum has soft thick patches of hair on either side. The pronotal lobes are paper thin, and almost see-through, extending anteriorly, toward the head. The front-facing and side surfaces of the thorax (the omaulus) are also separated by a carina. **WINGS:** Two submarginal cells. **LEGS:** Arolium between front tarsal claws. **ABDOMEN:** In females, scopae are on the underside of the abdomen.

SIMILAR GENERA: With their yellow and black markings, *Dianthidium* look similar to other Anthidiini, though they are the only ones with the distinctive thin margin on the pronotal lobes. They can be distinguished from *Anthidium* by the teeth: *Anthidium* have five teeth, while *Dianthidium* have three teeth. Also, *Anthidium* are generally larger. *Anthidiellum* are more similarly sized, but have four teeth and curved subantennal sutures. *Trachusa* lack the paper-thin pronotal lobes seen in *Dianthidium* as well as the sharp edges at the back of the head, and between the front and side of the thorax. In *Paranthidium* the front and middle tibiae are significantly modified so that there is a shallow, polished depression (see *Paranthidium* for more details).

— *Dianthidium curvatum*

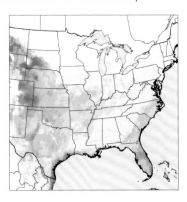

SIZE: Small; 7 mm. **PHENOLOGY:** April through October. **FLORAL HOSTS:** Has a preference for flowers in the Asteraceae. **RANGE:** This is the most commonly seen of the eastern *Dianthidium.* Missouri east to the coast; North Carolina south through Florida. **NESTING:** Nests in dense aggregations in the soil, with nest cells often attached to plant roots. Occasional nests are in vertical banks. *D. curvatum* uses sand grains held together by plant resin to construct nest chambers. Species may share nest entrances, but not nest chambers.

IDENTIFICATION: Small yellow and black bee. **HEAD:** In both sexes, the clypeus is usually yellow, but some female specimens have yellow only on the sides of the clypeus. Yellow markings continue up the sides of the face, but end abruptly at the top of the compound eyes. Mandibles are entirely black, with three teeth in both sexes. The lateral ocelli are small compared with those of other *Dianthidium* species. **THORAX:** Maculations on the front half of the scutum are variable; may be all black, or with a line of yellow at the anterior margin extending to the sides. The axillae and the scutellum are yellow.

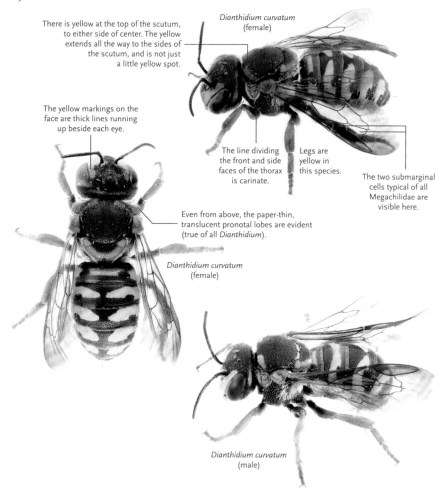

There is yellow at the top of the scutum, to either side of center. The yellow extends all the way to the sides of the scutum, and is not just a little yellow spot.

Dianthidium curvatum (female)

The yellow markings on the face are thick lines running up beside each eye.

The line dividing the front and side faces of the thorax is carinate.

Legs are yellow in this species.

The two submarginal cells typical of all Megachilidae are visible here.

Even from above, the paper-thin, translucent pronotal lobes are evident (true of all *Dianthidium*).

Dianthidium curvatum (female)

Dianthidium curvatum (male)

WINGS: Smoky. **ABDOMEN:** Tergal segments have yellow spots on the sides, separated by black in the middle. In males T6 may have significant yellow or red markings, or may be entirely black.

SIMILAR SPECIES: There are four subspecies of *D. curvatum*. In the East, *Dianthidium curvatum curvatum* and *Dianthidium curvatum floridiense* occur. *Dianthidium curvatum floridiense* occurs in Florida only. *Dianthidium curvatum curvatum* is mostly black, while *D. c. floridiense* has more red on its body and especially its legs. *Dianthidium c. floridiense* also has a small spine on the forecoxa that is absent in the other subspecies. It is slightly larger than *D. c. curvatum,* and has a larger second mandibular tooth in males. This bee exhibits an extraordinary amount of rust-red on the thorax and abdomen.

PARANTHIDIUM

— SUBFAMILY: Megachilinae
— TRIBE: Anthidiini

OVERVIEW: Small yellow and black bees, seen in midsummer as they collect pollen from the Asteraceae on which they specialize. Nest in the ground, often in sandy soil. May nest in small aggregations of a dozen or so individuals.

IN THE WORLD: Worldwide there are seven species, all in North and Central America. In the U.S. and Canada there is one species with three subspecies; two of these subspecies occur east of the Mississippi River (*P. jugatorium lepidum,* occurring mostly in the southeastern U.S., and *P. j. jugatorium*, which occurs mostly in the northeastern U.S.).

CLEPTOPARASITES: Unknown, maybe *Stelis.*

IDENTIFYING FEATURES: HEAD: The mandible has three or four teeth, but not five. In females, the mandible is broad at the base, and extremely narrow at the beginning. THORAX: The propodeal triangle is extraordinarily punctate. WINGS: Two submarginal cells. LEGS: There is an arolium; on the fore- and midtibia there is no tibial spine arising from the end (apex) of the tibia. Instead, the outer apical tibial margin is gently curved, creating the edge of a spoonlike indentation that runs along the tibia. ABDOMEN: In males, T7 has three lobes, with the middle lobe longer and broader than those on either side. In females, scopae are on the underside of the abdomen.

SIMILAR GENERA: *Dianthidium* look very similar to *Paranthidium*. The carina that is so evident at the back of the head in *Dianthidium,* however, is lacking in *Paranthidium*. In addition, while both genera have thin projections (lamellae) extending forward from the pronotal lobe, they are very short in *Paranthidium*, as opposed to the more obvious projections of *Dianthidium*. The shape of the fore- and midtibiae in *Paranthidium* is distinctive; it is rounded and scooplike, which is not the case for any other Anthidiini in eastern North America.

— *Paranthidium jugatorium*

SIZE: Small; 8–9 mm. PHENOLOGY: Late summer, July through early September. FLORAL HOSTS: Appears to specialize on Asteraceae. RANGE: Minnesota east to New York, south to Arkansas, Louisiana, and Georgia. NESTING: Holes in the ground; may make their own in sandy soil, or may use preexisting, including old nest burrows of other bee species. Pebbles are brought to the nest and used to form mini scree slopes that separate nest cells. Very little resin is used.

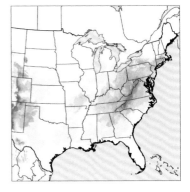

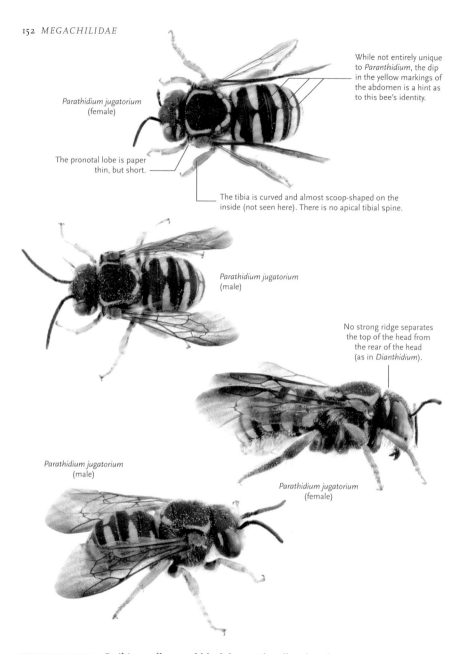

Parathidium jugatorium
(female)

While not entirely unique to *Paranthidium*, the dip in the yellow markings of the abdomen is a hint as to this bee's identity.

The pronotal lobe is paper thin, but short.

The tibia is curved and almost scoop-shaped on the inside (not seen here). There is no apical tibial spine.

Parathidium jugatorium
(male)

No strong ridge separates the top of the head from the rear of the head (as in *Dianthidium*).

Parathidium jugatorium
(male)

Parathidium jugatorium
(female)

IDENTIFICATION: Striking yellow and black bee with yellow bands running across each abdominal segment. Bands are separated in the middle by black, but the width of the black diminishes toward the apex of the abdomen. As this is the only species in the eastern U.S., other characters are included in the genus description above.

SIMILAR SPECIES: There is only one species of *Paranthidium* in the U.S. For similar genera, see above.

STELIS

— **SUBFAMILY:** Megachilinae
— **TRIBE:** Anthidiini

OVERVIEW: *Stelis* are uncommon small to medium-sized bees with variable coloration ranging from jet-black to dark with yellow-and-orange-striped abdomens. These bees are cleptoparasites on a wide array of bee genera and parasitize other Megachilidae. When a host bee is away from the nest, a female *Stelis* enters the nest and deposits one or two eggs on the pollen mass left by the host for her own offspring. The *Stelis* larva kills the host bee's offspring and then eats the pollen.

IN THE WORLD: Worldwide there more than 100 species; the majority are found in the Northern Hemisphere. In the U.S. and Canada there are 51 species, with 11 occurring in the East.

IDENTIFYING FEATURES: Rounded dark bees, often with dark yellow, cream, or orange markings on the face, edges of the thorax, and abdomen. Like all other Megachilidae, they have two submarginal cells, though as a cleptoparasite, they lack pollen-collecting hairs on their abdomen or anywhere else. **HEAD:** The preoccipital ridge is not a carina. **THORAX:** The scutum and the surface of the tergal segments on the abdomen both appear extremely roughened with thick, dense punctures. **LEGS:** There is an arolium between the tarsal claws, which are cleft. On the midtibia, there are two spines at the apex (tip). **WINGS:** The second recurrent vein meets the submarginal cells *behind* the vein defining the second submarginal cell. **ABDOMEN:** In males, there are no spines or protrusions on T6 or T7.

SIMILAR GENERA: The body shape of *Stelis* appears similar to *Osmia* or some other Osmiini. Look for yellow or ivory markings, especially on the abdomen, the roughened integument, and the cleft tarsal claws (which are not split in Osmiini).

Distinguishing between species of *Stelis* is difficult, involving minute characters that grade into each other. We highlight one common, relatively easily identified species here.

— *Stelis louisae*

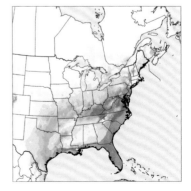

SIZE: Small; 8 mm. **PHENOLOGY:** March through late August. **FLORAL HOSTS:** As cleptoparasites, they do not visit flowers for pollen. They can be found collecting nectar from a wide array of flowering species. **RANGE:** Florida and Texas north to Kentucky and Virginia. **NESTING:** Parasitizes *Megachile* and other members of the family Megachilidae. **IDENTIFICATION:** Smaller dark bees with highly variable markings. **HEAD:** The clypeus may be yellow, entirely black, or some mix of both. The area near the compound eye is usually yellow.

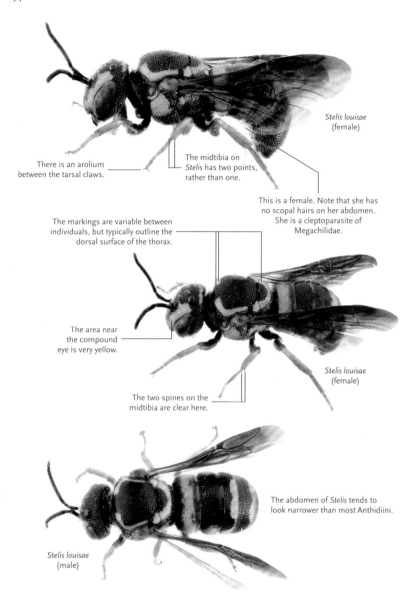

Stelis louisae
(female)

There is an arolium
between the tarsal claws.

The midtibia on
Stelis has two points,
rather than one.

This is a female. Note that she has
no scopal hairs on her abdomen.
She is a cleptoparasite of
Megachilidae.

The markings are variable between
individuals, but typically outline the
dorsal surface of the thorax.

The area near
the compound
eye is very yellow.

Stelis louisae
(female)

The two spines on the
midtibia are clear here.

The abdomen of *Stelis* tends to
look narrower than most Anthidiini.

Stelis louisae
(male)

THORAX: Yellow outlines the outer margins of the scutum and the scutellum.
ABDOMEN: The bee may have red, yellow, or ivory markings. In females, T6 has
a tuft of stiff, long, dark hair at the center. Some males also possess this tuft. In males,
T7 possesses a central ridge that runs perpendicular to the rim of the segment.
SIMILAR SPECIES: *Stelis grossa* has similar markings but is rare and restricted
to Florida.

TRACHUSA

— SUBFAMILY: Megachilinae
— TRIBE: Anthidiini

OVERVIEW: Robust bees, often large, not always as yellow and black as some of the other Anthidiini, though more so than other Megachilidae. Often slightly hairy. The dietary preferences for most species are unknown, but some appear to be specialists. Ground nesters. Inside nests, cells are separated using either leaf material, resin, pebbles, or soil. Occasionally nest in aggregations.

IN THE WORLD: With more than 50 species worldwide, *Trachusa* can be found throughout the Northern Hemisphere, and a few species also occur in Africa. There are 19 species in North America, with 5 occurring east of the Mississippi River.

CLEPTOPARASITES: *Stelis* and *Coelioxys*.

IDENTIFYING FEATURES: HEAD: The head rounds gently from top to back, with no carina separating the faces. The head is thick, with the ocelli near the middle of the top of the head rather than the back. In males, there are yellow markings on the clypeus and usually beside each compound eye. **WINGS:** The second recurrent vein comes very close to meeting the second submarginal vein straight on. There are two submarginal cells. **LEGS:** The midtibia is wide, nearly as wide as the hind tibia, with rounded edges and a blunt projection, rather than a ridge or spine. The hind tibia has small bumps covering its surface. The tarsal claws are split so that there are two teeth. There is an arolium, but it is much smaller than in many Anthidiini genera. **ABDOMEN:** The anterior face of T1 has a ridge where it folds to the dorsal face, creating a concave surface. There is no pygidial plate. In males, the final tergal segment curls strongly under, so that it is difficult to see. In females, pollen is collected in scopae on the sternal segments.

SIMILAR GENERA: *Trachusa* look similar to other anthidiines, including *Anthidium*, *Dianthidium*, and *Paranthidium*. The larger size is a clue, as is the lack of projections, lamellae, or ridges on the body. The midtibia, though not the easiest body part to see, is distinct in *Trachusa*, being relatively wide.

— *Trachusa dorsalis*

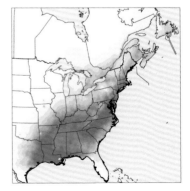

SIZE: Medium to large; 13–15 mm.
PHENOLOGY: Late summer, August through September. **FLORAL HOSTS:** Unknown, may specialize on Fabaceae (pea family), with numerous records for *Strophostyles*. **RANGE:** New Jersey south to Georgia. Continues west through Louisiana but absent from the Midwest.
IDENTIFICATION: Stout bee with yellow and black markings throughout. **HEAD:** In males, the clypeus and all areas adjacent, as well as the mandibles, are yellow. **THORAX:** Scutum is mostly black, with yellow lining the sides near the tegula.

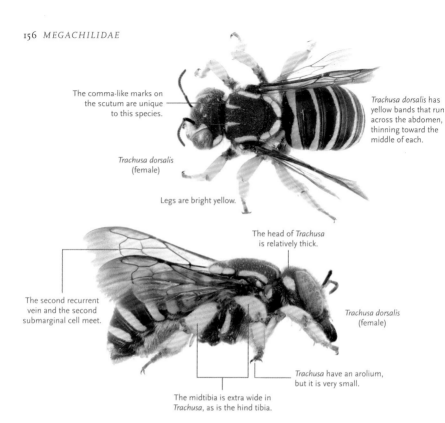

The comma-like marks on the scutum are unique to this species.

Trachusa dorsalis has yellow bands that run across the abdomen, thinning toward the middle of each.

Trachusa dorsalis (female)

Legs are bright yellow.

The head of *Trachusa* is relatively thick.

The second recurrent vein and the second submarginal cell meet.

Trachusa dorsalis (female)

Trachusa have an arolium, but it is very small.

The midtibia is extra wide in *Trachusa*, as is the hind tibia.

Extending from the front of the thorax back to midway are two yellow commas, one on either side of center. **LEGS:** Yellow, with midtibia appearing thickened. **ABDOMEN:** Yellow markings are thicker to the sides of each tergite, and thinner in the middle.

SIMILAR SPECIES: There are five *Trachusa* species in the East. *Trachusa dorsalis* is among the largest, and the only one with comma-like marks on the scutum. *Trachusa ridingsii* is all black on the thorax and has yellow hair bands running along the apex of each tergal segment. *T. zebrata* has an entirely black scutum, but yellow markings on other sections of the thorax. The other two *Trachusa* are rare, smaller, and possess some combination of yellow and black markings, but never yellow commas as seen in *T. dorsalis*.

LITHURGOPSIS

— **SUBFAMILY:** Lithurginae
— **TRIBE:** Lithurgini

OVERVIEW: Large dark bees with oversized heads, usually seen deep inside cactus blossoms. Mostly late spring through summer bees. North American species collect pollen only from cactus flowers; the closely related non-native species *Lithurgus chrysurus* collects pollen from the also non-native star thistle (*Centaurea*), which is from the Mediterranean. All *Lithurgopsis* nest in wood, often dead wood.

IN THE WORLD: Worldwide there are roughly 10 species of *Lithurgopsis*, all of which occur in North and South America. The closely related genus *Lithurgus*, with 36 species, is more widely distributed. In eastern parts of North America there is one species from each genus.

CLEPTOPARASITES: No known bee parasites.

IDENTIFYING FEATURES: Large solid black bee with light white stripes on the abdomen; appears slightly elongate. HEAD: In females, there is a strong protuberance between the antennal sockets, entirely above the clypeus. From a distance this looks like a black bald spot above the clypeus; up close the 3-D nature of the structure is evident. WINGS: Two submarginal cells. LEGS: On the fore- and midtibiae are coarse teeth running in two parallel rows, creating a groove on the tibia. In males, there is an arolium. ABDOMEN: Females have a central spine in place of a pygidial plate; scopal hairs are on the sternal segments of the abdomen. In males, on the abdomen, there is a well-developed pygidial plate.

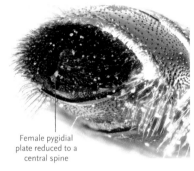

Female pygidial plate reduced to a central spine

SIMILAR GENERA: *Megachile* look similar but lack the protuberance on the face in females. In males, the spinelike pygidial plate seen in *Lithurgopsis* is unique. *Lithurgus* can be hard to distinguish from *Lithurgopsis*. The arolia seen in male *Lithurgopsis* is absent in *Lithurgus*. And in females, the protuberance on the face includes the clypeus as well as the area above it in *Lithurgus*, but not in *Lithurgopsis*.

— *Lithurgopsis gibbosa*

SIZE: Large; 15–18 mm.

PHENOLOGY: March through July, earlier in southern part of range.

FLORAL HOSTS: Pollen specialist on *Opuntia* (prickly pear); visits a wide array of flowers for nectar. RANGE: Florida north to North Carolina. Absent from Mississippi basin, but occurs in Texas, north to Kansas. Not commonly seen in much of the East. NESTING: Nest in holes in wood; capable of chewing the wood themselves to make new nests or larger nesting spaces in preexisting tunnels.

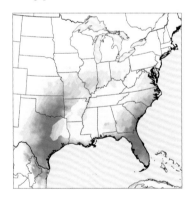

IDENTIFICATION: Large dark bee, with modest white stripes on abdomen. Body is matte-black. HEAD: In females, the area above the clypeus sticks out notably, as a curved thick ridge. In males, the area above the clypeus is not significantly raised, but is heavily pitted. The face is slightly oblong. Mandible has three teeth, with the middle one more elongate than the other two. WINGS: Slightly darkened. ABDOMEN: In females, scopal hairs are light orange.

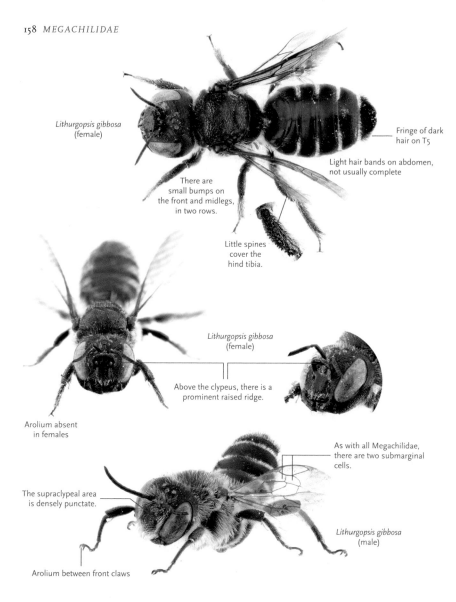

Lithurgopsis gibbosa
(female)

Fringe of dark
hair on T5

Light hair bands on abdomen,
not usually complete

There are
small bumps on
the front and midlegs,
in two rows.

Little spines
cover the
hind tibia.

Lithurgopsis gibbosa
(female)

Above the clypeus, there is a
prominent raised ridge.

Arolium absent
in females

As with all Megachilidae,
there are two submarginal
cells.

The supraclypeal area
is densely punctate.

Lithurgopsis gibbosa
(male)

Arolium between front claws

SIMILAR SPECIES: *Lithurgopsis littoralis* overlaps with *L. gibbosa* for some of the latter's western range. Both are pollen specialists on *Opuntia* and so both can be seen flying at the same time of year. The protuberance on the face of *L. littoralis* is flatter, when viewed from the front, and the sides are more developed than the middle. *Lithurgus chrysurus* also overlaps with *Lithurgopsis gibbosa*, but for only some of the eastern portion of the latter's range. *Lithurgus chrysurus* specimens have no arolium, have a second flagellar segment that is longer than the first, and in females, the facial protuberance is wedge-shaped, so that it angles gradually from its high point between the antennae to the base of the clypeus.

APIDAE

Apidae is a family of extremes and contrasts. For example, while it is among the most diverse families in North America and includes many of our easier to recognize bees, it also includes its share of seldom-seen genera. And while many Apidae are large and fuzzy and fast fliers, there are entire subfamilies that are small and nearly hairless. Bees in the family Apidae span the spectrum of behaviors from highly social species with a queen, workers, and clear division of labor, to completely solitary species. Apidae also contains the largest proportion of cleptoparasitic species of any family. There are nearly 6,000 species and 200 genera in the world and they occur on every continent. In North America there are more than 1,000 species in 50 genera. The vast majority of North American Apidae nest in the ground, though a few, like the carpenter bees, nest above ground. Among North American species are a large proportion of specialists as well as many generalists.

While not native to North America, the most famous species in the family is undoubtedly *Apis mellifera* (the western, or European, honey bee). This species is the only bee north of the Mexican border to make honey, live in large hives with tens of thousands of workers, and die after stinging. The honey bee has become a key player in many agricultural systems as it is often used for orchard and crop pollination. Also found in the family are squash bees, carpenter bees, bumble bees, digger bees, and long-horned bees.

IDENTIFICATION: Because the family is so diverse, unifying characters are not immediately evident. It is often easier to identify the genus than the family; many of the characteristics used to identify members of Apidae are small differences in specific parts of the mouth. These can be hard to see. All bees in the Apidae family have a long tongue. While not true for all genera, most are very hairy, and females often have dense, very long scopal hairs on their hind legs. Larger species also often have a reduced jugal lobe.

In long-tongued bees, like those in Apidae, the first two segments of the labial palps are elongated and are much longer than the second two segments.

TAXONOMY: Worldwide there are nearly 6,000 species in the Apidae family, distributed on every continent and species-rich wherever they occur. In North America, species are divided among three subfamilies (these three subfamilies are the only subfamilies in Apidae around the world) and numerous tribes: Apinae, primarily the medium to large-sized fuzzy bees; Nomadinae, comprising entirely cleptoparasites; and Xylocopinae, the small and large carpenter bees. Details for the subfamilies are listed below.

SUBFAMILY XYLOCOPINAE

There are two genera, each in its own tribe, in this subfamily. In the tribe Xylocopini are *Xylocopa,* large, shiny, black bees. In the tribe Ceratinini are the significantly smaller but also shiny *Ceratina.* See the text below for more characteristics.

SUBFAMILY APINAE

There are 26 genera in this subfamily in North America, with 19 in the eastern U.S. While there is considerable morphologic diversity in the look of the Apinae, almost all females have slender hairs along the apical margin of S6 that get denser toward the center. In many groups the clypeus protrudes markedly from the face. In noncleptoparasitic tribes, the pygidial plate, pygidial fimbriae, and prepygidial fimbriae are present. Scopal hairs are restricted to the hind tibia and basitarsus.

— **ANTHOPHORINI:** All are robust bees, fast-flying, with copious hair. On the wings there are no hairs, so that the cells are completely bare. This group consists of two genera, *Habropoda* and *Anthophora.*

— **APINI:** While the Apini are well represented in other parts of the world, in North America this tribe is represented by just one species: *Apis mellifera.* It can be distinguished from other Apidae (and Apinae) by the corbicula in females (which are more commonly seen than males) and the hairy compound eyes. On the hindwing, there is a jugal lobe.

— **BOMBINI:** The Bombini are represented by one genus in North America, *Bombus,* which also contains the subgenus *Psithyrus,* the cleptoparasitic bumble bees. They are the other corbiculate Apidae, but they have no jugal lobe. Their compound eyes are not hairy.

— **CENTRIDINI:** Large, bold bees that fly fast and are hairy. On the head, the first flagellar segment is often longer than the scape. On the wing, there is only a very small stigma. On the legs, there is no arolium (seen commonly in many Apidae). There is one genus: *Centris.*

— **EMPHORINI:** Medium to large bees, with lots of hair. In males, the antennae are short. On the head in both sexes, the vertex is gently curved, and stands out above the ocelli. This tribe is found only in the Americas, and in eastern North America two genera are common (*Ptilothrix* and *Melitoma*), while a third genus, *Diadasia,* is more common in the western U.S. and Canada.

— **ERICROCIDINI:** Medium to large strikingly patterned cleptoparasites. Cleptoparasites of *Centris.* They, like their hosts, are more common in the West. There is one genus in North America: *Ericrocis* (not covered in this book).

— **EUCERINI:** Medium to large hairy bees, usually with pale hair bands. In males of many species the antennae are very long. On the tongue, if it can be seen, the paraglossa is very long, often reaching to the end of the second segment of the labial palpus. On the head, the vertex is flat, so that the ocelli poke up a little. In North America there are 212 species in 14 genera. In the eastern U.S. can be found *Eucera,* which includes a number of subgenera that used to be separate genera: *Cemolobus, Eucera* sensu strictu, and *Peponapis.* Other genera include *Florilegus, Svastra, Melissodes,* and *Tetraloniella,* which is not featured in this book.

— **EUGLOSSINI:** These are the orchid bees, rarely seen even in their native range. The species here have extraordinarily long proboscises and brilliant green bodies. There is one genus in North America: *Euglossa.*

— **EXOMALOPSINI:** Small to moderately sized hairy bees with pale hair bands on the abdomen. On the head, next to each compound eye, there is a row of long, stout hairs, which is not seen in other Apidae genera. This group consists of *Exomalopsis* and *Anthophorula,* both of which are rare in the East and not included here.

— **MELECTINI:** Strikingly colored cleptoparasitic bees. Larger than many other cleptoparasites, and also fuzzier. In North America there are three genera. Only two, *Xeromelecta* and *Melecta,* are seen in the East, and rarely. The western genus is *Zacosmia.* None of the Melectini are featured in this book.

— **OSIRINI:** Includes one genus, *Epeoloides.* This bee has only been seen half a dozen times in the last 50 years in the East. It is not included in this book.

— **PROTEPEOLINI:** Includes one genus, *Leiopodus,* which occurs only along the border of Mexico with the U.S. It is not included here.

SUBFAMILY NOMADINAE

All bees in this subfamily are cleptoparasites, lacking scopal hairs, and often with patches of appressed hairs on the thorax and abdomen. Many of these tribes have in them only one genus. With a few exceptions, most are rarely seen, and many genera do not occur in the East.

— **AMMOBATINI:** In North America, represented by one genus, *Oreopasites,* seen only in the western U.S. It is not included in this book.

— **AMMOBATOIDINI:** Consists of one genus in North America, *Holcopasites.* These are small and coarsely punctate, with a red abdomen and patches of pale, flattened white hairs, like polka dots.

— **BIASTINI:** One genus of very small bees, *Neopasites,* found in North America, and only in the West. This genus is not described in this book.

— **BRACHYNOMADINI:** A tribe better represented in South America; in North America, one genus occurs, in the arid Southwest: *Brachynomada.* It is not included in this book.

— **EPEOLINI:** Stout, strikingly colored, black and white bees with pointed abdomens. The axillae are elongated into points that hang over the scutellum. Two genera: *Epeolus* and *Triepeolus.*

— **HEXEPEOLINI:** Consists of one genus, *Hexepeolus,* found only in the southwestern U.S. This genus is not described in this book.

— **NEOLARRINI:** Only one genus of very small bees, found in the western United States, east as far as North Dakota and some of Texas. *Neolarra* is not included here.

— **NOMADINI:** Only one genus, *Nomada.* Unlike other genera included in the Nomadinae, *Nomada* are relatively common. They are slender, wasplike, often with thickened antennae. Colors include some combination of red, white, yellow, and black.

— **TOWNSENDIELLINI:** Contains one genus of black and white bees, *Townsendiella,* found only in arid areas of the western United States. It is not included here.

XYLOCOPA

— **SUBFAMILY:** Xylocopinae
— **TRIBE:** Xylocopini

OVERVIEW: Species in this genus are among the largest in North America. With shiny black bodies, loud wings, discourteous behavior, and a propensity for nesting communally in wood close to human domiciles, they are hard to miss. Carpenter bees can be seen from March through October; one of the few bees with adults that can overwinter. They are generalists that prefer large open flowers, but will "steal" nectar from those with narrow corollas by cutting a hole at the base of the flower to get to it. Nest in dead wood, especially tree stumps; one of the few bees to chew their own holes. Often nest in gables, soffits, gazebos, decks, and other wood structures near homes. Nests are long galleries, used for multiple generations, but elongated each year to accommodate new members.

IN THE WORLD: More than 400 species worldwide, well represented on every continent. In the U.S. and Canada there are 9 species, with 2 occurring in the East. One is restricted to Florida, but the other is abundant and widespread throughout.

CLEPTOPARASITES: No bee parasites known.

IDENTIFYING FEATURES: Large, often shiny black to bluish-black bees. Easy to recognize. **HEAD:** In males, the lower half of the face has bright yellow markings. The head overall is round—wider than long or subequal; the malar space is very short. **THORAX:** In North American species, the thorax of both males and females is often covered with black hair (but see, for example, *X. virginica*). **WINGS:** The marginal cell is very elongated, tapering to a point at both ends. The second submarginal cell is narrowed, almost triangular in shape, with the margin closest to the marginal cell much narrower than the bottom margin. **LEGS:** In females, scopal hairs are stiff stout brushes of black hair. **ABDOMEN:** With less hair than the thorax; hairs may be light or dark. **SIMILAR GENERA:** Bumble bees (*Bombus*) are often mistaken for *Xylocopa*. The yellow integument on the faces of the males distinguishes those individuals from bumble bees. And the shiny abdomen, lacking distinct hair bands on T2–T5, distinguishes them from female bumble bees, which have a hairy abdomen (note: in southern Florida there is a subspecies of *X. virginica* that has small tufts of white on the sides of T5 and T6). In addition, bumble bees carry pollen in a shiny corbicula, whereas female *Xylocopa* have stout thick scopa on their hind legs. The head of the bumble bee is often longer than it is wide, whereas *Xylocopa* have very round heads.

Xylocopa virginica

SIZE: Large; 17–23 mm. **PHENOLOGY:** Almost year-round in southern areas of their range. March through November in other areas. **FLORAL HOSTS:** Polylectic, visiting a wide variety of plants for pollen and nectar. Often seen cutting holes in the base of flowers with narrow floral tubes in order to suck nectar out of plants into which it cannot fit. **RANGE:** Throughout the Midwest, north to New England, and south to Florida. **NESTING:** Cavity nesters, often seen in man-made structures creating large galleries, with multiple individuals working in the same area. **IDENTIFICATION:** Overly large bee that flies throughout the summer. Often multiple individuals are seen at once as females use same nest entrance, and males patrol. **HEAD:** The malar space is very short, almost nonexistent. The

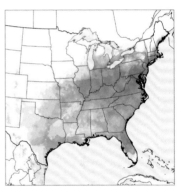

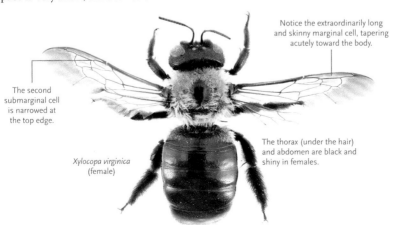

Notice the extraordinarily long and skinny marginal cell, tapering acutely toward the body.

The second submarginal cell is narrowed at the top edge.

The thorax (under the hair) and abdomen are black and shiny in females.

Xylocopa virginica
(female)

The thorax and first section of the abdomen sport dense blonde hairs.

The abdomen is very shiny in *Xylocopa*.

Xylocopa virginica
(female)

There are thick stout scopal hairs on the hind legs.

Unlike bumble bees, *Xylocopa* males have pale faces.

Males have eyes that look like they are about to touch at the top.

T5 and T6 have stout black bristles.

Xylocopa virginica
(male)

genal area is thick, and consequently so is the whole head. In males, the eyes nearly meet at the top and the lower half of the face is creamy yellow, though the antennal scapes are dark. **THORAX:** Hair is blonde. The integument is shiny black beneath. **WINGS:** Dark. **LEGS:** In females, stout dark-colored scopal hairs occur on the tibia. **ABDOMEN:** The integument is black and shiny, though in males it may appear to have slight purple tints. The first tergal segment may have light blonde hair, but typically there is little hair beyond this (*Xylocopa virginica texana* has short, light-colored hair on much of the abdomen).

SIMILAR SPECIES: In Florida there is an additional species of *Xylocopa*. *Xylocopa micans* males have a green/blue tint, while females appear light purple. In males, the antennal scape is yellow on the underside, and the legs have some light hairs on them. In females, there are no lighter-colored hairs on the sides of the thorax, as in *X. virginica*. *Megachile sculpturalis* is another large dark bee that flies at the same time and nests in wood. On the wing, there are only two submarginal cells in *M. sculpturalis*. On the abdomen, in females of *M. sculpturalis*, scopal hairs occur on the underside, rather than on the legs as in *X. virginica*. And the overall appearance of *M. sculpturalis* is longer and narrower than the hulky appearance of *Xylocopa*.

CERATINA

— **SUBFAMILY:** Xylocopinae
— **TRIBE:** Ceratinini

OVERVIEW: Small bees, but often extremely abundant. Shiny gunmetal green/black bodies, with white markings on the face. All species are generalists and can be seen on a wide variety of flowers, including weedy plant species. *Ceratina* nest in the pithy stems of last year's flowering forbs and especially shrubs (*Sumac, Sambucus,* etc.). Females overwinter as adults in small tunnels in stems and excavate that same tunnel into a nest in the spring.

IN THE WORLD: Around 350 species around the world, 25 species in North America, and 5 species in the eastern U.S. and Canada.

CLEPTOPARASITES: In North America, none known.

IDENTIFYING FEATURES: Mostly hairless gunmetal green/black bees of small size. **HEAD:** Usually yellow markings on the lower portion of the clypeus; in males more prominent, and often with a line up the center of clypeus, like an upside-down T. **THORAX:** Elongated. **WINGS:** Three submarginal cells. **ABDOMEN:** Same width as the thorax. The apex of the abdomen often comes to an abrupt point. Each tergal segment constricts at its apex, giving the abdomen edges a wavy appearance.

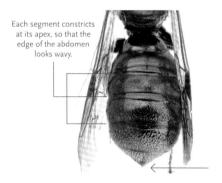

Each segment constricts at its apex, so that the edge of the abdomen looks wavy.

SIMILAR GENERA: The small size and dark coloration can make them appear similar to *Hylaeus* and *Lasioglossum* (especially *L. [Dialictus]*). *Hylaeus* have two submarginal cells, and the overall body shape is skinnier. In males, the markings on the face are distinctive. In *Hylaeus* the males have yellow next to each compound eye; in *Ceratina* the yellow is restricted to the clypeus, usually in the center. *Hylaeus* abdomens do not constrict to a sudden point, and they are not as shiny as *Ceratina*. *Lasioglossum* (*Dialictus*) do not have yellow on their faces. They tend to be greener, and often have noticeable hair bands on the abdomen. The basal vein on *Ceratina* can appear arcuate, as in *L. (Dialictus)*, which can be confusing. The facial markings, hair bands, and abdominal shape should be sufficient characters to distinguish the two.

Females of many eastern *Ceratina* species are part of a species complex, meaning there is considerable variation in features occurring within one species, and also much overlap in morphological features between different species, which makes identification difficult. It may not be possible, even with a microscope, to verify the identity of some eastern *Ceratina*.

Ceratina calcarata

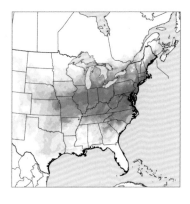

SIZE: Small; 5–8 mm. **PHENOLOGY:** March through late October. **FLORAL HOSTS:** Polylectic, visiting many plants for pollen and nectar. **RANGE:** North Dakota east to Maine, incorporating southern Canada, and south through Texas and Georgia. **NESTING:** Hollow plant stems.

IDENTIFICATION: Dark blue-green and relatively shiny. **HEAD:** In females, the clypeus may have a small ivory line in the middle; in males, the clypeus is almost completely ivory, in a broad upside-down T-shape. The face has deep punctures but is very shiny between. Very few punctures on underside of head. In males, antennal segments 2 and 3 are broader than long. **THORAX:** Few punctures on the scutum, even on the posterior half. **WINGS:** Slightly darkened. **LEGS:** In males, the hind femurs are very angled. In females, the front femur is completely dark, usually with no dot of ivory coloring at the front. **ABDOMEN:** In males, the end of T7 is flattened into a broad and elongated lip.

SIMILAR SPECIES: *Ceratina calcarata* females are nearly indistinguishable from *C. dupla* females; identification is best determined through association with males present at the same location. In general, the females of *C. calcarata* have few punctations on the back half of the scutum; female *C. dupla* have more even and dense punctation on the back half of the scutum.

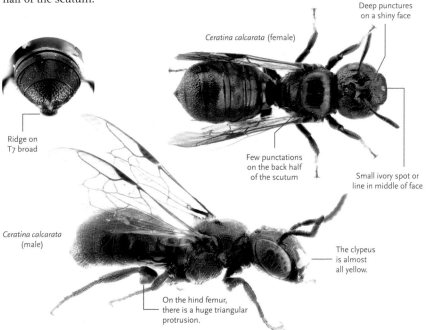

Deep punctures on a shiny face

Ceratina calcarata (female)

Ridge on T7 broad

Few punctations on the back half of the scutum

Small ivory spot or line in middle of face

Ceratina calcarata (male)

The clypeus is almost all yellow.

On the hind femur, there is a huge triangular protrusion.

Males can be distinguished by the strong, almost tooth-like angle on the hind femur found in *C. calcarata,* which is absent from *C. dupla* males. *Ceratina strenua* also looks similar, but is best distinguished by its smaller size and more greenish hue. In females, the front tibia of *C. strenua* has a small ivory stripe at the base, which is often missing, or is merely a spot, in *C. calcarata. Ceratina strenua* males have a narrow ridge on T7, as *C. calcarata* does, but it is broad, and takes up at least half of the tergal segment.

Ceratina dupla

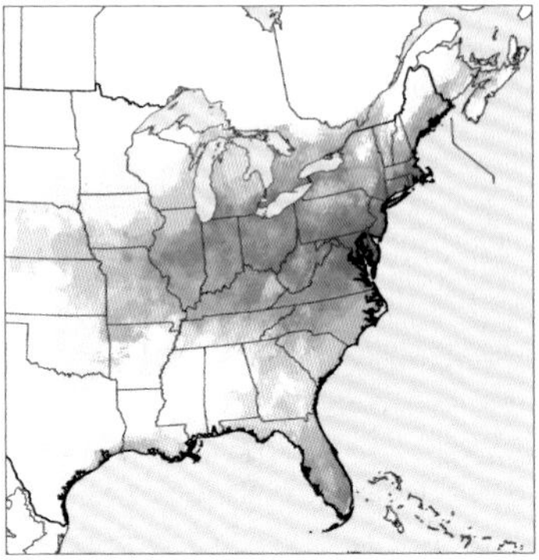

SIZE: Small; 6–8 mm. **PHENOLOGY:** March through October. **FLORAL HOSTS:** Generalist, seen on a wide variety of flowering plants. **RANGE:** Widespread throughout the eastern U.S. and Canada. **NESTING:** Nests in hollow plant stems, including teasel (*Dipsacus*). **IDENTIFICATION:** Blue-green metallic bee, leaning more toward green than deep blue. **HEAD:** In females, the clypeus has a long, central ivory line; in males the clypeus is largely all ivory. The head is regularly punctate, with just a few impunctate areas (compare with other eastern *Ceratina*). **THORAX:** The scutum is also evenly pitted, with small pits, and only a small central area that is bare of pits. **WINGS:** Slightly darkened. **LEGS:** In males, the hind femur is not at all angled, but may be slightly expanded at the base; the inner and outer surfaces of

Punctures on the back half of the scutum even and dense

Ceratina dupla (female)

Ceratina dupla (male)

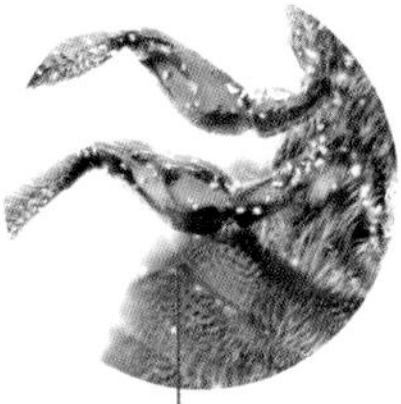

Lacking the tooth-like angle on the hind femur.

the femur are sharply distinguished from each other by a strong ridge. In females, the front femur is completely dark, with no dot of ivory coloring at the front. **ABDOMEN:** In males, there is a small carina at the center of T7 that appears as a very small hump. **SIMILAR SPECIES:** *Ceratina mikmaqi* is an eastern species that is very difficult to distinguish from *C. dupla*. They overlap in most locations in the northeastern portion of their ranges and have previously been considered variations of one species. They nest in similar materials, but *C. mikmaqi* is seen a little later in the year than *C. dupla* (which may be bivoltine, at least in some regions). The most distinguishing feature between the two are features of the hind femur, which exhibits a stronger ridge separating the inner and outer surfaces in *C. dupla*. *Ceratina dupla* is also similar in appearance to *C. calcarata*. See *C. calcarata* for more information.

Ceratina strenua

SIZE: Petite to small; 4.5–6.5 mm.
PHENOLOGY: May through October or even November at southern locations. **FLORAL HOSTS:** Generalist, found on many different flowering plants. **RANGE:** Widespread throughout eastern North America; absent from Florida. **NESTING:** Plant stems.
IDENTIFICATION: Very small blue-green bee. **HEAD:** In females, there are few pits, with the clypeus almost entirely impunctate, giving the face an overall shiny appearance. The middle of the clypeus has a long ivory mark. In males, the clypeus is almost entirely yellow. **LEGS:** In females, the front femur

Ivory stripe on the front tibia

Ivory spot at the base of the tibia

Tooth-like angle on the hind femur

Lip on T7 is narrow.

Ceratina strenua (female)

Ceratina strenua (male)

has a small white spot at its apex. In males, there is a white stripe extending the length of the front tibia. The hind femur has a strong triangular protrusion at about the middle. **WINGS:** Smoky, but less so than in other *Ceratina*. **ABDOMEN:** In males, T7 has a narrow lip, longer than it is wide.

SIMILAR SPECIES: Few male *Ceratina* in the East have a strong protrusion on the hind femur. This character alone should distinguish at least male *Ceratina* from all but *C. calcarata*. Between these two, the difference in the shape of the ridge on T7 is distinctive; in *C. strenua* it is narrow and elongate, while it is broad and shorter in *C. calcarata*. In females, the ivory stripe on the front tibia is unique. One species in Florida, *C. floridana,* shares this character, but that species is significantly larger, and much bluer in coloration.

DIADASIA

— **SUBFAMILY:** Apinae
— **TRIBE:** Emphorini

OVERVIEW: Hairy, fast-flying bees seen most often in early to midsummer. All species are specialists; in North America, these bees specialize on just one of five plant families (Asteraceae, Onagraceae, Convolvulaceae, Cactaceae, and, most commonly, Malvaceae). Bees nest in the ground, with many species creating elaborate turrets, periscopes, or chimneys over their nest openings, which are usually in hard-packed dry earth.

IN THE WORLD: North, Central, and South America; amphitropically distributed so the genus occurs on either side of the tropics, but seldom within the tropics. About 45 species altogether, with 30 in the U.S. and Canada. Four species occur east of the Rocky Mountains. While common in the Midwest, they are seldom seen east of the Mississippi River.

CLEPTOPARASITES: No bee parasites known.

IDENTIFYING FEATURES: Bees of variable size, from 5 to 20 mm; fuzzy. **HEAD:** Narrower than width of thorax when viewed from above. Eyes often with bluish tinge. Face appears consistently oval, rounded on top, and not flattened as in some other Apidae. The tongue is relatively short; when extended, not reaching even to the middle of the thorax. The first flagellar segment of the antennae is short—less than twice as long as width. **THORAX:** In males, the propodeal region is bare of hair, and usually heavily polished. **LEGS:** There is an arolium between the front claws. In many females, the front legs have long dense hairs on the base of the front femur, and the scopal hairs on the hind legs all curve up and in at their tips. In males, the claws of the hind legs are usually broad and rounded. **ABDOMEN:** Many species have distinct apical hair bands running across the terga. Though difficult to see, on S2 there is a raised lateral line that is produced at its middle.

There is no easily accessible published key to North American *Diadasia*, so identifying *Diadasia* to species can be difficult. With so few species in the East, host plant can help narrow down possible options.

SIMILAR GENERA: May look similar to other large fuzzy Apidae. Can be distinguished from most by smaller head width, and the rounded vertex (Eucerini, for example, are flattened across the top of the head). The wing venation is also unique—Anthophorini and Eucerini species lack the longer cubital cell, and the distance between the two portions of the lower vein of the radial cell is more or less equal in other bee groups. Scopal hairs, though dense in all very fuzzy Apidae, distinctly curl in for *Diadasia*. Finally, the raised ridge on the second sternal segment is unique, among Apidae, to *Diadasia*, though it is difficult to see.

Diadasia enavata

SIZE: Medium to large; 14–16 mm.
PHENOLOGY: May through September, when sunflowers (*Helianthus*) are in bloom. **FLORAL HOSTS:** Strict specialist on sunflowers *(Helianthus)*; may be seen on occasion foraging for nectar on other plants, especially other Asteraceae. **RANGE:** This bee has the largest distribution of any of the 30 species of *Diadasia* found in the U.S. and Canada. Found across the Midwest, from southern Manitoba south through Texas and northern Mississippi; west to the California coast. **NESTING:** Ground-nesting.
IDENTIFICATION: Large, pale, fuzzy bee seen frequently on sunflowers. **HEAD:** Narrower than the width of the thorax. From the front, the

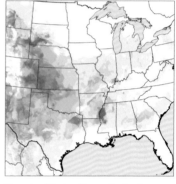

The vertex of the head is curved rather than flat as in similar-looking bees (like *Anthophora*).

Diadasia enavata
(female)

The head is narrower than the width of the thorax.

The thorax is covered in pale gold hair, more or less dense depending on the age of the specimen.

Diadasia enavata
(female)

Scopal hairs are numerous, thin, and wispy.

The scopal hairs are thick, feathered, and each one curves in just a little.

On the female, there are long curved hairs on the femur.

The clypeus doesn't protrude very far from the face.

There is an arolium between the claws in *Diadasia*.

Diadasia enavata
(male)

head appears rounded at the vertex, gently doming above the ocelli so that they do not seem to stick out from the head. The mandibles are dark at their bases. **LEGS:** In females, the tibial spurs are straight, or just slightly curved at the very tip. On the front legs of females, the hairs of the basitarsus are very long, with feathery branches when viewed under a microscope or with a hand lens. **ABDOMEN:** The propodeal enclosure is very shiny, with no pits, and no sculpting of any kind. On T3 and T4, the hair is pale, with no appressed dark hairs anywhere.

SIMILAR SPECIES: There are four species of *Diadasia* in eastern North America, including much of the Midwest. *Diadasia afflicta* and *D. diminuta* are both specialists on poppy and globe mallows (*Callirhoe* and *Sphaeralcea*), which is where they are mostly seen. These species are much smaller in size than *D. enavata*. *Diadasia australis* is a cactus specialist, mostly on prickly pear (*Opuntia*) and seldom seen as one moves east.

MELITOMA

— **SUBFAMILY:** Apinae
— **TRIBE:** Emphorini

OVERVIEW: Medium to large dark bee often seen foraging in *Ipomoea* flowers during the summer months, especially early in the morning. All *Melitoma* are specialists, with the majority specializing on flowers in the Convolvulaceae, especially *Ipomoea*. All species are ground nesters, with many preferring to nest in vertical banks or even adobe walls.

IN THE WORLD: Around a dozen species occur, all in the Americas. Of these, 4 are found in North America, with 3 occurring in the Midwest and locations further east.

CLEPTOPARASITES: Maybe *Triepeolus* and *Epeolus*.

IDENTIFYING FEATURES: HEAD: *Melitoma* have rounded heads, as in other Emphorini, with the vertex evenly curved above the level of the ocelli. The head is narrower than the width of the thorax. The tongue is exceedingly long, extending almost to the end of the thorax, when under the body. **THORAX:** In most species, there are dark and light hairs intermixed, creating a patchwork of dark and light areas across the top of the body. In males, even the propodeal region is covered in thick hair. **LEGS:** Scopal hairs are long and feathery. **WINGS:** The long vein that separates the cubital cell from the radial cell is intersected by the cubital vein near the end, rather than near the middle (as in *Diadasia*). **ABDOMEN:** S2 does not possess a sharply angled projection.

SIMILAR GENERA: Looks very similar to *Ptilothrix,* and often can be found on the same plants as *Ptilothrix* too. The most notable difference is that *Ptilothrix* has a large arolium between the claws, while *Melitoma* does not. Can also resemble *Diadasia*, but in *Diadasia* S2 is strongly angled, and the hair patterns are very different. May also be confused with a dark bumble bee (*Bombus*). The scopal hairs, which are long and feathery in *Melitoma*, are very distinct from the flat, shiny corbicula seen in bumble bees.

Melitoma taurea

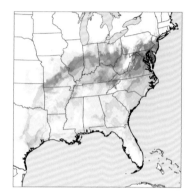

SIZE: Small to medium; 9–12.5 mm.
PHENOLOGY: Mid-June through mid-September (may be earlier in Florida). **FLORAL HOSTS:** Specialist on morning glory (*Ipomoea*). May visit other flowers for nectar. **RANGE:** Kansas, eastern Texas, and Iowa, east to Georgia and northern Florida, north to New Jersey. **NESTING:** Most often seen nesting in vertical banks of hard-packed soil. Females bring water to the nesting site to moisten the soil and may then use the soil they excavate from the nest to create "chimneys" over the nest entrance.

IDENTIFICATION: Overall dark appearance, medium to large in size. **HEAD:** The clypeus is all black and sticks out from the head when viewed in profile. The antennal scapes are completely black in both sexes. **THORAX:** The body is covered with fine pale hairs, intermixed with black on the scutum and the scutellum so that it almost appears longitudinally striped or patchy. **LEGS:** Scopal hairs are dark, thick, and heavily branched, with branches lighter in color than the stalks. **ABDOMEN:** Short appressed white hairs, thicker at the base of each tergal segment, form white stripes, which can be seen when the bee is head-down in the corolla of *Ipomoea*.

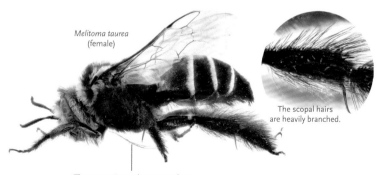

Melitoma taurea
(female)

The scopal hairs
are heavily branched.

The tongue is very long, extending
nearly to the end of the thorax.

The head is narrower than the width of the thorax.

Bright white hair bands on abdomen

Long feathery scopal hairs

Distinct light and dark pattern on the thorax

Melitoma taurea (female)

The patterns of light and dark hair on the thorax are unique.

Ariola present

The legs of males are long.

Melitoma taurea (male)

SIMILAR SPECIES: May overlap with *Melitoma grisella* at the western edge of its range. *Melitoma grisella* has only pale hairs on the top of the head, between the compound eyes, while *M. taurea* has a mix of light and dark hairs. Similarly, the thorax, especially the scutum and scutellum of *M. grisella* is covered entirely with pale yellow hairs, while in *M. taurea* the hairs are both light and dark. *Melitoma marginella* overlaps with *M. taurea* just in Texas; *M. marginella* is a subtropical bee more common in Mexico. The two can be distinguished by the much-oranger pubescence on the head of *M. marginella* than on *M. taurea*.

PTILOTHRIX

— **SUBFAMILY: Apinae**
— **TRIBE: Emphorini**

OVERVIEW: Large, dark, hairy bees. Presumed to be specialists, mostly on plants in the mallow family (Malvaceae). *Ptilothrix* are solitary ground nesters. Nests are usually on flat ground or gently sloping banks, with short turrets, and balls of sculpted earth around them. They use water to soften and form the soil around their nests, and can be seen landing on water to gather droplets to bring back to their nesting site.

IN THE WORLD: *Ptilothrix* occurs only in North, Central, and South America. Found north and south of tropical regions, it is considered amphitropical. There are around 13 species, but only 3 in North America. In the eastern U.S. and Canada, only 1 species occurs.

CLEPTOPARASITES: Maybe *Triepeolus* and *Epeolus*.

IDENTIFYING FEATURES: Large bees, usually dark colored; many species have strong apical hair bands across each tergal segment (note: the eastern species of *Ptilothrix* does not have these). **HEAD:** The vertex is gently curved so that the ocelli fall below the profile of the back of the head. The clypeus is black and lightly polished. On the antennae, the first flagellar segment is at least two times as long as it is wide. **THORAX:** Very hairy, so that the integument, including the propodeal area, is hard to see. **LEGS:** No arolium between the tarsal claws. In females, the scopal hairs are thick, long, and very feathery. **ABDOMEN:** S2 is smoothly curved, with no strong angle. **SIMILAR GENERA:** Eastern species of *Xylocopa* have similar hair patterns to eastern *Ptilothrix*. The larger size of *Xylocopa* should help. The scopal hairs on *Xylocopa* are stout and sparse, unlike the thick and feathery hairs of *Ptilothrix*. In males, the clypeus of *Ptilothrix* is black, but in *Xylocopa* males it is yellow or ivory. *Bombus* can also be similarly colored, but possess a corbicula in place of feathery scopal hairs. *Diadasia* may also appear somewhat similar in size and general shape. *Ptilothrix* are slenderer, and lack the arolia seen in *Diadasia*. The second sternal segment of *Diadasia* is angular, not curved as it is in *Ptilothrix*.

Ptilothrix bombiformis

SIZE: Medium to large; 12.5–17.5 mm. **PHENOLOGY:** Mid-June through August, when *Hibiscus* bloom.

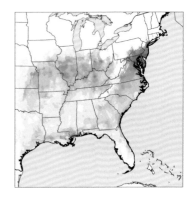

FLORAL HOSTS: Specialist on native *Hibiscus*, though may be seen on some cultivars, and may occasionally be seen in *Ipomoea* flowers. **RANGE:** Kansas to Maine, south to Maine, south to Florida and eastern Texas. **NESTING:** Nests near marshes and other swampy areas, usually in roads, parking pull-outs, or levees.

IDENTIFICATION: Large bee with gray/blonde hair on the thorax. **HEAD:** Light yellow hairs are intermixed with dark hairs between the antennae and on the vertex, which is gently rounded. The malar space is small to nearly nonexistent. The clypeus in both sexes is black. **LEGS:** Appear relatively long compared with the body size. **ABDOMEN:** Though many species of *Ptilothrix* have white stripes on the abdomen, the hair banding on *P. bombiformis* is all black hairs. **SIMILAR SPECIES:** No other species of *Ptilothrix* occur in the eastern U.S.

Ptilothrix bombiformis
(female)

Relatively long legs

Head covered with dark hairs, with light hairs intermixed near the antennae

Very short malar space

No arolia

Ptilothrix bombiformis
(male)

Thorax is
dirty blonde.

Abdomen is covered
in thick dark hair, all
of uniform length.

Ptilothrix bombiformis
(female)

Long legs with long
scopal hairs on the
basitarsus

EUCERA

— SUBFAMILY: Apinae
— TRIBE: Eucerini

OVERVIEW: Larger bees, often noticed because of the protruding clypeus, or the long antennae in males. Some species are distinctly spring, but with multiple unique subgenera, there are also summer and fall species. The genus includes specialists (with many on Asteraceae) and generalists. All nest in the ground, usually in modest holes with little externally visible modification.

IN THE WORLD: Found around the world, with 220 species distributed mostly in the Northern Hemisphere: Japan through Central Asia, west to Spain and the Canary Islands. In the U.S. there are six subgenera, many of which used to be genera (number of U.S. species listed in parentheses): *Synhalonia* (55 species), *Cemolobus* (1 species), *Peponapis* (6 species), *Tetraloniella* (6 species), *Xenoglossa* (4 species), and *Syntrichalonia* (1 species). In the eastern U.S. there are 15 species, belonging to the subgenera *Synhalonia* (7 species), *Cemolubus* (1 species), *Peponapis* (2 species), *Tetraloniella* (3 species), and *Xenoglossa* (2 species). Several of these bee groups occur only, or just barely, into the Midwest. We highlight 5 of the 15 eastern species, choosing ones that are common across the eastern U.S. and eastern Canada.

CLEPTOPARASITES: *Triepeolus*.

IDENTIFYING FEATURES: Large, fuzzy bees. HEAD: The clypeus sticks out notably from the face, and is often yellow. The proboscis is very long. In males, the antennae are long and completely black. WINGS: In North American species, there are three submarginal cells. Small erect hairs occur inside the cells on the wing.

ABDOMEN: There are often abdominal stripes. When present, they are at the base of each tergal segment, and often wrap around to the sternal segments underneath.

SIMILAR GENERA: *Melissodes* are similar in appearance. The difference between the two can be hard to see. *Melissodes* have tegulae that are pointed at the anterior end, but rounded at the posterior end, giving them a tear-drop shape. *Eucera* have round tegulae.

This is a difficult character to see in fuzzy specimens and hair may need to be scraped aside. In general, *Melissodes* fly later in the year and are smaller than most eastern *Eucera*. *Habropoda* may also appear similar, and fly at the same time. In the East there is only one *Habropoda* species; its wings are not hairy inside the cell margins, as *Eucera* wings are.

Recently, species of *Eucera (Synhalonia)*, *Peponapis*, *Xenoglossa*, *Cemolobus*, and a host of others in various eucerine bee genera were found to be similar enough to each other, and different enough from everything else, to warrant putting them all in the same genus, and making the old genus names into subgenera. Thus, the squash bee *Peponapis* is now *Eucera (Peponapis)*. The characters describing the bee have not changed, only its name to more accurately reflect its relationships with other bees. Nonetheless, coming up with general characters that unite the bees in the same genus has become more complicated. Be patient with yourself as you learn to distinguish between these subgenera. Below are a few key points for the subgenera covered in this book.

Eucera (Synhalonia): Three submarginal cells. Includes all *Eucera* sensu strictu in North America. Next to each compound eye there is no strong carina, especially toward the lower half of the face (as is seen in other Eucerini). Also, the hair bands on tergal segments of the abdomen often run underneath, and across each sternal segment

Eucera (Cemolobus): The apex of the clypeus has three distinct lobes. Bees in this subgenus are found on *Ipomoea* and *Calystegia* flowers.

Eucera (Peponapis): Extremely protuberant clypeus. Bees are usually seen in or near squash flowers.

Eucera (Xenoglossa): On the antennae in males, the first flagellar segment is significantly longer than the second. In most *Eucera*, the first flagellar segment is very short. In females and males, there is a tooth on the inner margin of the mandible, right near the base. Often seen in or around squash flowers.

Eucera (Synhalonia) atriventris

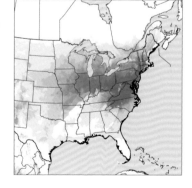

SIZE: Medium to large; 13–15 mm. **PHENOLOGY:** March through July. **FLORAL HOSTS:** Generalist, but commonly seen on Fabaceae and also *Penstemon*. **RANGE:** Pennsylvania and New York west to Minnesota and Iowa. South to Georgia and North Carolina. **NESTING:** Ground-nesting bee.

IDENTIFICATION: Medium-sized fast-flying bee with dark abdomen and gray or blonde hair on the thorax. **HEAD:** Clypeus sticks out far from the face; punctures on clypeus are coarse and distinct. In males, clypeus and labrum are yellow. The mandibles are also slightly

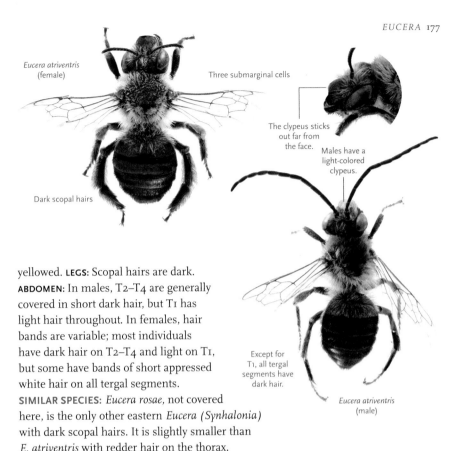

Eucera atriventris
(female)

Three submarginal cells

The clypeus sticks
out far from
the face.

Males have a
light-colored
clypeus.

Dark scopal hairs

Except for
T1, all tergal
segments have
dark hair.

Eucera atriventris
(male)

yellowed. **LEGS:** Scopal hairs are dark.
ABDOMEN: In males, T2–T4 are generally
covered in short dark hair, but T1 has
light hair throughout. In females, hair
bands are variable; most individuals
have dark hair on T2–T4 and light on T1,
but some have bands of short appressed
white hair on all tergal segments.
SIMILAR SPECIES: *Eucera rosae,* not covered
here, is the only other eastern *Eucera (Synhalonia)*
with dark scopal hairs. It is slightly smaller than
E. atriventris with redder hair on the thorax.

Eucera (Synhalonia) hamata

SIZE: Medium to large; 13–17 mm.
PHENOLOGY: April through
August. **FLORAL HOSTS:** Broad
generalist seen on many
flowering plants.
RANGE: Maryland west to Wisconsin, Kansas, and
Colorado, and south to Georgia and the Florida
Panhandle. **NESTING:** Ground nester, sometimes
among dense vegetation. May nest in
aggregations.
IDENTIFICATION: Medium-sized fast-flying bee
with light white stripes on abdomen and auburn/gray hair on thorax. **HEAD:** Clypeus
sticks out far from the face. Punctures on clypeus are coarse and distinct, but very
close together. In males, clypeus and labrum are yellow. The mandibles are also slightly
yellowed. **LEGS:** Scopal hairs are light-colored, and simple, with no branches. In both
sexes, the hind tibial spur is strongly hooked at its end, curving sharply and suddenly

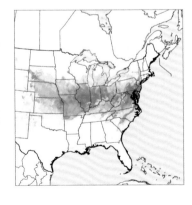

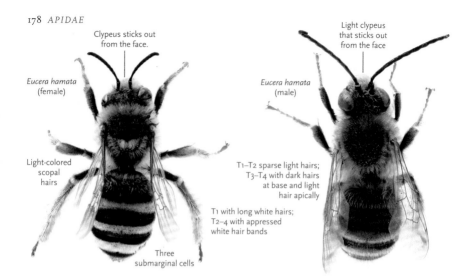

Eucera hamata (female)

Clypeus sticks out from the face.

Light-colored scopal hairs

Three submarginal cells

Eucera hamata (male)

Light clypeus that sticks out from the face

T1–T2 sparse light hairs; T3–T4 with dark hairs at base and light hair apically

T1 with long white hairs; T2–4 with appressed white hair bands

inward. **ABDOMEN:** In females, distinct white hair bands run across the base of the second through fourth tergal segments. The anterior face of T1 is coated in thick, long, white hairs. In males, T1 and T2 are generally covered in short, sparse hair that is a mix of light and dark hairs; there are no distinct hair bands. In

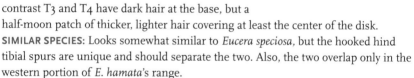

contrast T3 and T4 have dark hair at the base, but a half-moon patch of thicker, lighter hair covering at least the center of the disk. **SIMILAR SPECIES:** Looks somewhat similar to *Eucera speciosa*, but the hooked hind tibial spurs are unique and should separate the two. Also, the two overlap only in the western portion of *E. hamata*'s range.

Eucera (Cemolobus) ipomoeae

SIZE: Medium; 12–15 mm.
PHENOLOGY: June and July.
FLORAL HOSTS: Specializes on *Ipomoea* and *Calystegia*. Males can be found inside these flowers in the morning. It is one of only a handful of bees to visit *Ipomoea* flowers exclusively, so the plant association can be useful in identifying this bee; however, of the *Ipomoea* visitors, this is the least commonly seen. **RANGE:** Rarely seen; flies very early in the

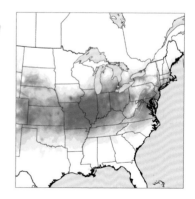

morning or late in the evening. Occurs from North Carolina west through Illinois and Missouri (one record in Colorado). South through Georgia. **NESTING:** Unknown, but presumably a ground-nesting bee.

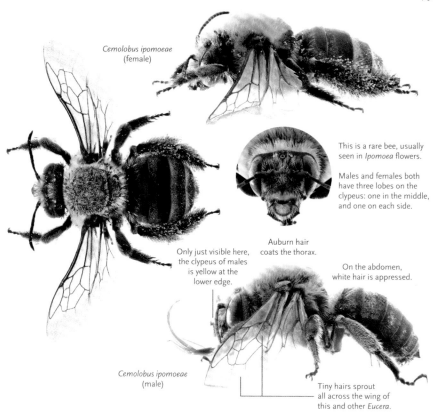

Cemolobus ipomoeae
(female)

This is a rare bee, usually seen in *Ipomoea* flowers.

Males and females both have three lobes on the clypeus: one in the middle, and one on each side.

Auburn hair coats the thorax.

Only just visible here, the clypeus of males is yellow at the lower edge.

On the abdomen, white hair is appressed.

Cemolobus ipomoeae
(male)

Tiny hairs sprout all across the wing of this and other *Eucera*.

IDENTIFICATION: Medium-sized, robust bee with auburn hair on the thorax and appressed hair bands on the segments of the abdomen. **HEAD:** In both sexes, the lower margin of the clypeus has three distinct lobes that are large enough to be visible with the naked eye, or in photographs. In males, and relative to other *Eucera*, the antennae are short, barely extending to the tegulae. Also in males, the first flagellar segment is significantly longer than the second. Finally, the clypeus of males is yellow at its base. **LEGS:** Scopal hairs are thick, widely separated. **ABDOMEN:** Strong white stripes of appressed, almost silvery hairs run the width of each tergal segment. The integument underneath is polished. In males, on the abdomen, T6 has a lateral tooth; this can be difficult to see.

SIMILAR SPECIES: This is the only member in its subgenus and can be easily distinguished by the uniquely shaped clypeus, and the floral host associations.

Eucera (Peponapis) pruinosa

SIZE: Medium; 12–14 mm. **PHENOLOGY:** June through August. **FLORAL HOSTS:** Specializes on *Cucurbita* (squash and pumpkins). Common inhabitant of gardens with squash and pumpkin. Males can be found in these flowers in the morning or late evening, even once the flower is wilted. Females usually forage in the early morning.

RANGE: Widespread across the United States; rare in the Pacific Northwest.

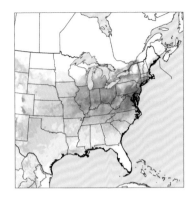

NESTING: Ground nester; often seen in the vicinity of the squash plants it visits.

IDENTIFICATION: Larger fast-flying bee seen in the early morning on pumpkin and squash flowers. HEAD: Clypeus sticks out from face and is about as tall as the width of the compound eye. In males, there is a yellow circular or triangular spot right in the center of the clypeus. The antennae in males are somewhat long, extending just past the wing bases. THORAX: Uniformly hairy with umber-colored hair. LEGS: Scopal hairs are light brown, and widely spaced. ABDOMEN: Strong frosty hair bands, slightly appressed, run across the abdomen in both males and females.

SIMILAR SPECIES: *Eucera (Xenoglossa) strenua* is also commonly found in squash flowers, but some differences are apparent. See *E. strenua* for specifics.

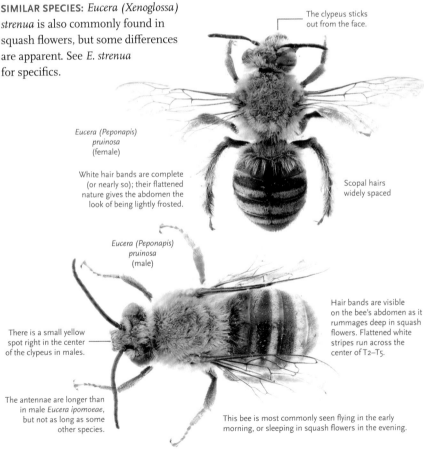

The clypeus sticks out from the face.

Eucera (Peponapis) pruinosa (female)

White hair bands are complete (or nearly so); their flattened nature gives the abdomen the look of being lightly frosted.

Scopal hairs widely spaced

Eucera (Peponapis) pruinosa (male)

There is a small yellow spot right in the center of the clypeus in males.

The antennae are longer than in male *Eucera ipomoeae*, but not as long as some other species.

Hair bands are visible on the bee's abdomen as it rummages deep in squash flowers. Flattened white stripes run across the center of T2–T5.

This bee is most commonly seen flying in the early morning, or sleeping in squash flowers in the evening.

Eucera (Xenoglossa) strenua

SIZE: Medium to large; 14–18 mm. **PHENOLOGY:** June through September. **FLORAL HOSTS:** Specializes on *Cucurbita*. Common inhabitant of gardens with squash and pumpkin, and most often seen in the morning, when squash blossoms are open. Males can be found in these flowers in the morning or late evening in wilted flowers. **RANGE:** Widespread across the United States; absent from northern states, including North and South Dakota, Montana, Idaho, Wyoming, and Minnesota. **NESTING:** Ground nester; often seen in the vicinity of the squash plants it visits.

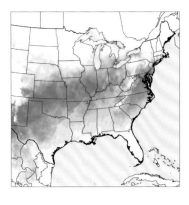

IDENTIFICATION: Orange fuzzy bee with frosty white stripes on the abdomen. Most commonly found in squash blossoms, but larger than *E. pruinosa*. **HEAD:** Clypeus sticks out from face and is about as tall as the width of the compound eye. Labrum and mandibles in female are yellow, while clypeus is mostly black, but it may have yellow at its rim. In males, labrum, mandibles, and clypeus are yellow. The antennae in males are long. In both sexes the first flagellar segment is about as long as the second and third segments combined. **THORAX:** Thickly covered in auburn hair. **LEGS:** Scopal

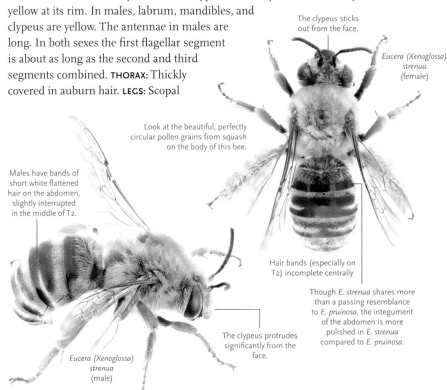

The clypeus sticks out from the face.

Eucera (Xenoglossa) strenua (female)

Look at the beautiful, perfectly circular pollen grains from squash on the body of this bee.

Males have bands of short white flattened hair on the abdomen, slightly interrupted in the middle of T2.

Hair bands (especially on T2) incomplete centrally

Though *E. strenua* shares more than a passing resemblance to *E. pruinosa*, the integument of the abdomen is more polished in *E. strenua* compared to *E. pruinosa*.

The clypeus protrudes significantly from the face.

Eucera (Xenoglossa) strenua (male)

hairs are long, and exceptionally widely spaced. In males legs are orange. **ABDOMEN:** In females, T1 is covered in erect hairs, at least basally. Appressed hair bands run across T2–T4 but are interrupted in the center, especially on T2.

SIMILAR SPECIES: Looks very similar to *Eucera (Peponapis) pruinosa*, but is slightly bigger, and with yellow mandibles. *Eucera (Xenoglossa) kansensis* overlaps with *E. strenua*, especially in the Midwest. In *E. kansensis,* the clypeus of females is yellow to white, with the coloration covering about half the total surface of the clypeus. In males of *E. kansensis,* the legs are a red/brown color.

FLORILEGUS

— **SUBFAMILY:** Apinae
— **TRIBE:** Eucerini

OVERVIEW: *Florilegus* are medium-sized bees with a slight bit of iridescence on the tergal segments. They are relatively rare but can be seen on *Pontederia* in May through August. Nests in the ground.

IN THE WORLD: Found in the Americas, with 11 species in the West Indies and Central and South America, but only one species in the United States.

CLEPTOPARASITES: Unknown, likely *Triepeolus*, which cleptoparasitizes many Eucerini.

IDENTIFYING FEATURES: Long-horned bees with a mild iridescence on the tergal segments, in both sexes. **HEAD:** The eyes angle slightly away from each other, and the carina along the inner margin of the eyes is slightly raised and polished. If the mouthparts can be seen, there are five segments to the maxillary palpi instead of four or six; the mouthparts of the maxilla and mentum have hooked hairs. In females, the face is very wide, with a black clypeus. In males, the clypeus is all yellow. Also in males, the antennae are long, extending beyond the end of the thorax. **LEGS:** Scopae are heavily feathered, and long. On the forelegs, the femur is notably thickened. **ABDOMEN:** Tergal segments are dark in appearance but have a slight metallic sheen in the light. At a minimum, T2 and T3 have thick basal segments that are not interrupted in the middle. The basitibial plate in females is bare, with no hairs obscuring it. T6 has thin lateral teeth on either side. In males, the tergal hair bands are often interrupted in the middle, especially on T2 and T3. Also in males, if it can be seen, T6 is a long ridge that extends beyond the edges of the plate. T7 has a strong angle to either side of the pygidial plate (this can be hidden by the dense hair on T6).

SIMILAR GENERA: *Florilegus* looks similar to *Melissodes* and it is easy to confuse the two. In *Florilegus*, there is a tooth along the inner margin of the mandible of both males and females that is distinct. This is usually seen only when the mandible is open. Also in females, the scopal hairs are more heavily branched in *Florilegus* than in *Melissodes*. See genus description of *Melissodes* for more distinguishing features.

Florilegus condignus

SIZE: Medium; 11–12 mm.
PHENOLOGY: June through August (and early September in Florida, which may have two generations). **FLORAL HOSTS:** Oligolectic, specialist on *Pontederia*. **RANGE:** New Jersey south to mid-Florida, west to New Mexico, Colorado, and Nebraska. Particularly abundant in the Great Plains. **NESTING:** Nests in the ground, about 6 inches deep, with a preference for sandy soils. There is usually a tumulus associated with the nest entrance, and nests may be in loose aggregations. Males often sleep together in aggregations on grass stems.
IDENTIFICATION: As there is only one species in the U.S., characteristics are listed in Identifying Features for the genus.
SIMILAR SPECIES: See similar genera; there is only one U.S. species.

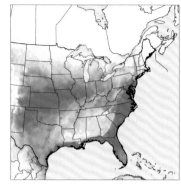

Florilegus condignus
(female)

Florilegus condignus
(male)

Yellow clypeus

Femur thickened

There is a slight metallic sheen to, especially, T1 in *Florilegus*...

...while T2 and T3 have wide apical bands of appressed hair.

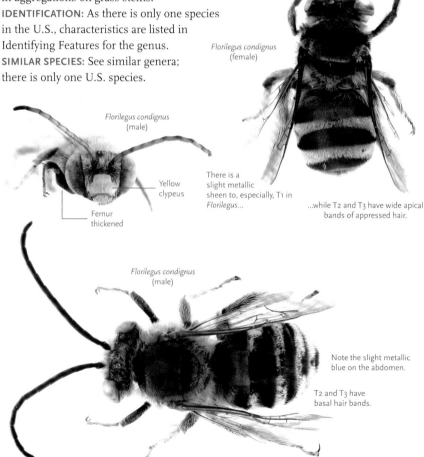

Florilegus condignus
(male)

Note the slight metallic blue on the abdomen.

T2 and T3 have basal hair bands.

MELISSODES

— **SUBFAMILY:** Apinae
— **TRIBE:** Eucerini

OVERVIEW: *Melissodes* are fast-flying fall bees in which the males have extremely long antennae. Many are specialists on plants in the sunflower family. *Melissodes* females nest in the ground, and may nest in aggregations.

IN THE WORLD: Worldwide there are around 125 species, distributed almost entirely in the new world. Nearly 100 species occur in North America, and 30 species are found in the East.

CLEPTOPARASITES: *Triepeolus, Epeolus,* possibly *Melecta* or *Xeromelecta.*

IDENTIFYING FEATURES: Medium-sized bees that fly fast. **HEAD:** In males, antennae are long and often extend back at least to end of scutellum. The clypeus of males is pale or yellow. In both sexes, the first segment of the antennae is less than half as long as the second segment. The maxillary palpi, on the mouthparts, are four-segmented (this is hard to see without a microscope). **THORAX:** Tegula is teardrop-shaped, tapering to a point at the anterior end (this can be very hard to see and may require the removal of hair from the region with the tip of a pin). **WINGS:** Marginal cell is long, curving gently away from the wing margin, and the entire surface, even inside the cells, is covered with minute stiff hairs. **LEGS:** Scopal hairs may be branched or simple, but are thick. On the abdomen, bands of hair often run across each tergal segment. In many species the hair on the fourth tergal segment is separated in the middle, giving the band a notched look. In males, there is a small tooth to either side of the pygidial plate.

SIMILAR GENERA: *Eucera, Florilegus* and *Svastra* are other Eucerini that look very similar to *Melissodes* species. Of these, only *Melissodes* has teardrop-shaped tegulae. It also has four-segmented maxillary palpi; *Eucera* and *Florilegus* do not have four-segmented maxillary palpi. In *Eucera,* the clypeus usually sticks out substantially from the face. *Florilegus* is a rarer species and often has a slight metallic sheen to the abdomen that is not seen in *Melissodes*. In *Svastra,* some species have four-segmented palpi. They tend to be larger bees, though, with broad thick hair bands on the abdomen, and flattened, branched hairs frequently intermixed with other hairs.

Melissodes bimaculata

SIZE: Medium; 11–15 mm.
PHENOLOGY: July through September. **FLORAL HOSTS:** Polylectic, but often seen on Asteraceae. **RANGE:** Widespread across the East. **NESTING:** Ground-nesting, often in aggregations. Males commonly seen sleeping together on grass stems.
IDENTIFICATION: Medium-sized black bee.
HEAD: In males, the antennae are long, extending

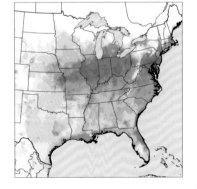

Black hairs on the head, thorax, and abdomen

Melissodes bimaculata (female)

Clypeus protrudes

White spots on the sides of T4

Light-colored scopal hairs

Melissodes bimaculata (male)

Black and white hairs on the face

Black hairs on abdomen with white patches on sides of T2–T5

Yellow clypeus

back past the end of the thorax. The clypeus is yellow. The hairs on the head range from all black, to a mix of white and black together. **LEGS:** Scopal hairs are long, feathered, and light-colored. In males, the hairs on both the mid- and hind legs range from black to bright white. **ABDOMEN:** In females, T1–T3 are covered in short black hair; T4 has unique white patches of hair to either side of center. T5 and T6 are black. In males, most hairs on the tergal segments are black, with no true hair bands, but patches of white hair on the sides of T2 through T5 are common. On T4, when viewed from the side, there is a band of dark, sparse, slightly longer hairs that stand up from the integument slightly.

SIMILAR SPECIES: Several other species show some dark hairs on the scutum or scutellum, including *M. apicata, M. denticulata, M. subillata,* and *M. tincta.* In males, *M. bimaculata* has entirely dark hair on the gena; other species have light hair here. *Melissodes bimaculata* also lacks strong white hair bands running across the tergal segments. None have the white patches seen in female *M. bimaculata* on T4.

Melissodes comptoides

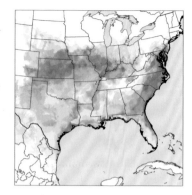

SIZE: Medium; 10–13 mm.
PHENOLOGY: Late July through October. Earlier in more southern regions. **FLORAL HOSTS:** Generalist, seen on a wide variety of flowering plants. **RANGE:** Widespread throughout the eastern U.S.; more common in southern states than northern. Missing from Great Lakes. **NESTING:** Ground-nesting, often in aggregations.

IDENTIFICATION: Medium-sized lighter-colored *Melissodes*, though color varies greatly in this species, and southern species and eastern species are darker than those of the Midwest. **HEAD:** The clypeus does not protrude significantly from the head in profile. The inner margins of the eyes converge. The vertex is covered in a mix of light and dark hairs. In males, the labrum is light-colored. Also in males, the first antennal segment is significantly shorter than the second, though the antennae overall are long, ending posterior of T1. **THORAX:** In females, the scutum and scutellum are covered entirely in lighter hairs, with no dark hairs mixed in. On the sides of the thorax, however, the hairs are dark. **LEGS:** Scopal hairs are heavily branched. The inner side of the hind basitarsi and tibiae are often dark rusty brown to black. **ABDOMEN:** White hair bands run across each tergal segment, set back from the rim enough that the rim itself is visible below. In females, T2 and T3 are heavily punctate, but shiny in between pits. T4 has a strong white band that may be interrupted medially by a tuft of darker hairs.

SIMILAR SPECIES: Appears very similar to *M. communis* (not covered here). *M. communis* can be distinguished by the longer first flagellar segment in the males, and the lack of punctation on T2 and T3 in females.

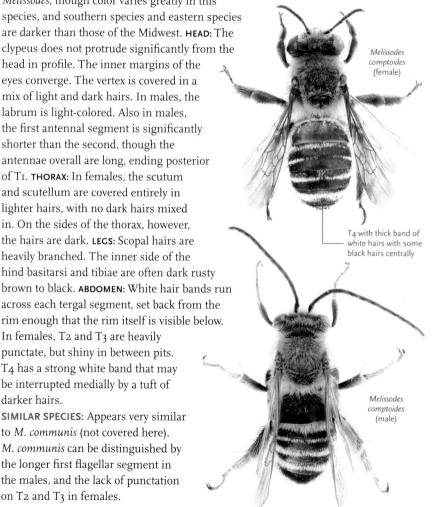

Melissodes comptoides (female)

T4 with thick band of white hairs with some black hairs centrally

Melissodes comptoides (male)

Melissodes denticulata

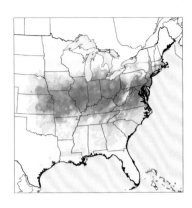

SIZE: Small to medium; 9–11 mm.
PHENOLOGY: Late June through
September. **FLORAL HOSTS:** Asteraceae
specialist, perhaps strong preference for
Vernonia. **RANGE:** New England west through
Great Lakes region and North Dakota. South
to Texas and northern Florida. **NESTING:**
Ground-nesting, often in aggregations.
IDENTIFICATION: Medium-sized light-colored
Melissodes. **HEAD:** Clypeus does not protrude
significantly from the head in profile. On the
vertex, the hairs are all dark, though the face may have lighter hairs. In females, the
clypeus is black; in males, clypeus and labrum are both white, though some black occurs
at the top of the clypeus. Also in males, the first flagellar segment of the antenna is a
little less than half as long as the second segment. **THORAX:** Hairs are mostly dark, though
the edges of the thorax are lined with lighter-colored hairs. **WINGS:** Slightly smoky.
LEGS: Scopal hairs are white, long, heavily branched, and wavy. In males, the hairs on
the legs are notably shorter than those of other *Melissodes*. **ABDOMEN:** White hair bands
run across the tergal segments, though these are often widely interrupted, or the hair
color gets darker, medially. In males, the apex of each tergal segment is thin, almost to
the point of being see-through. T6 in males with a distinct apical spines, laterally.
SIMILAR SPECIES: *Melissodes vernoniae* (not included here) looks very similar to
M. denticulata. On the whole, *M. vernoniae* is larger in size and lighter in vestiture.

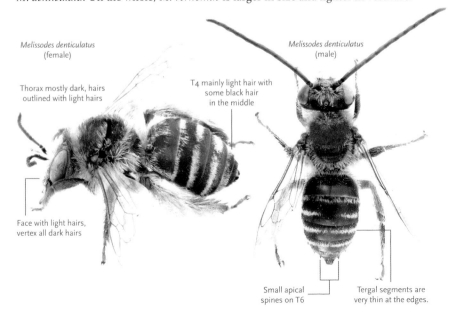

Melissodes denticulatus
(female)

Melissodes denticulatus
(male)

Thorax mostly dark, hairs
outlined with light hairs

T4 mainly light hair with
some black hair
in the middle

Face with light hairs,
vertex all dark hairs

Small apical
spines on T6

Tergal segments are
very thin at the edges.

It lacks dark hairs intermixed on the sides of the thorax, and the wings are lighter and clearer. Males of *M. vernoniae* have shorter antennae, but longer first flagellar segments. *Melissodes denticulatus* occurs much further east than *M. vernoniae*, which is restricted to the plains, ranging as far east as Illinois.

Melissodes desponsa

SIZE: Medium; 11–14 mm.
PHENOLOGY: June through September. **FLORAL HOSTS:** Asteraceae specialist; preference for *Cirsium* and other thistles. **RANGE:** Southern Canada south to Alabama, west to Oklahoma. Common north to New England.
NESTING: Ground-nesting, often in aggregations.
IDENTIFICATION: Medium to large *Melissodes*.
HEAD: The clypeus protrudes significantly from the face. If the mouthparts are extruded, the long blade of the galea can be seen; it is nearly twice the length of the clypeus. The vertex is all light-colored hairs. In males, the labrum is black, though the clypeus is yellow. The inner margins of the eyes appear parallel to each other.
THORAX: Most of the hair is light in color, though the sides of the thorax are dark.
WINGS: Slightly smoky. **LEGS:** Scopal hairs are heavily branched, and auburn-colored. **ABDOMEN:** In males, the hairs are all black. In females, there are no hair bands on T2–T4, only scattered black hairs, giving the abdomen a heavily polished look.
SIMILAR SPECIES: The heavily protruding clypeus and distinct hair patterns across the thorax and abdomen distinguish this species from other eastern species.

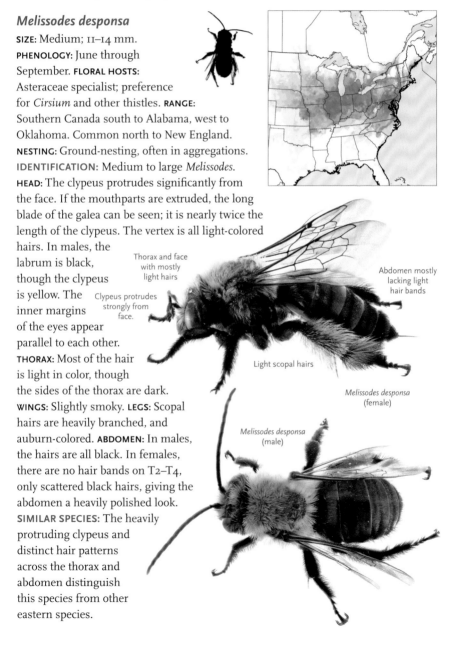

Thorax and face with mostly light hairs

Clypeus protrudes strongly from face.

Abdomen mostly lacking light hair bands

Light scopal hairs

Melissodes desponsa (female)

Melissodes desponsa (male)

Melissodes trinodis

SIZE: Small to medium; 9–11 mm.
PHENOLOGY: July through September.
FLORAL HOSTS: Asteraceae specialist; preference for *Helianthus*.
RANGE: Southern Canada south to Florida, west to Colorado and southern Texas.
NESTING: Ground-nesting, often in aggregations.
IDENTIFICATION: Medium-sized *Melissodes,* often with rusty to orange-colored thorax. **HEAD:** In males, the clypeus is yellow, as are the labrum and the bases of the mandibles. The vertex

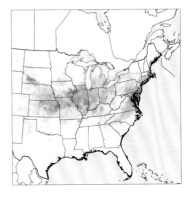

consists of all light-colored hairs. **THORAX:** Hairs are bright to pale orange/red, with no dark hairs mixed in. **LEGS:** Scopal hairs are bushy, straw-colored, and very branched. **ABDOMEN:** In females, hair patterns are variable. Stripes, either light-colored or orange/red run across T2–T4. These tend to be thinner laterally, and thicker in the middle. They do not occur right at the apex of each segment.
SIMILAR SPECIES: *Melissodes agilis* (not covered here) looks similar to *M. trinodis,* with females differing in the darker overall color, and the lack of reddish-brown hairs. In males, the base of the mandibles is black in *M. agilis* and the wings are darker.

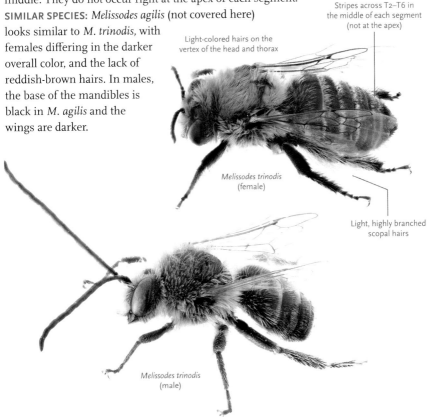

Stripes across T2–T6 in the middle of each segment (not at the apex)

Light-colored hairs on the vertex of the head and thorax

Melissodes trinodis (female)

Light, highly branched scopal hairs

Melissodes trinodis (male)

SVASTRA

— **SUBFAMILY:** Apinae
— **TRIBE:** Eucerini

OVERVIEW: Large fast-flying bee with a lot of hair, which is often strikingly colored. Scopal hairs are robust, and wings are often smoky. Many species are specialists (*Helianthus, Oenothera*). Ground nesters, sometimes in small aggregations.

IN THE WORLD: Twenty-three worldwide, all found in the New World; more than 20 of these are found north of the equator. In North America there are 16 species; 5 of these occur in the East.

CLEPTOPARASITES: *Triepeolus*.

IDENTIFYING FEATURES: HEAD: Malar space is almost nonexistent; there is very little space between the eye and the beginning of the mandible. The clypeus is relatively flat. In males, the antennae are long, but not overly so, ending near the back of the thorax. In males and females, the first flagellar segment is less than half the length of the second one, but longer than it is wide. **THORAX:** The tegulae are oval-shaped. On the metanotum there is often a tuft of hair that is longer than the hair around it. **ABDOMEN:** There are basal hair bands on T2 and often T3 and T4, and these are covered with flattened, branched hairs.

SIMILAR GENERA: *Melissodes* are closely related and share a similar appearance though are smaller on average than *Svastra*. Antennae in male *Melissodes* are longer than in male *Svastra*. In both sexes, *Melissodes* have a clypeus that sticks out further in profile. Hair bands on the abdomen of *Melissodes* are more pronounced. *Eucera* also appear more similar, but do not overlap much with *Svastra,* which fly in the fall, while many *Eucera* are spring bees. Other similar genera are specialists on flowers that differ from those where *Svastra* are most commonly seen: *Florilegus* is restricted to *Pontederia,* and *Eucera* (*Peponapis*) occurs on *Cucurbita* species.

Svastra obliqua

SIZE: Medium to large; 14–16 mm. **PHENOLOGY:** July through September. **FLORAL HOSTS:** Specialist on sunflowers (*Helianthus*) but may visit other composites as well. **RANGE:** From California to New York, largely absent from the Northeast. Less common in northern states though occasionally found in southern Canada. **NESTING:** Solitary, nest in the ground, preferring bare dirt. Often nest in aggregations, and several females may share a nest entrance.

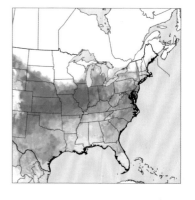

IDENTIFYING FEATURES: Large bee with copious hair, contrastingly colored across the body. There are two distinct color forms of *S. obliqua*. One is nearly all dark, while the other has patches of both light and dark hair. Both are described here. **HEAD:** Eyes are large, wider than the genal area. In males, the clypeus is bright yellow. **THORAX:** The scutum is covered in thick tawny hair, which fades to black at the posterior end. In females, the sides of the thorax are dark in color. In males, the sides of the thorax are tawny in color. **WINGS:** Dark and smoky. **LEGS:** In males, the inner surface of the hind basitarsus is covered with dark rust-colored hairs. In females, scopal hairs are highly feathered, and pale in color. **ABDOMEN:** In females, T2 has a band of tawny appressed hairs running across the middle of the segment. T3 has a hair band comprising simple hairs that narrows toward the midline but does run across the middle of the segment. T4 has a thick light-colored hair band, with no interruptions. The pygidial plate is V-shaped. In males, bands run evenly across each tergal segment, midway through the segment. Also in males, T7, if visible, lacks lateral spines.

SIMILAR SPECIES: There are five species of *Svastra* in the East. Of these, *S. obliqua* is the most widely distributed, and most likely to be seen. *Svastra atripes* has dark scopal hairs instead of pale-colored ones. *Svastra compta* has simple scopal hairs instead of the branched ones seen in *S. obliqua*. And *S. aegis* and *S. petulca* both lack any dark-colored patches on the side of the thorax, beneath the tegula, while *S. obliqua* is either entirely, or at least partially, dark-colored.

Svastra obliqua obliqua
(female)

Svastra obliqua caliginosa is a much darker subspecies, with no complete hair bands on the abdomen.

T4 with thick complete hair band

Svastra obliqua
(male)

ANTHOPHORA

— **SUBFAMILY:** Apinae
— **TRIBE:** Anthophorini

OVERVIEW: Conspicuous fast-flying bees, medium to large in size. Often hover in front of flowers, tongue extended, adjusting their legs. The thorax is hairy, and hair may be black, red, or (most commonly) gray. Seen spring through fall. Almost all *Anthophora* nest in the ground or in vertical banks (see *A. terminalis* for an exception), either in aggregations or singly. Some *Anthophora* construct small mud chimneys over their nest entrances.

IN THE WORLD: There are more than 400 species found around the world, mostly in the Northern Hemisphere. Nearly 60 species occur in the U.S. and Canada, and 12 are found in the Midwest and East.

CLEPTOPARASITES: *Melecta, Zacosmia, Xeromelecta, Coelioxys, Oreopasites.*

IDENTIFYING FEATURES: *Anthophora* are medium to large hairy bees that fly remarkably fast. Typically gray in color, they collect pollen on their hind legs. **HEAD:** The vertex appears flattened, not rounded (as in Emphorini). In males there are extensive yellow or white markings on the clypeus and often also the antennal scapes and/or the mandibles. **WINGS:** Three submarginal cells and, importantly, the first recurrent vein intersect the second submarginal cell near the middle. The wings are bare in the veined area (the cells are bare), but very hairy at the edges. The third submarginal cell in *Anthophora* is more or less square (compare with *Habropoda*). **LEGS:** In males, there are often modifications, like long brushes of hair. Both males and females have arolia.

SIMILAR GENERA: *Habropoda* look so similar to *Anthophora* that wing venation is the only certain way to distinguish them. In *Habropoda*, the first recurrent vein intersects exactly at the junction of the second and third submarginal cell, creating a plus sign (+) on the wing. The third submarginal cell is fairly curved at the posterior end. *Bombus* females also look similar, but collect pollen in corbicula, not in scopal hairs. The faces of *Bombus* tend to be longer, and males (which are less commonly seen) do not possess yellow coloration. On the hindwing, *Bombus* lack a jugal lobe. *Melissodes* and other Eucerini may seem similar in size and hairiness. The antennae of male Eucerini are significantly longer than in male Anthophora. Also, the Eucerini have small hairs on the wings, while Anthophorini wings are hairless in the area where the veins are.

Anthophora abrupta

SIZE: Medium to large; 11–17 mm. **PHENOLOGY:** March through September. **FLORAL HOSTS:** Generalists seen foraging on many different plants. Often fly in the spring, or early morning. **RANGE:** Texas and Florida (not as common in Florida) north through southeastern Canada. **NESTING:** Gregarious nester with many females building nests in close proximity to each other. Often nests in vertical banks, or sometimes even found in adobe bricks. **BEHAVIOR:** Males chew parsnip stems (*Pastinaca*) and sop up the juices onto hairs on the labrum, and the row of hairs on the lower edge of the clypeus. The juice is mixed with other secretions by the bee and dabbed onto objects in its territory to mark the edges. Known for their docile nature, seldom sting. **IDENTIFICATION:** Tawny to straw-colored thorax with black hairs on the head and abdomen.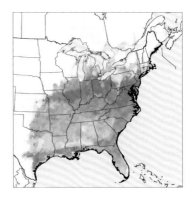

HEAD: The clypeus is strongly protruding. The gena is the same width as the eyes. Males have a yellow clypeus, yellow scapes, and yellow next to the compound eyes. The clypeus has a distinctive line of dark hairs running along its lower edge; the labrum of males is also unique, with flattened hairs that are not visible without a high-powered microscope. In females, the clypeus is roughened between pits. **THORAX:** Dirty blonde thick hair covers the scutum and scutellum. **WINGS:** Slightly cloudy. **LEGS:** Scopal hairs on hind tibia are black. **ABDOMEN:** In males, there is no pygidial plate.

SIMILAR SPECIES: *Anthophora bomboides* is very similar in appearance and belongs to the same subgenus (*Melea*). Most notably, *A. bomboides* often has more yellow hairs on the head and abdomen than *A. abrupta*. In addition, in females, the clypeus is shiny between punctations in *A. bomboides*. In males, there is no black "mustache" of hair running along the apical margin of the clypeus in *A. bomboides,* as there is in *A. abrupta.*

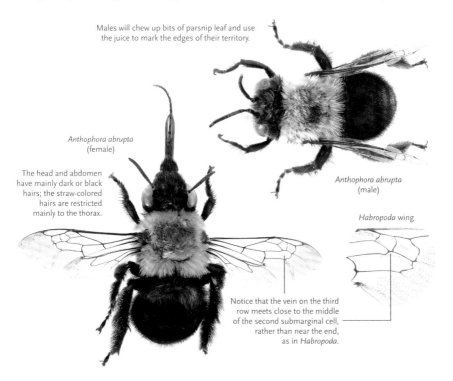

Males will chew up bits of parsnip leaf and use the juice to mark the edges of their territory.

Anthophora abrupta (female)

The head and abdomen have mainly dark or black hairs; the straw-colored hairs are restricted mainly to the thorax.

Anthophora abrupta (male)

Habropoda wing

Notice that the vein on the third row meets close to the middle of the second submarginal cell, rather than near the end, as in *Habropoda*.

Anthophora bomboides

SIZE: Medium; 12–15 mm.

PHENOLOGY: April through July.

FLORAL HOSTS: Generalist.

RANGE: *Anthophora bomboides* ranges across the U.S. with various subspecies predominating in different regions.

NESTING: Gregarious nester, but solitary. Often nesting in vertical banks.

IDENTIFICATION: *Anthophora bomboides* shows great variation in the color patterns of the thorax and especially the abdomen. Individuals may exhibit yellow, red, orange, or tawny hair on any or all of T1–T4, depending on the individual and the subspecies. **HEAD:** The clypeus is strongly protuberant. The gena is the same width as the eyes. Males have a yellow clypeus, yellow scapes, and a small bit of yellow beside the clypeus.

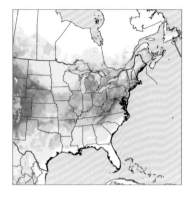

In females, the clypeus is polished and shiny between pits. **THORAX:** Scutum shiny with large pits. **WINGS:** Slightly cloudy. **LEGS:** Scopal hairs on hind tibia are black. **ABDOMEN:** In males, there is no pygidial plate.

The head, thorax, and T1 on the abdomen have straw-colored hairs. Black hairs are restricted mainly to the abdomen.

Anthophora bomboides
(female)

SIMILAR SPECIES: There are five subspecies of *A. bomboides. Anthophora bomboides bomboides* is the most commonly seen along the east coast of the U.S., ranging as far south as northern Florida, and north throughout Alberta. *Anthophora b. sodalis* can be found throughout the Midwest but ranges as far west as northern California and British Columbia, Canada. It differs mostly in the degree of redness on the abdomen. Despite this variation in hair coloration, *A. bomboides* can *typically* be distinguished from the similar-looking *A. abrupta* by the characters listed under *A. abrupta*.

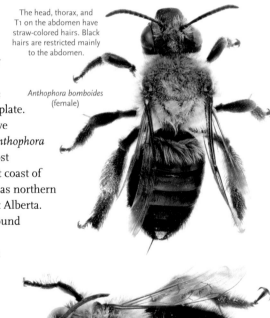

Anthophora bomboides
(male)

Anthophora terminalis

SIZE: Medium; 10–13.5 mm.
PHENOLOGY: Early June through September. **FLORAL HOSTS:** Generalist, visiting a wide variety of plants for pollen and nectar, but may have preference for those with long corolla tubes. **RANGE:** Occurs across the U.S. In the East, can be found from Alabama, Tennessee, and North Carolina, north to Manitoba, Ontario, and Quebec. **NESTING:** These are the only *Anthophora* that nest in excavated cavities instead of in the ground. They can be found in beetle burrows in rotting logs and inside larger plant stems.

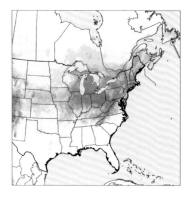

IDENTIFICATION: Large, fast-flying, dark bee. The thorax and abdomen sport light gray hair, beneath which the integument can be clearly seen. **HEAD:** The gena is narrower than the width of the compound eye. In males, the clypeus is all yellow, and the yellow runs up above the clypeus to the antennal sockets, as well as in a strip next to each compound eye. The scapes and mandibles are black. **THORAX:** Light straw-colored hair intermixed with black covers the thorax. **ABDOMEN:** Tergal segments have bands of short white hair at the apex of each. In females, the end of the abdomen has bright orange stiff hairs that are visible in flight or as they burrow into flowers.

SIMILAR SPECIES: May appear similar to *A. abrupta* and *A. bomboides* as they are similar size and fly at the same time. The orange tip is unique to female *A. terminalis*, and the antennal scapes of male *A. terminalis* lack yellow, which is seen in males of the other two species.

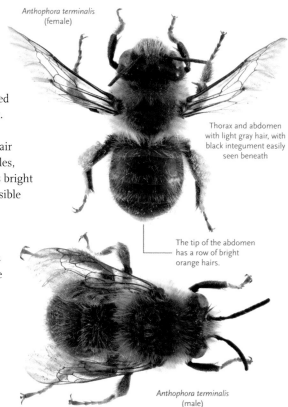

Anthophora terminalis
(female)

Thorax and abdomen with light gray hair, with black integument easily seen beneath

The tip of the abdomen has a row of bright orange hairs.

Anthophora terminalis
(male)

HABROPODA

— **SUBFAMILY:** Apinae
— **TRIBE:** Anthophorini

OVERVIEW: *Habropoda* is a genus of large bees (12–16 mm) commonly seen throughout the East in the early spring. *Habropoda* nest in the ground, usually individually, but they are sometimes found in aggregations. Many of them are oligolectic, collecting pollen from only one or two flowering plant genera, or just one family. **IN THE WORLD:** Worldwide, there are more than 50 species. In the U.S. and Canada there are 21 species, but only one of them frequents the eastern states. **CLEPTOPARASITES:** Most commonly *Melecta pacifica*, but also *Xeromelecta, Epeolus,* and *Triepeolus.*
IDENTIFYING FEATURES: *Habropoda* are large fuzzy bees that fly in the spring. In overall appearance, they resemble *Anthophora* to such an extent that wing venation may need to be used to distinguish them (see similar genera). **HEAD:** Between the compound eyes, the vertex is very flat. In males there are often significant yellow or white markings on the clypeus, the antennal scape, and even the mandibles. **THORAX:** Often hairy. Tegulae are rounded, and more or less symmetrical. **WINGS:** Three submarginal cells. The first recurrent vein meets the line dividing the second and third submarginal cells straight on, forming a plus sign (+) or an X. The wings are bare in the veined area, but very hairy at the edges. **LEGS:** In males, there are often modifications, like long brushes of hair. Both males and females have an arolium. **ABDOMEN:** Variously hairy, but often the color of T1 matches that of the thorax.
SIMILAR GENERA: *Anthophora* species, which are in the same tribe, look remarkably similar, and it may require a microscope to be certain of identity. In *Habropoda,* the vein that forms the edge of both the second and third submarginal cells meets the first recurrent vein squarely on, forming a plus sign (+). In *Anthophora,* the first recurrent vein meets the middle of the second submarginal cell, forming a T instead. *Habropoda* tend to fly earlier in the year. In the East, *Habropoda laboriosa* most resembles *Anthophora abrupta. Bombus* are large and hairy but lack yellow faces (as seen in male *H. laboriosa*). At the time of year when *Habropoda* are flying, the most common bumble bees seen are queens, which are significantly larger than female *Habropoda. Habropoda* do not have yellow or orange hair bands on the abdomen. *Eucera* are also fuzzy and big. The scopal hairs of *Eucera* that fly at the same time are longer than those of *H. laboriosa.* Their wings are hairy throughout, rather than just outside the veins. And male *Eucera* have very long antennae.

Habropoda laboriosa

SIZE: Medium to large; 14–16 mm. **PHENOLOGY:** February in southern states, and March in later states, through April and May, respectively. **FLORAL HOSTS:** Polylectic, but with a strong preference for *Vaccinium* (blueberry) flowers and *Gelsemium* (jessamine) flowers. **RANGE:** Widespread; New England south to Florida, west to Mississippi and Illinois. **NESTING:** Ground-nesting bee.

IDENTIFICATION: Hefty bees with considerable blonde to gray hair, especially on the thorax and T1. **HEAD:** The clypeus protrudes notably from the face. In males it is ivory to bright white in color. White extends up, from the clypeus as a thin line next to the compound eye. From straight on, the vertex is flattened, and not domed. In males, the antennae are short—about the same length as in females and all black. **THORAX:** Covered in evenly

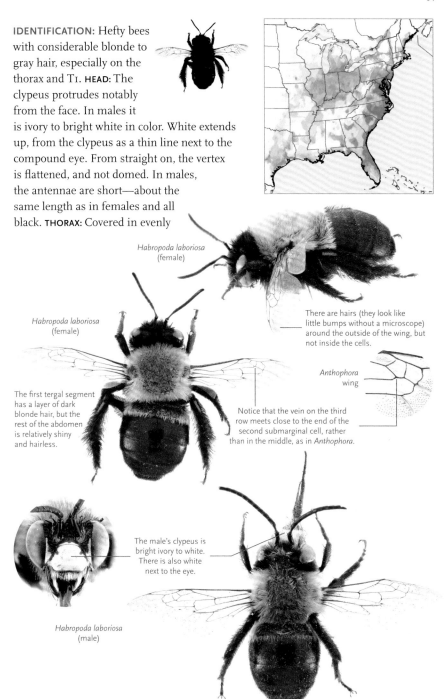

Habropoda laboriosa
(female)

Habropoda laboriosa
(female)

There are hairs (they look like little bumps without a microscope) around the outside of the wing, but not inside the cells.

Anthophora wing

The first tergal segment has a layer of dark blonde hair, but the rest of the abdomen is relatively shiny and hairless.

Notice that the vein on the third row meets close to the end of the second submarginal cell, rather than in the middle, as in *Anthophora*.

The male's clypeus is bright ivory to white. There is also white next to the eye.

Habropoda laboriosa
(male)

short, thick, orange to straw-colored hair. **LEGS:** Scopal hairs on hind tibia and basitarsus are black, brushy, and not long, though they do get longer toward the distal end. **ABDOMEN:** First tergal segment is colored the same as the thorax. The rest is covered in dark sparse hair, so that the shiny integument is visible. **SIMILAR SPECIES:** *Habropoda laboriosa* is the only *Habropoda* in the East.

CENTRIS

— **SUBFAMILY:** Apinae
— **TRIBE:** Centridini

OVERVIEW: Medium to large, fast-moving bee, some species with bright red eyes and extremely brushy pollen-collecting hairs on the hind legs of females. Most species are specialists, though a few generalists occur. Many species collect floral oil, in addition to pollen, from flowers. Ground-nesting species that often occur in aggregations of a dozen to several thousand.

IN THE WORLD: Around 225 species around the world, in North and South America, mostly found in hot, tropical regions. Twenty-two species occur in the U.S. and Canada. Two species occur in the eastern U.S.

CLEPTOPARASITES: *Ericrocis.*

IDENTIFYING FEATURES: Large bees with robust scopal hairs. **HEAD:** The first flagellar segment of the antenna is longer than the scape. In many species, the eyes appear bright red or green while the bee is alive. **WINGS:** The outside edges are covered in short stiff hairs. The stigma is relatively small. The first submarginal cell is smaller than the second (there are three). **LEGS:** There is no arolium. The scopal hairs cover both the hind tibia and the basitarsus and are exceptionally thick and stiff. In many species, on the fore- and midlegs, there are large combs of flattened bristles near the tibial spurs, likely used in collecting oils from flowers.

SIMILAR GENERA: Few genera in the U.S. look similar to *Centris*. The large scopae, fast flight, and notable eye color are three features that make this bee unique. From a distance, *Centris* may appear similar to *Anthophora*. The density of the scopal hairs should separate the two. In addition, the first submarginal cell is bigger than the second submarginal cell in *Anthophora*.

Centris errans

SIZE: Medium; 11–14 mm. **PHENOLOGY:** March and April. **FLORAL HOSTS:** Mostly Malpighiaceae, especially *Byrsonima*, but can be seen visiting other flowers. **RANGE:** Florida and the Bahamas; relatively rare. **NESTING:** Ground-nesting bee. **IDENTIFICATION:** Medium-sized fast-flying bee. The head and thorax are amber-colored, and the abdomen is rusty red. **HEAD:** The face has yellow markings on and beside the clypeus, shaped like a trident. The clypeus sticks out slightly from the face, and there is a highly polished ivory line on the clypeus that has no pits. **WINGS:** Dark and smoky. **LEGS:** Red. In females, scopal hairs are thick, stout, and tawny-colored. On

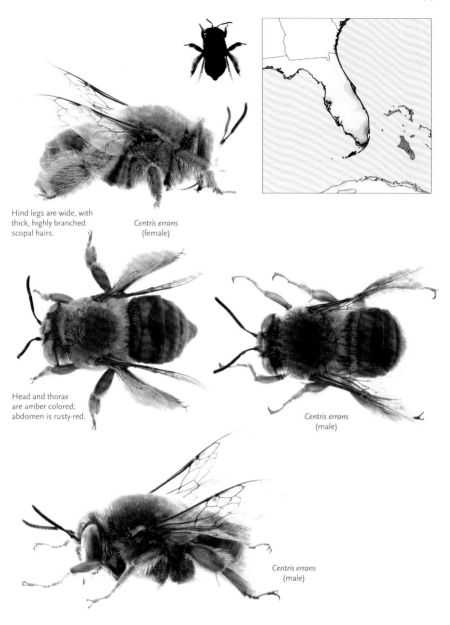

Hind legs are wide, with thick, highly branched scopal hairs.

Centris errans
(female)

Head and thorax are amber colored; abdomen is rusty-red.

Centris errans
(male)

Centris errans
(male)

the forelegs, there is a fringe of longer hairs, and a very short comb. **ABDOMEN:** Hairs are generally light in color, denser on T1 than on other segments.

SIMILAR SPECIES: In Florida, the newly present species *C. nitida* flies at the same time as *C. errans*. The two can be easily distinguished, though. *Centris nitida* is significantly smaller and has yellow hair on the thorax, and a black abdomen.

EUGLOSSA

— **SUBFAMILY:** Apinae
— **TRIBE:** Euglossini

OVERVIEW: Brilliant green, medium-sized bees with extraordinarily long tongues. They are usually associated with orchid pollination. Tropical orchids produce scent compounds specifically to attract male orchid bees. The male bee collects the scent compounds and, in the process, pollinates the orchid. Collected compounds are then used to attract females; the male perches on a branch and fans his wings while releasing the volatiles into the air near a female. The compounds produced by orchids are thus very species-specific, and certain male orchid bees are important in the pollination of certain orchid species.

The *Euglossa* introduced to Florida is well established, thriving, and expanding its range across southern Florida, even in the absence of its host orchids. This suggests that the males may not need the orchids as much as the orchids need the bees (obligate and facultative mutualisms, respectively). Males in Florida (and elsewhere) have been observed foraging for scent compounds on fungi, heavily scented non-native flowers, decomposing vegetation, and essential oils. Males will occasionally fight over stores of floral scent.

IN THE WORLD: Primarily Neotropical bees found from Mexico south to Paraguay, Brazil, and Argentina. There is one species north of the U.S.-Mexico border. It is an introduced species that arrived in North America sometime around 2003. It is now well established and occurs widely throughout the lower half of Florida.

CLEPTOPARASITES: None known.

IDENTIFYING FEATURES: Easy to recognize: bright metallic coloration and fast flight patterns. Males often hover for extended periods. **HEAD:** The tongue is at least half as long as the body, and can be seen below, or extended in front of, the body when the bee hovers. Males usually have yellow or ivory on the clypeus, mandibles, lower portions of the face, and the labrum. Head is often slightly wider than the thorax, and inner margins of compound eyes converge in many species. **THORAX:** Often with short sparse hairs. Punctation can be dense to sparse. Scutellum may extend beyond pronotum. Most species are bright green or blue, but a few have orange hair or integument. **LEGS:** Females do not possess scopal hairs but have corbiculae, and wet pollen masses may be seen adhering to the bees' hind legs. In males, the hind tibia is inflated and extremely large; scent compounds are stored inside this highly modified appendage. **ABDOMEN:** Usually lacking hair bands on tergal segments.

At the time of its discovery in Florida in 2003, *Euglossa dilemma* was thought to be *Euglossa viridissima*, but detailed studies revealed it to be the very similar-looking *E. dilemma*. *E. viridissima* does not appear to be in the U.S.

SIMILAR GENERA: In the U.S. and Canada, *Euglossa* may look somewhat similar to *Agapostemon*, but the larger body size and more robust stature are distinctive. The leg features (thickened, flattened tibiae) of both female and male *Euglossa* are unique to that genus, and not found in *Agapostemon* or any of the Augochlorini.

Euglossa dilemma

SIZE: Medium; 11–13 mm.
PHENOLOGY: Seen year-round in
Florida. **FLORAL HOSTS:** Polylectic,
visiting a wide array of flowering plants.
RANGE: Introduced. Found in Florida.
NESTING: Solitary cavity nester (trees, wood
stumps). Nests may contain up to 20 cells. Nests
are modified using plant resins.
IDENTIFICATION: In both sexes the bee is bright
metallic green, relatively hairless, and has dusky
wings. The bees are quick in flight, but will
hover in front of flowers for extended periods of time.
HEAD: The head of males contains ivory markings on
the mandibles, clypeus, and underside of the antennae.
Tongues of both species are extremely long, about
two-thirds the length of the body. Inner margins of
compound eyes slightly converging. **THORAX:** Emerald
green, with white hair on sides of thorax. Scutellum
elongated, overhanging metanotum. **WINGS:** Darkened.
LEGS: Males have wide, inflated-looking hind tibiae,
noticeable even in flight. In females, the
flattened hind tibiae, which may be packed
with matted pollen/nectar, are often clear
as they hover in the air. **ABDOMEN:** Widened
anteriorly, so that it is wider than
the thorax. Brilliant green.
SIMILAR SPECIES: There is only
one species of *Euglossa* in
eastern North America.

Euglossa dilemma
(male)

You can attract male orchid bees
to your yard if you live in southern
Florida. Leave out blotter paper
scented with clove or mint oils.

These black felty pads on the hind legs are
used to attract females, when scent
compounds are put on them.

Male *Euglossa* collect scents
from flowers and pack them
into the hollow area on
their back legs.

The edge of the clypeus and up near the
eye is lined with white/ivory in males.

Euglossa dilemma
(male)

The tongue of *Euglossa* is longer than
that of any other North American bee.

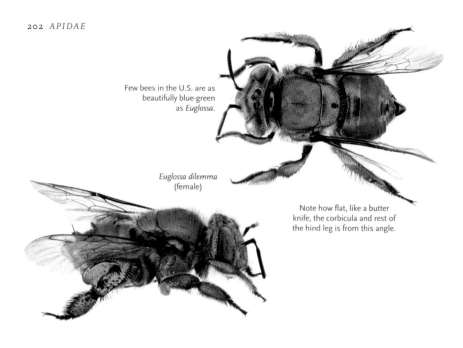

Few bees in the U.S. are as beautifully blue-green as *Euglossa*.

Euglossa dilemma (female)

Note how flat, like a butter knife, the corbicula and rest of the hind leg is from this angle.

BOMBUS

— **SUBFAMILY: Apinae**
— **TRIBE: Bombini**

OVERVIEW: Large, fuzzy bees, striped with black, yellow, and orange. Conspicuous flower visitors from early spring through the fall. Bumble bees are social bees with annual colonies. The phenology differs from species to species, and some colonies end the season much earlier than others.

Colonies begin anew each year, with large queens emerging in the early spring to initiate nesting. They are often observed in early spring flying slowly over the ground, examining various cavities for potential nesting sites. Chosen sites are often abandoned rodent burrows or hollow areas near grass tussocks; they have also been found in old flowerpots, bird boxes, and other places that provide shelter. The queen's first generation of daughters are small and develop within two months of the queen's initial flight. These daughters become the primary harvesters of pollen and nectar, while the queen stays home producing more brood. The next generations of daughters are larger than the first, so that the size of bumble bees seen foraging grows as the season progresses. By mid- to late summer, a colony could grow to include up to 500 individuals. At this time, the queen lays eggs that will become male bumble bees, and also eggs that will become next year's queens. Males leave the nest to find queens from other colonies. All worker bees in a season perish in the fall. Mated queens overwinter in hibernacula and emerge the following spring to start the cycle again. Because the colony is active across multiple seasons, bumble bees are generalists, though they may focus on one plant genus during a foraging flight.

IN THE WORLD: Around 260 species occur worldwide, found mostly in the Northern Hemisphere, with a few species in northern Africa, Central America, and South America. They are more common at higher elevations than lower. In North America, there are almost 50 species. In the eastern U.S. and Canada there are 28 species.

CLEPTOPARASITES: One subgenus, *Bombus (Psithyrus)*, parasitizes other *Bombus* species.

IDENTIFYING FEATURES: Generally large bee (some workers can be very small) with thick yellow and black hair on the head, thorax, and abdomen, where it often appears as stripes. Some species also have white, orange, or red stripes on the abdomen. Under the hair, the integument is completely black. **HEAD:** In males, the integument of the clypeus is never colored, but may have colored hairs covering the surface. In females the clypeus is hairless and usually polished. In many species the malar space is longer than wide, giving the face an elongated look. **THORAX:** Covered in thick hair, which may be all yellow or a mixture of yellow and black hairs. The location of patches of yellow and black hair are important for distinguishing species. **WINGS:** Usually dark, clear in some species. The jugal lobe is missing from the hindwing in all species. On the forewing the stigma is very short. There are three submarginal cells. **LEGS:** In females, there is a corbicula on the hind leg; the tibia is flattened, even slightly concave, and hairless, except for a fringe of hair around the outer edges (*Bombus* [*Psithyrus*] lack this character). The basitarsus is enlarged and rectangular. Hind tibial spurs are present. The tarsal claws are split. **ABDOMEN:** Tergal segments are colored in various combinations of yellow, black, red, and white. The combination is often a major factor used in distinguishing species.

One subgenus of *Bombus*, *Psithyrus*, parasitizes other species in the same genus. There are 29 species of *B. (Psithyrus)* in the world, with six in North America, all of which occur in eastern states and provinces. The overall form of this subgenus is similar to other *Bombus* species, but females lack a well-developed corbicula. Instead, the hind tibia in females is slightly convex, and hairy. Male *B. (Psithyrus)* can be distinguished by the notably smaller heads and the bare patches on T4–T6.

While many bumble bee species can be easily identified on the wing, there are also a number of *Bombus* species that are difficult to distinguish from each other; their hair patterns are variable, even in the same colony, and there is considerable size and morphological variation between queens, workers, and males.

SIMILAR SPECIES: The large size of *Bombus* queens gives them a similar appearance to *Xylocopa*. In female *Xylocopa*, the presence of scopal hairs is distinguishing. In male *Xylocopa*, the off-white markings are distinctive. In both, the rounder face of *Xylocopa* is telling. Several other large Apidae look similar to bumble bees. Some *Anthophora* species are orange and sized like female worker *Bombus*. The shorter malar space in *Anthophora*, scopal hairs (in females), and yellow face (in males) should differentiate the two. Also, the marginal cell in *Anthophora* is much shorter than in *Bombus*, and *Anthophora* have a jugal lobe, which *Bombus* do not.

worker

queen

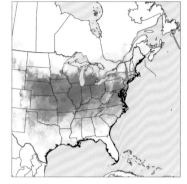

Bombus auricomus

SIZE: Queen: 18–20 mm; worker: 18–21 mm; male: 17–20 mm. **PHENOLOGY:** Queens are seen in late April and May. Workers are seen late May–July. New queens and males seen in August and September. **FLORAL HOSTS:** Very broad generalist. **RANGE:** Less common than other bumble bees, though it has a large range. Texas east to the Atlantic Seaboard, north to southern Ontario, west through Saskatchewan Province. **NESTING:** Colonies are small with 35–80 individuals. The queen lays eggs in separate cells, rather than together as other *Bombus* do.

IDENTIFICATION: Moderately sized bumble bee with short hair. **HEAD:** Vertex entirely yellow. Malar space only just longer than it is wide, so that the face is relatively short. In males, eyes are bulging, and converge at the top of the head. **THORAX:** The anterior half of the scutum (before the tegulae) is yellow; between the tegulae is a stripe of black. The scutellum is usually black, but may be yellow or a mix of the two colors. **WINGS:** Smoky. **ABDOMEN:** T1 is variable and may be all yellow, all black, or may include intermixed yellow and black hairs. T2–T3 are yellow. T4–T5 segments are black. In males, T1–T3 are yellow, T4–T6 black.

SIMILAR SPECIES:

Bombus pensylvanicus and *B. terricola* both look similar. *Bombus pensylvanicus* has all black hair on the vertex. Typically, *B. pensylvanicus* has yellow on T1, and the posterior portion of the thorax is all black, rather than a mix of black and yellow hairs. Between the two (*B. auricomus* and *B. pensylvanicus*), *B. auricomus* is more common. *Bombus terricola* is not featured in this book as it is relatively uncommon. If seen, it may be recognized by the slightly swollen clypeus.

Thorax is yellow with a thick black stripe between tegulae. The scutellum on this specimen is intermixed black and yellow hairs, though many are just black.

T2–3 are yellow. T1 and T4–T6 are black.

Bombus auricomis (female)

Hair on face black with yellow hairs on top of head

worker

queen

Bombus bimaculatus

SIZE: Queen: 17–22 mm; worker: 10–16 mm; male: 13–15 mm. **PHENOLOGY:** Queens are seen in early April (one of the earliest bumble bees to fly). Workers appear in early May and fly through August. Males appear in mid-June and fly through October. New queens appear in August–October. **FLORAL HOSTS:** Broad generalist. **RANGE:** Common. Widespread throughout the East, and frequent in urban environments. Less frequently seen in the Midwest. **NESTING:** Nest underground, in hollow logs, or occasionally in grass tussocks above ground. Underground nests are 0.3–1 m deep and consist of several brood areas seemingly randomly distributed.

T1 is yellow, and T2 is yellow centrally, appearing as two tufts or lobes.

Black head, yellow thorax with black or mixed hairs centrally between tegulae

Hair is long and uneven, making the bee look shaggy.

IDENTIFICATION:
Shaggy, medium-sized bumble bee. **HEAD:** Malar space is just longer than broad. The hair on the face is predominantly black, with

Bombus bimaculatus
(female)

only a little yellow (if any). On the vertex, hair is yellow. **THORAX:** Anterior and posterior sections of the thorax are yellow, but a black spot is usually present at the center/posterior edge of the scutum. **ABDOMEN:** T1 is yellow; T2 is yellow centrally, appearing as two tufts of yellow hair to either side of center. All other tergal segments have all-black hair. In males, T1 is all yellow, T2 is yellow medially, and T3–T6 are usually black but intermixed with yellow in some individuals. **SIMILAR SPECIES:** *Bombus impatiens* looks similar to *B. bimaculatus*. In *B. bimaculatus*, there is some yellow on T2, while *B. impatiens* is all black on T2.

Bombus (Psithyrus) citrinus

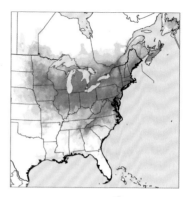

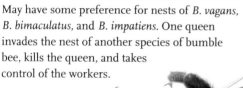

SIZE: Medium to large; 13–21 mm. **PHENOLOGY:** April through October. **FLORAL HOSTS:** Cleptoparasite; may be seen on any number of flowers when nectaring, but does not collect pollen. **RANGE:** Alabama and Georgia north to southern Canada, west to Iowa and North Dakota. **NESTING:** May have some preference for nests of *B. vagans*, *B. bimaculatus*, and *B. impatiens*. One queen invades the nest of another species of bumble bee, kills the queen, and takes control of the workers.

Abdomen variable: T1–T3 can be black, yellow, or mixed. T4–T6 are black.

Thorax yellow, sometimes with a black central spot

IDENTIFICATION: Light yellow bee of medium/large size. Hair is medium length. **HEAD:** Hair on face in both sexes is black, though a few yellow hairs may be intermixed.

The hind leg of *B. citrinus* lacks a corbicula. It is hairy and slightly convex, rather than hairless and polished and concave.

Malar space is short—making the head appear small. **THORAX:** All yellow, including the sides; some females, and all males, have a small black spot in the center of the thorax. **WINGS:** Smoky. **ABDOMEN:** Integument relatively shiny and visible through hairs. Typically the hair is all black, but there is much variation. T1–T3 may have yellow spots, or mixed yellow and black hairs. Sometimes T2–T3 are entirely yellow. T4–T5 are almost always black. In males, T1 is yellow, T2–T3 are intermixed, and T4–T6 are black. **SIMILAR SPECIES:** *Bombus citrinus* can be distinguished from other bumble bees by the fact that it looks like a bumble bee but has no corbicula. There are five species of parasitic bumble bee in the East. *Bombus citrinus* is the only one that regularly has a completely black thorax. Three nonparasitic species share similar patterning on the thorax: *Bombus affinis*, which typically has a band of red on the abdomen; *B. perplexus*, which has a longer face (malar space longer than it is wide) and is more consistently yellow on T1; and *B. vagans*, which has longer hair and always has a dark spot between the tegulae.

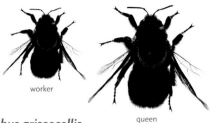

worker

queen

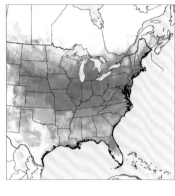

Bombus griseocollis
(female)

Bombus griseocollis

SIZE: Queen: 20–23 mm; worker: 10–18 mm; male: 15–18 mm. **PHENOLOGY:** Queens appear in May, and workers appear a month later and fly through September. Males can be seen from July through October. New queens appear in August and September. **FLORAL HOSTS:** Very broad generalist. **RANGE:** Found throughout North America. Seldom seen in the Southwest except at higher elevations. **NESTING:** Nests underground or in grass tussocks above ground. Colonies are small, no more than 50 workers. **IDENTIFICATION:** Larger bumble bee with short and even hair. **HEAD:** The malar spaces are clearly shorter than broad. Hair on the front of the face is black or sometimes mixed with light yellow. On the vertex, hair is black. In males, the eyes are bulging and converge slightly. **THORAX:** In both sexes, yellow, often with a black spot on the scutum. **ABDOMEN:** T1 is yellow. T2 is yellow or orange-brown, at least centrally. The apical margin of T2 is usually black hair, as are the apical margins of T3–T5. In males, T1 is yellow, T2 is medially yellow, and T3–T6 are black.

Thorax with yellow hair, sometimes with a black spot in the center

T1 is yellow, T2 is yellow or orangish-brown centrally, and T3–T5 are black.

SIMILAR SPECIES: Because the yellow hair on T2 is sometimes W-shaped, it can resemble *Bombus bimaculatus*. The difference is that T1 and T2 of *B. griseocollis* are usually brown, and the color doesn't extend to the edges of the tergal segments, as it does in *B. bimaculatus*. Also, the hair in *B. bimaculatus* is long and shaggy (not all the same length), and the malar space is longer than in *B. griseocollis*.

worker

queen

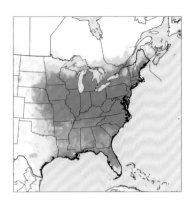

Bombus impatiens

SIZE: Queen: 17–21 mm; worker: 9–15 mm; male: 12–17 mm. **PHENOLOGY:** Queens appear in April through June, workers are abundant from May on. Males and new queens appear in July through the end of the flowering season. **FLORAL HOSTS:** Very broad generalist; may have a preference for thistles, goldenrods, and *Echinacea*. **RANGE:** Widespread in the East, including cities and urban areas; seen also in the West, but colonies there are introduced. **NESTING:** Nests underground.

IDENTIFICATION: Medium to large bumble bee with short, even hair; less variable hair patterns than other species. **HEAD:** The face is very round because the malar space is as wide as it is long. Hair on the face and the vertex is black, though with a few intermixed yellow hairs. In males, clypeus has yellow hair, but frons and vertex are black. **THORAX:** In both sexes, hair is all yellow, though there are some black hairs near the tegulae. **ABDOMEN:** In both sexes, T1 is yellow. T2–T6 are covered in black hair. **SIMILAR SPECIES:** *Bombus bimaculatus* is similarly light-colored on the thorax, but T2 has two distinct yellow spots on *B. bimaculatus*.

Bombus impatiens
(female)

Thorax covered
in yellow hair

T1 with yellow hair;
T2–T6 with black hair.

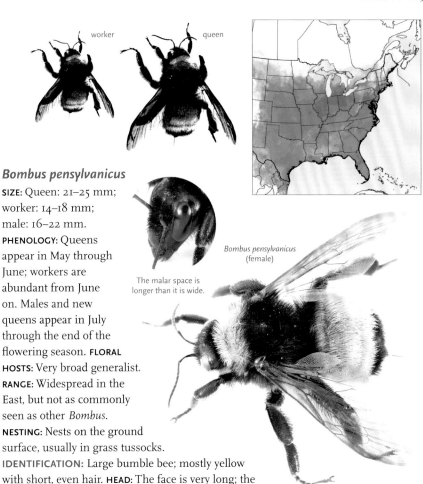

worker   queen

Bombus pensylvanicus
(female)

The malar space is
longer than it is wide.

Bombus pensylvanicus

SIZE: Queen: 21–25 mm;
worker: 14–18 mm;
male: 16–22 mm.

PHENOLOGY: Queens
appear in May through
June; workers are
abundant from June
on. Males and new
queens appear in July
through the end of the
flowering season. **FLORAL
HOSTS:** Very broad generalist.
RANGE: Widespread in the
East, but not as commonly
seen as other *Bombus*.
NESTING: Nests on the ground
surface, usually in grass tussocks.
IDENTIFICATION: Large bumble bee; mostly yellow
with short, even hair. **HEAD:** The face is very long; the
malar space is longer than it is wide. The vertex has
black hair, with no yellow mixed in. **THORAX:** Anterior
portion is yellow, with a black stripe between the wings. Posterior portion most often
black (though occasionally with mixed yellow hairs). **ABDOMEN:** T1 is usually black
basally and yellow at least along the apical margin, especially centrally; T2 and T3 are
yellow all the way across, and T4 and T5 are black. In males, T1–T4 are covered in long
yellow hairs. T5 is variably yellow or black. T6 and T7 are black.
SIMILAR SPECIES: *Bombus auricomus* and *Bombus terricola* both look similar. *Bombus
auricomus* is always yellow on the vertex. Typically, *B. auricomus* has a mix of yellow
and black hairs on T1 and T2, as does the posterior portion of the thorax. Between
the two (*B. auricomus* and *B. pensylvanicus*), *B. auricomus* is usually more common,
though this is not always the case (for example, in southern Ontario). *Bombus terricola*
is not featured in this book as it is relatively uncommon. If seen, it may be recognized
by the slightly swollen clypeus.

worker

queen

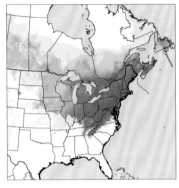

Bombus perplexus

SIZE: Queen: 16–21 mm; worker: 12–14 mm; male: 13–14 mm. **PHENOLOGY:** Queens appear in April through May; workers are abundant from May through August. Males and new queens appear in mid-June until the end of the flowering season. **FLORAL HOSTS:** Very broad generalist; commonly seen on *Lonicera, Prunus, Ribes, Vaccinium,* and other perennial shrubs. **RANGE:** Widespread in the Northeast and Great Lakes states, extending south through South Carolina. Absent from Missouri, Louisiana, Mississippi, and Alabama. **NESTING:** Nests on the ground surface or in underground rodent burrows.

IDENTIFICATION: Small bumble bee with long fuzzy hair. **HEAD:** Hair is mostly black on the face with some yellow at the vertex. The malar space is just longer than it is wide. In males, antennae are long, extending to the midpoint of the scutum if extended posteriorly. **THORAX:** Hair is almost entirely yellow. The sides of the thorax may be black or yellow. **ABDOMEN:** T1–T2 are yellow or occasionally light brown. T3 may be entirely yellow or may be yellow just in the center. T4 and T5 are black, or may have some white hairs. T1–T2 with yellow hair in males; T3–T6 with black.

SIMILAR SPECIES: *Bombus vagans* looks similar to *B. perplexus.* They can be distinguished by the yellower hair on *B. vagans*, the dark spot between the tegulae in *B. vagans* (all yellow in *B. perplexus*) and the entirely black T3 in *B. vagans. Bombus sandersoni* (not included in this book) is very similar to *B. perplexus* and is common in the northeastern United States. Between the two, *B. perplexus* has longer hair.

Long shaggy hair with all yellow hairs on the thorax

T1–T2 yellow, T3 can be black or yellow (especially centrally), and T4–T6 are black.

Bombus perplexus (female)

worker

queen

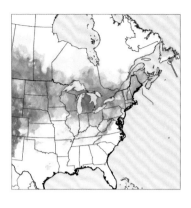

Bombus rufocinctus

SIZE: Queen: 16–18 mm; worker: 11–12 mm; male: 12–13 mm. **PHENOLOGY:** Queens appear May through June; workers are common June through September. Males and new queens appear in July. **FLORAL HOSTS:** Very broad generalist; commonly seen on *Cirsium, Aster, Trifolium, Solidago,* and *Melilotus.* **RANGE:** Common in the West, but found only in northern states toward the east, Minnesota and Wisconsin east to Maine. Common in southern Canada, but also found further north. **NESTING:** Nests on the ground surface or in underground burrows made by other organisms.

IDENTIFICATION: Small bumble bee with short hair. Highly variable in terms of color patterns, especially on the abdomen. **HEAD:** Hair on face black or yellow, but is nearly always yellow at the vertex. The malar space is shorter than it is wide, making the head very round for a bumble bee. In males, eyes are slightly bulging. **THORAX:** In both sexes, hair is yellow with a black stripe running between the tegulae. **ABDOMEN:** Color pattern variable with red or black hairs on parts of T3–T5. T1 is often yellow, and T2 is always yellow, usually all the way across the segment, but at a minimum it is yellow centrally. In males, T1–T2 and T5–T6 with yellow hairs; T3–T4 with black.

SIMILAR SPECIES: The color patterns of *B. rufocinctus* are so variable that it can be easily confused with a wide number of species. The small size, very round face, and consistently yellow T2 can help distinguish this species.

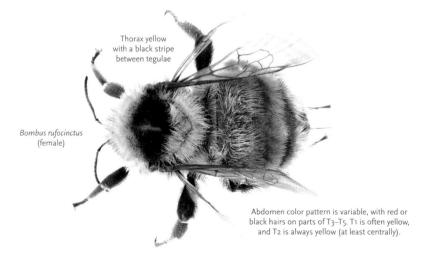

Thorax yellow with a black stripe between tegulae

Bombus rufocinctus (female)

Abdomen color pattern is variable, with red or black hairs on parts of T3–T5. T1 is often yellow, and T2 is always yellow (at least centrally).

Bombus ternarius

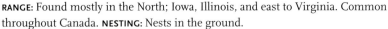

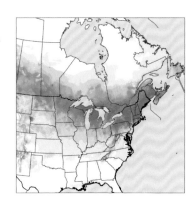

SIZE: Queen: 17–19 mm; worker: 8–13 mm; male: 10–13 mm. **PHENOLOGY:** Queens appear from April through May; workers are common May through September. Males and new queens appear from July until the end of the flowering season. **FLORAL HOSTS:** Very broad generalist; commonly seen on *Asclepias, Solidago, Rhododendron* (early in the year), and *Vaccinium*.
RANGE: Found mostly in the North; Iowa, Illinois, and east to Virginia. Common throughout Canada. **NESTING:** Nests in the ground.

IDENTIFICATION: Small bumble bee with short hair. **HEAD:** Hair is mostly black, with some yellow mixed in. The malar space is slightly shorter than it is wide, giving the head a relatively round appearance. In males, eyes slightly bulging, and converge toward the top. **THORAX:** In both sexes, hair is yellow anteriorly. There is a black triangle behind the black stripe on the tegula; yellow is on the sides of the metanotum and pronotum with black centrally. **ABDOMEN:** In both sexes, T1 is yellow, while T2 and T3 are bright orange. T4 is yellow. T5 is black.

SIMILAR SPECIES: Might look similar to *Bombus rufocinctus* individuals that are red on the abdomen. *B. ternarius* comes out earlier in the year and has a slightly longer face. The second tergal segment in *B. ternarius* is always red/orange, and not yellow as it is in most *B. rufocinctus*; however, there are some *B. rufocinctus* queens with red on T2.

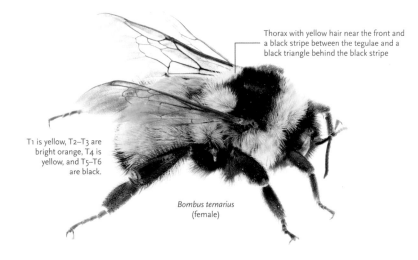

Thorax with yellow hair near the front and a black stripe between the tegulae and a black triangle behind the black stripe

T1 is yellow, T2–T3 are bright orange, T4 is yellow, and T5–T6 are black.

Bombus ternarius
(female)

worker

queen

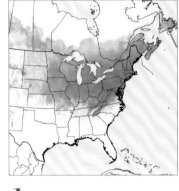

Bombus vagans

SIZE: Queen: 15–19 mm; worker: 6–16 mm; male: 11–13 mm. **PHENOLOGY:** Queens appear from April through May; workers are common May through September. Males and new queens fly from June through October.

FLORAL HOSTS: Very broad generalist; commonly seen on *Asclepias, Aster, Cirsium,* and *Spirea.*

RANGE: Widespread in northern states. Especially common in the Northeast (Connecticut through New Jersey) and south along the Appalachians. West to Missouri and Wyoming. Rare in the Pacific Northwest.

NESTING: May nest in grass tussocks or other areas above ground, or in rodent cavities in the ground. This bumble bee is more common in deeply forested areas than are most other bumble bees.

Long, shaggy yellow hair on the thorax with some black hairs centrally, sometimes forming a stripe

Bombus vagans (female)

Yellow hair on the sides of the thorax

T1–T2 are yellow, and T3–T6 are mainly black with occasionally some yellow hairs intermixed.

IDENTIFICATION: Medium-sized bumble bee with shaggy hair. **HEAD:** Hair is black with a few yellow hairs mixed in. The malar space is longer than wide, giving the head a long appearance. **THORAX:** In both sexes, hair is a mix of yellow and black with the black hairs concentrated between tegulae as a spot or stripe. On the sides, the thorax is yellow. **ABDOMEN:** In both sexes, T1–T2 are yellow and T3–T5 are black, but some specimens have intermixed yellow hairs. In some individuals, especially males, the tail is yellow.

SIMILAR SPECIES: Similar to *B. perplexus. Bombus vagans* has a black spot between the tegulae, and the vertex is black. Queens, and some worker individuals, of *Bombus affinis* share a similar patterning to *B. vagans,* with yellow on T1 and T2, a black spot between the tegulae, and a black vertex. These individuals can be distinguished from *B. vagans* by the swollen clypeus, evident in *B. affinis. Bombus sandersoni* (not included in this book) can also appear similar to *B. vagans.* Watch for the slightly shorter face of *B. sandersoni,* and the shorter hair all over the body.

Bombus affinis

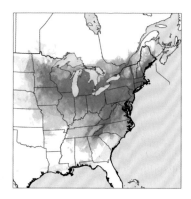

worker

queen

SIZE: Queen: 21–22 mm; worker: 11–16 mm; male: 13–17 mm. **PHENOLOGY:** Queens appear from May through June; workers are common June through September. Males and new queens fly from July through October. **FLORAL HOSTS:** Very broad generalist; commonly seen on *Asclepias, Aster, Helianthus, Solidago,* and *Lythrum.* **RANGE:** Rare.

This is an endangered species that is not commonly seen. A handful of records a year are recorded in northern states (Wisconsin, Minnesota, and Michigan, east to New York) and along the Appalachians. **NESTING:** Nests in rodent burrows underground. **IDENTIFICATION:** Large-sized bumble bee with medium to long hair. **HEAD:** Hair on the face is black. Hair on the vertex is black, with some intermixed yellow hairs. The clypeus protrudes dramatically from the face. The malar space is short, wider than long, so that the face is round instead of long. **THORAX:** Hair is yellow, with a black spot or black line between the tegulae. **ABDOMEN:** In both sexes, T1 is yellow. T2 is variable. In many individuals T2 is red at the apex, or may be red across its length; however, some individuals are yellow across all of the second segment. T3–T5 are black. In males, T2 is always partially red.

SIMILAR SPECIES: Looks similar to *B. griseocollis.* The clypeus in *B. griseocollis* does not protrude as it does in *B. affinis,* and the hair in *B. griseocollis* is much shorter than in *B. affinis.* Queen *B. affinis* can also be confused with *B. perplexus; Bombus perplexus* is yellow between the tegulae, while *B. affinis* queens are black between the tegulae. Individuals of *Bombus affinis* that are lacking in the red hair band can be confused with *B. vagans.* The hair of *Bombus vagans* is longer than in *B. affinis.*

Thorax hair is yellow, with a black spot or black line between the tegulae.

This is an endangered species and rarely seen.

T1 is yellow, and T2 is variable, often with orangish-red hairs, at least centrally, but sometimes yellow across all of the second segment. T3–T6 are black.

Bombus affinis (female)

APIS

— **SUBFAMILY:** Apinae
— **TRIBE:** Apini

OVERVIEW: Medium-sized amber-colored bees. Though many consider this the "quintessential" bee, it is not native to North America, and can be invasive. It shares few natural history characteristics with other bees found in this region. *Apis* are highly social species, living in colonies of up to 50,000 individuals. Within a colony, tasks are divided among female workers. Only one individual, the queen, actively produces offspring; she makes one mating flight, when she is mated with multiple males. This one mating flight is enough for her to lay fertilized eggs for the next five to seven years. In just one day, a queen may lay 1,000–2,000 eggs. She and her developing offspring are fed by workers. Depending on what these offspring are fed, they will develop into future queens or additional workers. Because they are perennial colonies, these bees are generalists; however, an individual bee may collect nectar or pollen from one kind of flower on a given trip.

IN THE WORLD: Seven species occur in the world. Most are found in Southeast Asia and India, but also tropical Africa. Two species, *Apis mellifera* and *A. cerana*, have been domesticated. *Apis mellifera* has been moved around the world and is widely used for pollination and honey production.

CLEPTOPARASITES: No other bee species are known to parasitize *Apis*.

IDENTIFYING FEATURES: Medium-sized bee with some fine hair on the thorax.

HEAD: Compound eyes are hairy. Inner margins of compound eyes converge toward the bottom. Mandibles are simple, with few notable teeth. **THORAX:** Covered in fine light auburn hair, through which the integument can be seen. **WINGS:** Marginal cell is extraordinarily long, extending almost to the end of the wing, and is rounded at the end. There are three submarginal cells, which end well back from the wing apex; the second is triangular in shape, rather than cuboidal. **LEGS:** In females pollen is collected on a corbicula. As the bee flies, the wet pollen mass may be visible, even if the corbicula is hard to discern. Hind legs often hang below the body in flight. The hind basitarsus is about as wide as long. There are no hind tibial spurs. **ABDOMEN:** Honey-colored with variable striping on the abdomen (some species have white stripes).

SIMILAR GENERA: *Apis* may look similar to *Andrena* or *Colletes* because of their size, overall body shape, and similar coloration. The flattened hind legs, hairy compound eyes, and unique wing venation of *Apis* are distinguishing characteristics.

Apis mellifera

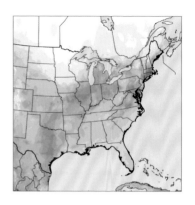

SIZE: Queen: 18–20 mm; worker: 10–15 mm. **PHENOLOGY:** Seen from very early in the year all the way through the flowering season. **FLORAL HOSTS:** Very broad generalist. **RANGE:** Non-native bee introduced several hundred years ago, with populations originating in many areas throughout the Eastern Hemisphere. Now widespread throughout eastern North America, especially in rural areas. **NESTING:** Nests in hives; most often hives are man-made, but feral colonies can also be found in hollow trees, and other large cavities.

IDENTIFICATION: See genus description for features; this is the only species in North America. Most individuals seen are females. In flight, females often hang their legs below the body, rather than holding them up tightly like many other bees do. **HEAD:** Males (drones) have large eyes that almost touch on top of the head. **ABDOMEN:** Shiny, may be variably colored from all black to very light colored, but usually with dark bands running across at least the first two tergal segments. **SIMILAR SPECIES:** *Apis mellifera* is the only species of *Apis* in North America. For similar genera, see above. There are nearly 24 subspecies of *Apis mellifera* subspecies that occur throughout the United States and Canada. One in particular, *Apis mellifera scutellata*, is known for its aggressive behavior, and is commonly called the "Africanized bee" or "killer bee." *Apis mellifera scutellata* bees cannot be recognized by appearance—genetic testing must be done.

Apis mellifera coloration ranges from light orange to dark brown.

Compound eyes covered with long hairs

Apis mellifera (female)

Marginal cell is very long, extending nearly to the end of the wing

Hind legs with corbicula (flattened, smooth area on the hind tibia with long hairs that wrap around it)

Apis mellifera (female)

Drones (males) have large eyes that almost touch on the top of the head.

Apis mellifera scutellata (sometimes called "killer bees") bees are morphologically indistinguishable from other subspecies.

Apis mellifera (male)

Apis mellifera scutellata (female)

NOMADA

— **SUBFAMILY:** Nomadinae
— **TRIBE:** Nomadini

OVERVIEW: Striking red or red and yellow parasitic bees seen in abundance in the spring and early summer. Most are nest parasites of *Andrena* species and are frequently seen hovering just above the ground, looking for nest entrances. With no need to collect pollen, this group has no floral preferences. Occasionally seen in the evening or early morning "sleeping," with bodies taut, legs tucked up, grasping a plant stem with their mandibles.

IN THE WORLD: *Nomada* is a species-rich genus, with more than 700 species found around the world. Though found on every continent, they are rare in the tropics of South America and sub-Saharan Africa. There are nearly 300 species in North America, with more than 60 in the East.

HOSTS: In North America mostly bees in the genus *Andrena,* but also *Agapostemon, Halictus, Lasioglossum, Melitta, Exomalopsis,* and *Colletes.*

IDENTIFYING FEATURES: Nearly hairless red and yellow bee, narrow-bodied and wasplike. They range in size from petite, to larger than a honey bee. **HEAD:** The base of the mandible is wider than the eye. **THORAX:** The scutum is overly rounded, rather than flat. **WINGS:** The marginal cell is very pointed and ends right on the wing margin. There are either two or three submarginal cells (usually three); the width of the first submarginal cell is equal to the widths of the second and third submarginal cells together. **ABDOMEN:** In females, S5 has a tuft of bristles to either side of center. The sixth tergal segment, which is barely visible, has a tuft of hair to either side of the pygidial plate.

Nomada are notoriously difficult to identify to species. While some subgenera are distinct, there are many species that have defied being placed in a subgenus with any certainty. For a handful of species, only one sex has been described. Furthermore, there appears to be significant variation in the color patterns of individuals even within one species. Below, we have pulled out just two species that can be more easily identified. For others, we refer you to the key listed in the references, which includes just 37 of the more than 60 found in the East. A note on *Nomada:* distinguishing males and females is more difficult than other bees because they lack scopal hairs. Counting antennal segments must be done with caution, because in many males the pedicel is nestled *inside* the apex of the scape and can be missed (resulting in a count of 12 antennal segments when there are 13). Make sure to also count tergal segments, as females have six exposed, while males have seven.

SIMILAR GENERA: No other bee genus exhibits the striking red and yellow markings seen on the body of *Nomada.* They are more likely to be mistaken for wasps than for other bee genera. *Brachynomada* (not included in this book), which are very rare, may appear similar but lack any yellow markings, and they are entirely black or black and red. The mandibles of *Brachynomada* are about the same width as the compound eye.

Nomada articulata

SIZE: Small to medium; 8–10 mm.
PHENOLOGY: April through late June.
HOSTS: *Andrena*. **RANGE:** Widespread
across North America.
IDENTIFICATION: Petite, wasplike bee with very
little hair, usually predominately red in color
with yellow markings, but may be nearly black
with yellow markings. **HEAD:** Head wider than
long, with coarse dense pits. Clypeus shinier
than the rest of the face. From the side, the gena

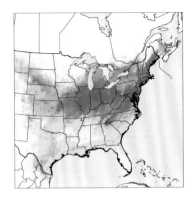

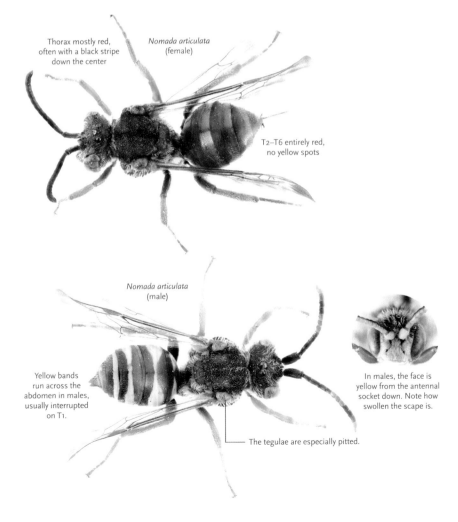

Thorax mostly red,
often with a black stripe
down the center

Nomada articulata
(female)

T2–T6 entirely red,
no yellow spots

Nomada articulata
(male)

Yellow bands
run across the
abdomen in males,
usually interrupted
on T1.

In males, the face is
yellow from the antennal
socket down. Note how
swollen the scape is.

The tegulae are especially pitted.

is wider than, or about the same width as, the compound eye. In females, antennal flagellar segment 1 is longer than segment 2. In males, the antennal scape is very swollen. The lower half of the face, including the underside of the scape, is yellow. **THORAX:** Scutum is heavily roughened and mostly red or black; if red, there may be a line of black right down the center. The sides of the thorax are covered in very fine white hairs. The tegulae are distinctly punctate. The propodeum is primarily red, with some light white hairs covering the segment. **LEGS:** On the hind tibia in females there is a row of four or five very short bristles, hidden beneath fine white hairs. **ABDOMEN:** In females, T2–T4 are entirely red, with no yellow maculations, though the color becomes lighter on the margins of tergal segments. In males, yellow markings are evident on the sides of T1 and T2, and run completely across T4–T6.

SIMILAR SPECIES: *Nomada articulata* is hard to distinguish from *N. australis,* which is less common; *N. australis* has the first and second flagellomeres equal in length in females and long flattened hairs on the hind tibia. *Nomada parva* may also appear similar in coloration. *Nomada parva* is much smaller and is likely parasitic on *Panurginus* instead of *Andrena*. On the abdomen, there are no pits on T2–T3. In males, the rear tibia has a unique long yellow stripe down its length. The face appears much shorter than it is wide, especially compared with other *Nomada*.

Nomada luteoloides

SIZE: Small; 9–10 mm.
PHENOLOGY: April through May.
HOSTS: *Andrena*. **RANGE:** Widespread across eastern North America, ranging as far west as Minnesota, Illinois, and Mississippi. North to southern Ontario.
IDENTIFICATION: Striking black and yellow bee with few hairs, and a wasplike appearance. **HEAD:** Antennae may appear with a slight reddish hue. From the side, the compound eye is as wide as the gena, which ends in a carina at the back

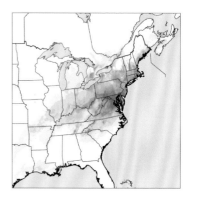

of the head (may be hard to see unless specimen is pinned). In males, the side of the scape that faces the head when the antennae are up is completely dark. Clypeus, which is yellow, protrudes slightly from face and is polished. If the labrum can be seen, there is a small projection right at the center of its apex. **THORAX:** The pronotal color may be light yellow, as are the tegula. The bulk of the scutum is dark: black, brown, or with patches of red. The scutellum is developed into two yellow bumps that stick out slightly from the overall outline of the thorax. The rear face of the propodeum is primarily yellow. **LEGS:** Yellow, but may have some red patches. In females, on the hind tibia there are five, or in some cases fewer, spines, and all of them are strongly curved to the side. **ABDOMEN:** In females, each segment has yellow bands with no interruption in the bands, except on T1, which may be slightly broken in the middle. Overall, there is minimal pitting and an overall shiny appearance.

The yellow spots on the scutellum in males are small.

Nomada luteoloides (male)

Note that the back of the scape is dark.

The gena is not as thick as the compound eye.

Nomada luteoloides (female)

On the hind tibia there are five thick spines that curve inward.

Just visible here, there is a small lip where the gena ends at the back of the head.

The thorax is primarily black or brown, with two yellow bumps near the back end.

Nomada luteoloides (female)

Abdomen with yellow and black/brown bands that are not interrupted

SIMILAR SPECIES: *Nomada imbricata* has an overall similar appearance. In males, the part of the scape that faces the head when the antennae are up is completely dark in *N. luteoloides*, but has a light stripe running through the dark patch in *N. imbricata*.

EPEOLUS

— SUBFAMILY: Nomadinae
— TRIBE: Epeolini

OVERVIEW: *Epeolus* are boldly marked black and white chunky bees. They are small to medium in size, but generally inconspicuous. The hair is white, appressed, and scalelike on a matte-black body. They are most common in the late summer and fall. They have no floral preferences and can be seen on a wide array of flowering plants.

IN THE WORLD: There are more than 100 species of *Epeolus* around the world, widely distributed on all continents. Around 32 species can be found in North America, and 17 of these occur in the East.

HOSTS: *Colletes.*

IDENTIFYING FEATURES: Modest-sized black and white or red/black and white bee with appressed lines and patches of hair on the head, thorax, and abdomen. Not fuzzy at all. HEAD: *Epeolus* are characterized by having three short segments on their maxillary palpi, instead of four or five, though these are difficult to see. THORAX: The scutum appears arched instead of flat, as in most bees. The axillae are drawn into long points that hang over the scutellum. Usually with two lines of appressed hairs, starting at the anterior edge of the scutum and extending halfway back. WINGS: The marginal cell is rounded at the tip. ABDOMEN: Appressed hairs create white lines running across each tergal segment. On T6 the pygidial plate is wide and short. Just anterior to the pygidial plate is a pseudopygidial area, usually covered with a patch of differently colored, even silvery, appressed hairs. The hairs on the edges of S6 in females are cone-shaped.

SIMILAR GENERA: *Triepeolus* can look very similar to *Epeolus*, and distinguishing the two without close inspection may not be possible. Overall, *Epeolus* are smaller than *Triepeolus*. Small male species of *Triepeolus* may be distinguished from male *Epeolus* only by looking at characters on the genitalia. For females, the pygidial plate is key: in *Epeolus* it is wider than it is long, with a pseudopygidial area that is shaped like a half-moon. In *Triepeolus* the pygidial plate is longer than it is wide, with the pseudopygidial area equally elongated.

Epeolus scutellaris

SIZE: Small; 7–10 mm. PHENOLOGY: July through September. FLORAL HOSTS: No preferred flowers; does not collect pollen. RANGE: Virginia north through Maine and Nova Scotia west to North Dakota.
NESTING: Parasitizes ground-nesting *Colletes.*
IDENTIFICATION: HEAD: Gena is thick, at least a third, if not more, the width of the eye. The lateral ocelli are close to the preoccipital carina. THORAX: Pronotal collar black. Scutum dark brown to black, though there may be hints of

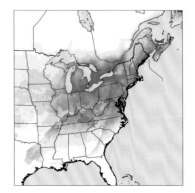

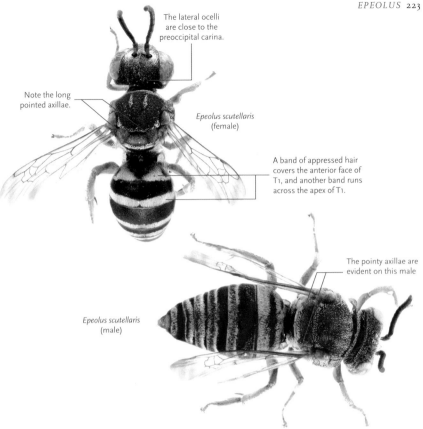

The lateral ocelli are close to the preoccipital carina.

Note the long pointed axillae.

Epeolus scutellaris (female)

A band of appressed hair covers the anterior face of T1, and another band runs across the apex of T1.

The pointy axillae are evident on this male

Epeolus scutellaris (male)

lighter color around the outer edges. In females, two white lines of appressed hair run down the scutum, just on either side of center. The scutellum may be either red or black. The axillae, which are usually red, are straight and long, extending back to the edge of the scutellum. They are not curved toward the middle of the scutellum, and are wide, overlying about half of each side of the scutellum. From the side, the scutellum is flattened, and not thickened or inflated in any way. **LEGS:** Lighter yellow to red color. **ABDOMEN:** In both sexes, the integument is all dark brown to black. The anterior face of T1 is covered in short white appressed hairs, which run to the sides of the segment. Here, they may connect with the basal hair band that also runs to the sides. T2 has an apical hair band that runs across the whole segment; it may or may not be interrupted in the center. The pseudopygidium (just anterior to the pygidium) is covered with light brownish hairs surrounded by light white hairs that cover the rest of the fifth tergal segment. Hair bands are stronger in females than in males.

SIMILAR SPECIES: *Epeolus pusillus* shares many characters with *Epeolus scutellaris*. Large differences include the size, with *E. scutellaris* being larger than *E. pusillus*, and darker in color, due to the lack of white appressed hairs on the sides of the thorax and the anterior face of T1.

TRIEPEOLUS

— **SUBFAMILY:** Nomadinae
— **TRIBE:** Epeolini

OVERVIEW: Medium-sized bees; matte-black bodies with bold white stripes made of matted hair. Cleptoparasites on *Melissodes* and other fall-flying Eucerini. No floral preferences as they do not collect pollen; frequently seen hovering near the ground where their hosts may be nesting. In the evening and early morning may be found grasping plant stems with their mandibles, legs tucked up beneath the body.

IN THE WORLD: There are more than 140 species of *Triepeolus* around the world. Absent from Africa, central Asia, India, and Australia, but found in South America, Europe, northern Asia, and North America. There are more than 100 species north of the Mexican border. Around two dozen of those occur in the eastern U.S. and Canada.

HOSTS: *Melissodes,* other Eucerini.

IDENTIFYING FEATURES: Matte-black bee with striking white patches of appressed hairs running across the abdomen and thorax. **HEAD:** Face is wider than it is long, and covered with thick or thin very matted hairs. Antennae are stout, and flagellar segments are black, but in some species the scape and pedestal are red. On the mouthparts, if they can be seen, the maxillary palpi consist of three segments.

THORAX: Axillae at the posterior end of the scutum are sharply pointed and protrude posteriorly over the scutellum almost to the propodeum. Hair patterns on the scutum are bold, and many species appear as though they have a "smiley face" stamped on them. **LEGS:** Often red, or with reddish areas. **WINGS:** Marginal cell is long and narrow. **ABDOMEN:** Variously striped with stark white flattened hairs. Pseudopygidial area is long; often longer than it is wide.

SIMILAR GENERA: Looks very similar to *Epeolus,* and may be indistinguishable without viewing the genitalia. Overall, *Epeolus* are smaller and there are differences in the pygidial plates that can help (see *Epeolus* for more information). On the wings, the marginal cell of *Triepeolus* is narrower and longer than that of *Epeolus;* both genera would need to be on hand to see the difference.

Triepeolus lunatus

SIZE: Small to medium; 9–14 mm.
PHENOLOGY: May through October.
HOSTS: *Melissodes,* especially *M. bimaculata.* **RANGE:** Coast to coast; rare in the Northwest and the extreme Northeast (Maine, New Hampshire, etc.). Found in eastern Canada as far north as southern Ontario.
IDENTIFICATION: Medium-sized bee with black integument (southern species may have some red), and white to ivory appressed patches of hair throughout. **HEAD:** Female has thick

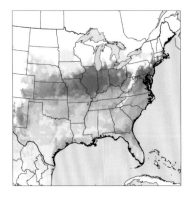

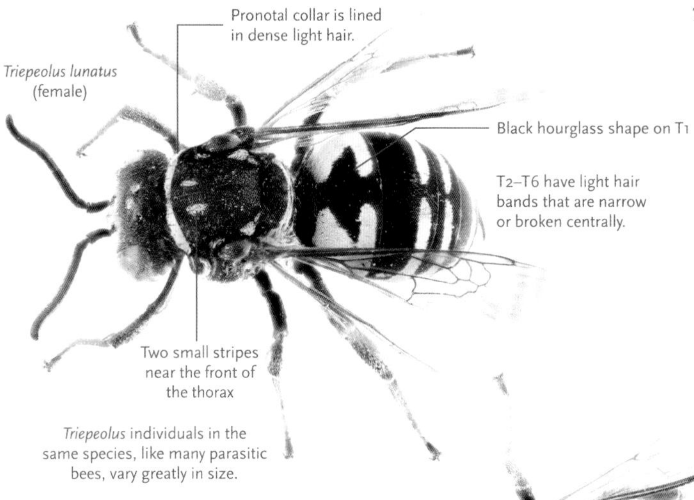

Triepeolus lunatus
(female)

Pronotal collar is lined
in dense light hair.

Black hourglass shape on T1

T2–T6 have light hair
bands that are narrow
or broken centrally.

Two small stripes
near the front of
the thorax

Triepeolus individuals in the
same species, like many parasitic
bees, vary greatly in size.

Triepeolus lunatus
(male)

hair sprouting near antennal bases. Males have lighter, almost silvery hair covering the whole face. On the clypeus, there is a raised ridge running down the middle. **THORAX:** Two stripes occur to either side of center, beginning posterior to the pronotal collar. The pronotal collar is lined in dense ivory-colored hair. The posterior rim of both the scutum and the scutellum possesses a band of white hair outlining the edge. The tegulae are usually red (especially from southern locations). **LEGS:** Usually rusty red. **ABDOMEN:** T1 mostly covered in appressed white hair, missing from the center to form an hourglass black shape. T2–T4 have apical bands of appressed hair that end, or narrow, medially. T5 has light gray patches of hair pointing toward the center of the segment, where it meets a third patch of hair that starts at the apex of the segment. **SIMILAR SPECIES:** *Triepeolus* can be difficult to distinguish, and many species occur in the East that are not included in this book. Pay attention to the two hair bands that run across T1; in many species these are parallel, but in *T. lunatus* (and a handful of others), the bands are not parallel, so that the black areas in the center look triangular. *Triepeolus simplex* appears similar to *T. lunatus,* but the lateral lines on the scutum touch the pronotal collar in *T. simplex*; they do not touch in *T. lunatus.* Also, *T. simplex* does not have a ridge down the center of the clypeus.

Triepeolus remigatus

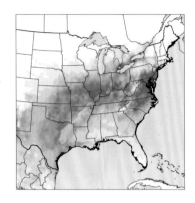

SIZE: Medium; 10–14 mm.
PHENOLOGY: Late May through September. **HOSTS:** *Eucera (Peponapis) pruinosa, Eucera (Xenoglossa) strenua,* and *Dieunomia heteropoda.*
RANGE: Coast to coast; absent from far northeastern states and northern states of the Midwest.
IDENTIFICATION: Matte-black bee with considerable white appressed hairs over entire body. **HEAD:** Face wider than long, shinier than other *Triepeolus.* The bases of the antennae may be reddish. **THORAX:** Pronotal collar is covered in thick, dense, ivory to white hair. The edges of the scutum are lined in a wide rim of appressed hair. Two lateral lines run down from the pronotal collar, which they touch, to either side of center. The posterior edge of the scutum is also lined with white hair, creating a central black area that looks like a head of broccoli, when viewed with the head aimed down. The tegulae are black. **ABDOMEN:** T1 is almost completely coated in yellow appressed hair, with a rhombus of black at the center, and a smaller triangle of black at the apex of the segment. In females, T2 has a wide semicircle of black at the base. In males, T2 is mostly black, surrounded by white hairs laterally and basally. In females, T3 and T4 have very wide hair bands that narrow only slightly in the center. T5 has two areas of light-colored appressed hair, laterally, and one brown area at the middle, along the apex; this hair is thicker and denser than the lighter-colored hair.

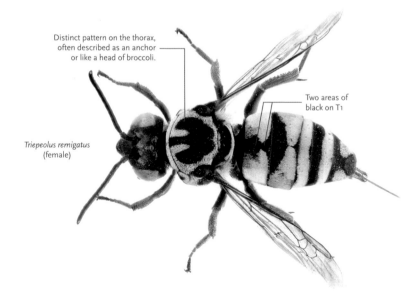

Distinct pattern on the thorax, often described as an anchor or like a head of broccoli.

Two areas of black on T1

Triepeolus remigatus
(female)

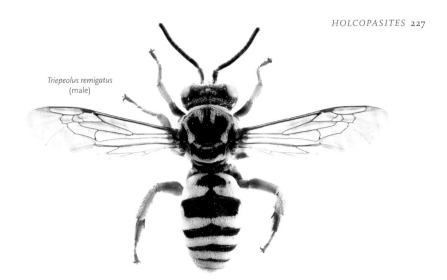

Triepeolus remigatus
(male)

SIMILAR SPECIES: Several *Triepeolus* species may look somewhat similar to *T. remigatus*, but this is the only species with its unique hair pattern on the scutum. *Triepeolus concavus* has yellow hair at the anterior half of the scutum, but this hair does not extend into two parallel lines. In addition, it does not have a triangle of black at the apex of T1.

HOLCOPASITES

— SUBFAMILY: Nomadinae
— TRIBE: Ammobatoidini

OVERVIEW: Small parasitic bees seen in the summer. They are relatively rare and seldom seen unless in the vicinity of a nesting site for their host. No floral preferences, and as often seen hovering above the ground looking for nest entrances as seen on flowers.
IN THE WORLD: Nineteen species are currently recognized; all occur in North America. Most are found in the western U.S., but three species occur in eastern states and Canada.
HOSTS: Andrenidae (*Calliopsis, Pseudopanurgus, Protandrena,* other Panurginae).
IDENTIFYING FEATURES: These are small pointy-ended bees covered in tiny rough punctures. HEAD: Antennae are located low on the face, just above the clypeus and clearly on the lower half of the face. THORAX: With white flattened hairs often in patches that look like spots. WINGS: Two submarginal cells. ABDOMEN: Red, or red and black, often with patches of flattened white hair. Males have a large pygidial plate, while females do not.
SIMILAR GENERA: *Sphecodes* have similar coloration between the thorax and the abdomen, but have three submarginal cells. *Ashmeadiella* can also be similarly colored, with white patterning on a red abdomen, and also have two submarginal cells. Female *Ashmeadiella* collect pollen on their abdomen, so scopal hair should be visible on those individuals. In both males and females of *Ashmeadiella* the head is much thicker, with a strong preoccipital carina, and the hair is not appressed as in *Holcopasites*.

Holcopasites calliopsidis

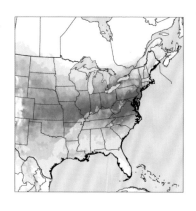

SIZE: Small; 5–6 mm. **PHENOLOGY:** June through August. **HOSTS:** Parasitic on *Calliopsis andreniformis*, and perhaps *Pseudopanurgus*. **RANGE:** Tennessee and Louisiana, north to southern Canada.

IDENTIFICATION: Small bees with red abdomen and reddish eyes. **HEAD:** The face is very short, with low antennae, occurring just above the clypeus. **THORAX:** The scutellum is raised, but not divided in any way by a groove. **WINGS:** Two submarginal cells. **ABDOMEN:** T2–T4 are marked by four white spots of appressed hair: two on either side of the center, and two toward the side. No lines of appressed hair exist. In males, there is a large pygidial plate, which is lacking in females.

SIMILAR SPECIES: There are three species of *Holcopasites* in the East. *Holcopasites calliopsidis* is the most widespread, but *H. illinoensis* and *H. heliopsis* overlap in range. In *H. heliopsis,* there are two lobes, lined in white appressed hairs, on the scutellum. In *H. illinoensis,* T2–T4 have a line of appressed hair at the basal end; the line gets thinner in the middle.

The body of *Holcopasites* bees is covered with flattened white hairs. In this particular species those hairs appear most notably as patches on the abdomen.

Holcopasites calliopsidis
(female)

The face is short with low antennae, which are attached just above the clypeus.

Notice the heavy punctation on the thorax.

Note that there are four patches of hair on each tergal segment: two just to either side of the middle, and two just before the segment wraps under the body.

The scutum is not raised into two lateral "knobs" in this species, as it is in similar looking *H. heliopsis*.

Holcopasites calliopsidis
(female)

There are two submarginal cells on the wing.

A KEY TO BEE GENERA IN EASTERN NORTH AMERICA

What follows is a dichotomous key to the bee genera of eastern North America that are included in this book.

Before you use this key to identify the genus of your insect, make sure that you are looking at a bee specimen. Look for four wings (two on either side) to rule out flies. Make sure there are no metallic silver-colored hairs on the face, and that the first segment of the abdomen is not elongated and thin. And look for the presence of branched hairs; these are usually present in multiple areas of the bee's body, but if in doubt, make sure to look near the pronotal lobe and on the propodeum.

A few notes on how to use a dichotomous key: First, information is presented in a series of couplets, as either/or statements. *Read both parts of a couplet completely* before making a decision. Remember that a bee must match *all* the information in a couplet, and not just some of it, unless explicitly stated as an either/or. Information is presented in a couplet in order from most important, and easiest to see, to least important, or most difficult to see. If, after reading both parts of a couplet, you are not sure which is more appropriate, try both. Run the bee through both parts. As the characters in other couplets are presented, it may become clear that the bee at hand does not fit the chosen path, and you can go back and try the other side of the couplet. Note also that characters presented in a couplet are not exclusive, in the sense that they apply only to the bees that will resolve in that couplet, and not to any that were broken out before that point. For example, if a couplet identifies *Anthidium* from other Anthidiini on the basis of its arolium, this does not exclude other bees that are not mentioned in the couplet from also having an arolium.

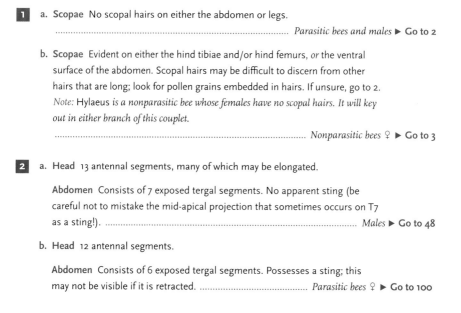

1   a. **Scopae** No scopal hairs on either the abdomen or legs.
.... *Parasitic bees and males* ▶ **Go to 2**

     b. **Scopae** Evident on either the hind tibiae and/or hind femurs, *or* the ventral surface of the abdomen. Scopal hairs may be difficult to discern from other hairs that are long; look for pollen grains embedded in hairs. If unsure, go to 2. *Note:* Hylaeus *is a nonparasitic bee whose females have no scopal hairs. It will key out in either branch of this couplet.*
.... *Nonparasitic bees* ♀ ▶ **Go to 3**

2   a. **Head** 13 antennal segments, many of which may be elongated.

     Abdomen Consists of 7 exposed tergal segments. No apparent sting (be careful not to mistake the mid-apical projection that sometimes occurs on T7 as a sting!). .... *Males* ▶ **Go to 48**

     b. **Head** 12 antennal segments.

     Abdomen Consists of 6 exposed tergal segments. Possesses a sting; this may not be visible if it is retracted. .... *Parasitic bees* ♀ ▶ **Go to 100**

3   a. **Hind leg** Hind tibia possesses a corbicula. It is polished, flattened, and
hairless, but surrounded by a fringe of hairs that curl toward its center.
Depending on the genus, may be greatly enlarged (*Figure 1*).
.... *Corbiculate bees (*sans *Bombus* subgenus *Psithyrus*)* ♀ ▶ **Go to 4**

  b. **Hind leg** Hind tibia does not form a corbicula. It is variously shaped, but not
flattened, hairless, or with a fringe of hairs curling in. .... ▶ **Go to 6**

Corbicula

Figure 2

Figure 1

No tibial spur

4   a. **Integument** Bee is brilliant green.

  Head Tongue is exceedingly long; if folded under the body, extends back at
least to the posterior end of the thorax (*Figure 2*). .... *Euglossa dilemma* ♀
Note: Occurs only in Florida and rarely.

  b. **Integument** Brown, amber, or black, but not brilliant green.

  Head Tongue is not so long that, when folded under the body, it extends back
to the posterior end of the thorax. .... ▶ **Go to 5**

5   a. **Hair** Tan, amber, or dark hairs, but no yellow hairs on body.

  Head Hairs protrude from the compound eyes (*Figure 3*).

  Wing Marginal cell is long, extending almost to the apex of the wing. There is
a pronounced jugal lobe on the hindwing (*Figure 4*).

  Hind leg Tibial spurs are absent (*Figure 1*). .... *Apis mellifera* ♀

Figure 3

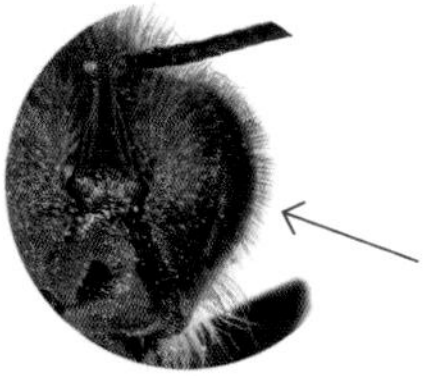

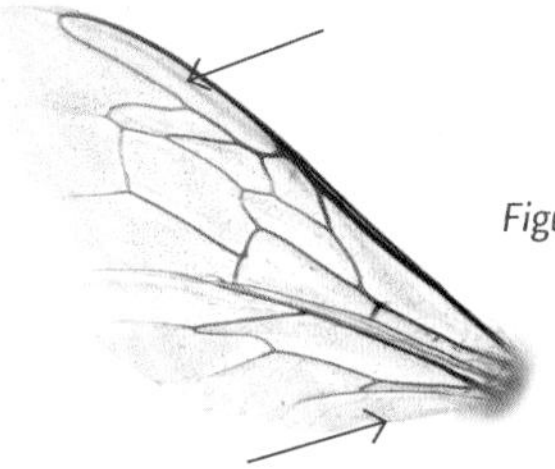

Figure 4

  b. **Hair** Some combination of yellow and black hair; may also include red or white stripes.

  Head Compound eyes are not hairy.

  Wing Marginal cell is slightly long, but on the hindwing, there is no jugal lobe (*Figure 5*).

  Hind leg Tibial spurs are evident (*Figure 6*). .... *pollen-collecting* **Bombus** ♀

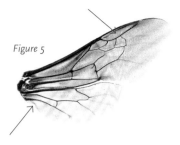

Figure 5

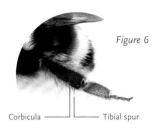

Figure 6

Corbicula ——————— Tibial spur

6 a. **Scopal hairs** Present on the underside of the abdomen, but not on the hind legs.

Wing Two submarginal cells. .... *nonparasitic Megachilidae* ♀ ▶ **Go to 7**

b. **Scopal hairs** Present on the hind leg; may be simple with few branches or dense and heavily branched. The abdomen may have a few scopal hairs laterally on T1, but overall lacks scopal hairs.

Wing May have 2 or 3 submarginal cells. .... ▶ **Go to 18**

7 a. **Head** Large knobs protrude from between the antennal sockets (*Figure 7*).

Mandible Has 3 teeth, with the middle one longer than the others (*Figure 7*).

Legs Numerous bumps (tubercles) on the outer surfaces of the hind tibiae, similar to crab legs on your dinner plate (*Figure 8*). Arolia absent between front claws.

Abdomen Pygidial plate reduced to small apical spine. .... *Lithurgopsis* ♀

b. **Head** No large knobs are evident between the antennal sockets.

Mandible May have any number of teeth, but the middle tooth is not significantly longer than the others.

Legs No tubercles on surface of the hind tibiae. An arolium may be present or absent.

Abdomen Pygidial plate present or absent, but not reduced to a small apical spine. .... ▶ **Go to 8**

Figure 7

Three teeth, middle one longer

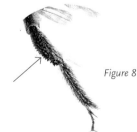

Figure 8

8   a. **Integument** Body with at least some yellow, ivory, and/or red markings, especially on the abdomen. In most species these markings are abundant and evident, but in a few species, the yellow or ivory maculations are restricted to the abdomen.

        Legs Tarsal claws are split or cleft.

        Wings Stigma is short. .... *nonparasitic* Anthidiini ♀ ▶ **Go to 9**

     b. **Integument** Body matte-black, or metallic blue or green, but never with yellow, ivory, or red maculations; however, hair may be colored yellow and red.

        Legs Tarsal claws are whole.

        Wings Stigma is elongated. .... ▶ **Go to 13**

9   a. **Legs** No arolium between the claws (*Figure 9*).

        Head Mandible has at least 5 teeth, usually 6 or more; many are small (*Figure 10*). .... ***Anthidium*** ♀

     b. **Legs** Arolium between the tarsal claws.

        Head Mandible has fewer than 5 teeth. .... ▶ **Go to 10**

Figure 9 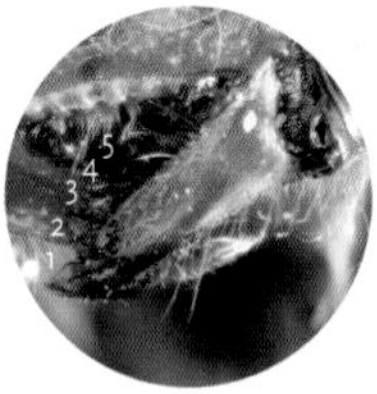   *Figure 10*

10   a. **Thorax** On the side of the thorax, the face that wraps from the side of the body around to the front (called the mesopleuron) is sharply angled, so that it looks like the edge of a box (strong omaular carina) (*Figure 11*). .... ▶ **Go to 11**
        Note: One Dianthidium *(D. texanum) occasionally seen in the East and not included in this book does not have a strong omaular carina. All other characters are consistent with* Dianthidium.

     b. **Thorax** On the side of the thorax, the mesopleuron is not sharply angled, but rounds gently from the lateral to the anterior face (*Figure 12*). .... ▶ **Go to 12**

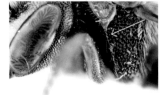

Figure 11

Figure 12

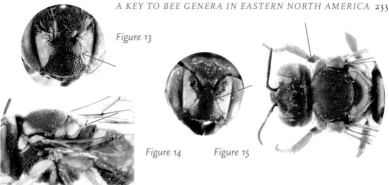

Figure 13

Figure 14 Figure 15

11 a. **Head** Subantennal suture curves strongly outward before connecting to clypeus. Strong preoccipital carina (*Figures 13 and 14*).

Thorax Scutellum extends posteriorly (backward) over the metanotum and pronotum as a broad shelf. Pronotal lobe may have a small carina, but it is not extended anteriorly as a nearly see-through plate (*Figure 14*). .... ***Anthidiellum*** ♀

b. **Face** Subantennal suture is a straight line between the antennal socket and the top of the clypeus (*Figure 15*). No strong preoccipital carina.

Thorax Scutellum ends before the metanotum and does not overhang the pronotum. Pronotal lobe very thin, almost see-through, and extending out toward the head. .... ***Dianthidium*** ♀

12 a. **Thorax** Pronotal lobe very thin and see-through, but also short.

Leg Hind tibia is not covered with small, simple bristles. .... ***Paranthidium*** ♀

b. **Thorax** Pronotal lobe rounded, and not thin and see-through.

Leg Hind tibia is covered in small, simple bristles (*Figure 16*). .... ***Trachusa*** ♀

13 a. **Legs** Arolia absent, always from hind legs, usually from all legs (*Figure 17*). .... ***Megachile*** ♀

b. **Legs** Arolia present (*Figure 18*). .... *Osmiini* ♀ ▶ **Go to 14**

Figure 16

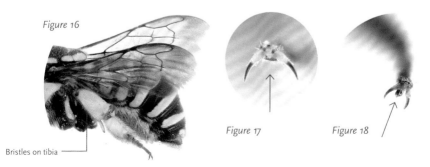

Figure 17   Figure 18

Bristles on tibia ⎯

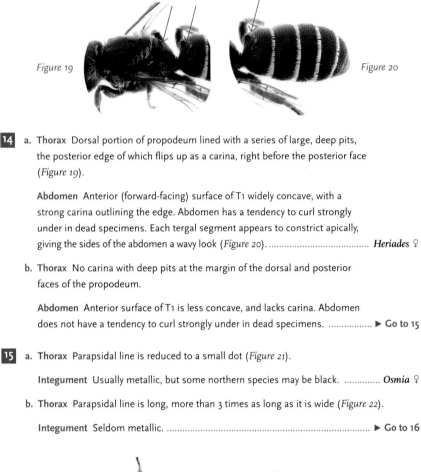

Figure 19   Figure 20

14   a. **Thorax** Dorsal portion of propodeum lined with a series of large, deep pits, the posterior edge of which flips up as a carina, right before the posterior face (*Figure 19*).

Abdomen Anterior (forward-facing) surface of T1 widely concave, with a strong carina outlining the edge. Abdomen has a tendency to curl strongly under in dead specimens. Each tergal segment appears to constrict apically, giving the sides of the abdomen a wavy look (*Figure 20*). .... ***Heriades*** ♀

b. **Thorax** No carina with deep pits at the margin of the dorsal and posterior faces of the propodeum.

Abdomen Anterior surface of T1 is less concave, and lacks carina. Abdomen does not have a tendency to curl strongly under in dead specimens. .... ▶ **Go to 15**

15   a. **Thorax** Parapsidal line is reduced to a small dot (*Figure 21*).

Integument Usually metallic, but some northern species may be black. .... ***Osmia*** ♀

b. **Thorax** Parapsidal line is long, more than 3 times as long as it is wide (*Figure 22*).

Integument Seldom metallic. .... ▶ **Go to 16**

Figure 21   Figure 22

16   a. **Thorax** Narrow and very elongated, so that the portion of the scutum anterior to the tegulae is as long as the portion posterior to them (*Figure 23*). .... ***Chelostoma*** ♀

b. **Thorax** Not elongated; the portion of the scutum anterior to the tegulae much less than the portion posterior to the tegulae. .... ▶ **Go to 17**

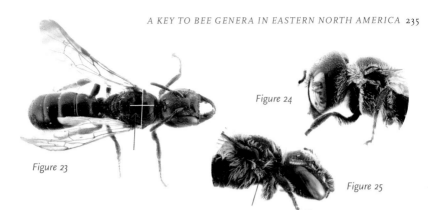

Figure 24

Figure 23

Figure 25

17 a. **Thorax** On the side of the thorax, the face that wraps from the side of the body around to the front (called the mesopleuron) is sharply angled, so that it looks like the edge of a box (strong omaular carina) (*Figure 24*). The anterior (forward-facing) portion of this plate is shiny and polished, while the lateral (side-facing) portion is punctate. .... ***Ashmeadiella*** ♀

   b. **Thorax** The mesepisternum rounds gently from the anterior to the lateral faces, and both are punctate to the same degree (*Figure 25*)............................... ***Hoplitis*** ♀

18 a. **Head** Two subantennal sutures run from each of the antennal sockets to the top of the clypeus (*Figure 26*). .... *Andrenidae* ♀ ▶ **Go to 19**
   Note: This may be hard to see in Andrena *females; verify by also looking for facial foveae and scopal hairs running up to the trochanters (see couplet 19).*

   b. **Head** One subantennal suture runs from each of the antennal sockets to the top of the clypeus. .... ▶ **Go to 23**

Figure 26

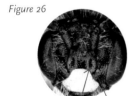

Figure 27

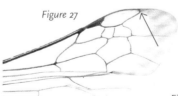

Figure 28

19 a. **Wing** Marginal cell is pointed, or very softly blunted right at the wing margin (*Figure 27*). There may be 2 or 3 submarginal cells.

   Head Facial foveae deep and pronounced beside each eye; filled with thick dense hairs (best viewed from above, looking along the plane of the face of the bee) (*Figure 28*).

Figure 29

   Scopae Extensive on the femurs and trochanters, in addition to the tibiae (*Figure 29*). In many species, the sides of the propodeum also have long hairs. ... ***Andrena*** ♀

b. **Wing** Marginal cell is abruptly cut off, and it often appears as though the cell is angling away from the wing margin (*Figures 30, 32, 34, 36*). There are 2 submarginal cells.

Head Hair is usually sparse on the face, and there may be significant yellow or ivory maculations. The facial foveae are mere shallow depressions without hair.

Scopae Scopal hairs variable, usually restricted to hind tibia and basitarsus, but not extending up onto the trochanters and underneath the body of the bee. On the sides of the propodeum there is no thick hair. .... *Panurginae* ♀ ▶ **Go to 20**

20 a. **Wing** Marginal cell is often so truncate as to appear as a square. The stigma is enlarged, almost as big as the marginal cell (*Figure 30*).

Size Minute: 4–8 mm. .... *Perdita* ♀

b. **Wing** Marginal cell is variable, but never so truncate as to appear square, and with an enlarged stigma.

Size Variable, but generally larger than 6 mm. .... ▶ **Go to 21**

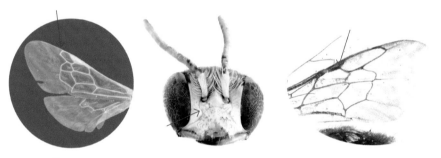

Figure 30 *Figure 31* *Figure 32*

21 a. **Head** Anterior tentorial pit is along the outer subantennal suture (*Figure 31*). Eyes, especially of live specimens, appear a light blue.

Wing Stigma is small and often narrow, about the same size as the prestigma (*Figure 32*).

Abdomen Tergal segments lined apically with thin bands of hair. S6 with tufts of dense, curving hairs at the apex. .... *Calliopsis* ♀

b. **Head** Anterior tentorial pit is at the junction of the epistomal and outer subantennal sutures.

Wing Stigma is larger than prestigma.

Abdomen Tergal segments lack apical hair bands. S6 without tufts of dense, curving hairs at the apex. .... ▶ **Go to 22**

22 a. **Thorax** On side of body, pre-episternal groove is missing (*Figure 33*).

   Wing First recurrent vein exactly meets the first transverse cubital (the vein separating the two submarginal cells) (*Figure 34*).

   Legs Forecoxa without large apical spine. .... ***Panurginus*** ♀

   b. **Thorax** On side of body, pre-episternal groove is visible (*Figure 35*).

   Wing First recurrent vein meets the middle of the second submarginal cell, not exactly meeting the first transverse cubital (*Figure 36*).

   Legs Forecoxa with large apical spine, with long hairs (this can be difficult to see). ....***Pseudopanurgus*** ♀
   Note: There is an additional genus found in North America called Pseudopanurgus *that is not included in this book. Based on the characters included here, it may key out as a* Pseudopanurgus; *between the two,* Pseudopanurgus *appears more robust, due to the wide anterior face of the mesepisternum. It also lacks a large, hairy, apical spine on the forecoxa.*

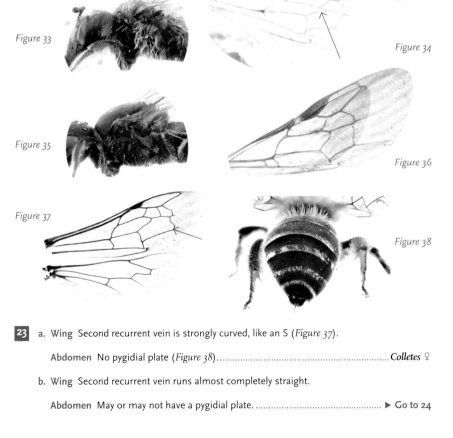

Figure 33

Figure 34

Figure 35

Figure 36

Figure 37

Figure 38

23 a. **Wing** Second recurrent vein is strongly curved, like an S (*Figure 37*).

   Abdomen No pygidial plate (*Figure 38*)..***Colletes*** ♀

   b. **Wing** Second recurrent vein runs almost completely straight.

   Abdomen May or may not have a pygidial plate. .... ▶ Go to 24

24 **a. Wing** Basal vein is strongly to moderately arced, rather than running as a straight line to the first submarginal cell (*Figure 39*). .... ▶ **Go to 25**

    b. Wing Basal vein is straight, not strongly arcing in toward the wing base before meeting the first submarginal cell. .... ▶ **Go to 31**

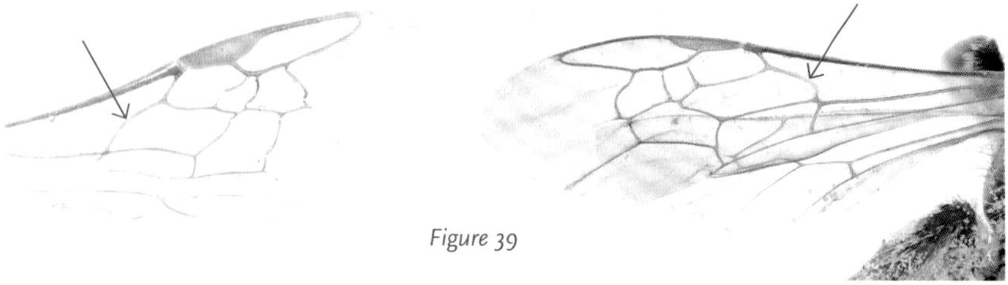

Figure 39

25 **a. Head** Usually a dot or line of yellow on the clypeus. Tongue is long (*Figure 40*).

    Wing Second submarginal cell is triangular, distinctly narrowing at the end nearest the wing margin.

    Abdomen Pygidial plate absent, though the tip of T6 may taper to a point. Each tergal segment is slightly constricted, so that the abdomen appears to have wavy edges (*Figure 41*). .... *Ceratina* ♀

    b. Head Never with a yellow dot on the clypeus. Tongue is short, tapering to a point.

    Wing Second submarginal cell is more or less square.

    Abdomen Often with hair bands running across the abdomen. Pygidial plate present. .... *pollen-collecting Halictinae* ♀ ▶ **Go to 26**

Figure 40   Figure 41

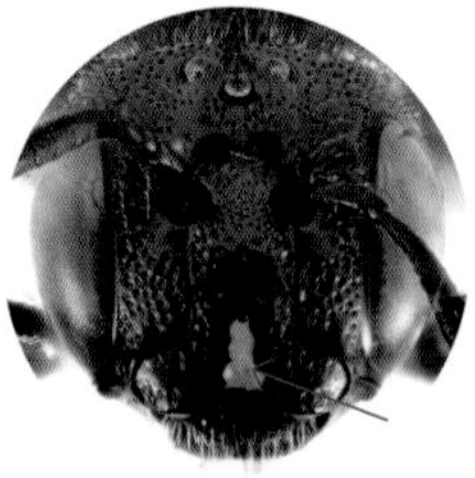

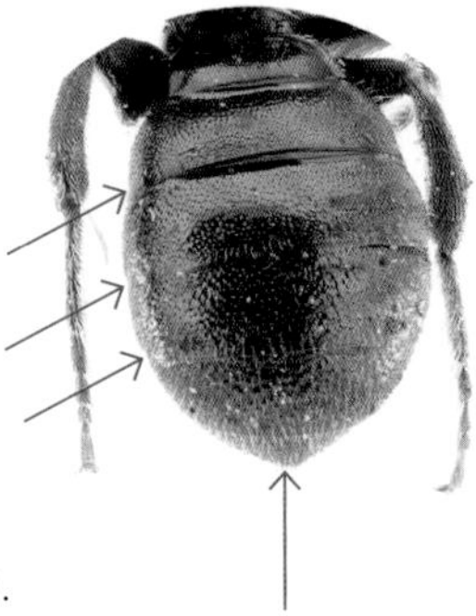

26 **a. Thorax** Bright polished green (*Figures 42 and 43*).

    Abdomen May be green, black, or yellow and brown. .... ▶ **Go to 27**

    b. Thorax May be lightly metallic green or coppery, but is not brilliantly so.

    Abdomen Brown, red, or black. .... ▶ **Go to 30**

27 **a. Head** Inner margin of compound eye without distinct notch; runs smoothly from bottom of face to the top.

Thorax The posterior surface of the propodeum is completely outlined by a strong carina (*Figure 42*). .... ***Agapostemon*** ♀

b. Head Inner margin of compound eye with distinct notch, usually just above the level of the antennal sockets.

Thorax The propodeum gently curves to its lateral and dorsal surfaces, with no clear carina completely encircling the posterior surface (*Figure 43*). .... *Augochlorini* ▶ **Go to 28**

Figure 42

Figure 43

28 **a. Thorax** Tegula is dented in on the interior side, forming a C-shape; not symmetric (*Figure 44*).

Legs Basitibial plate is very short, to the point of being barely visible. Hind tibial spurs are shaped like a little comb, with wide teeth.

Abdomen Apexes of T1 and T2 are lined with a row of short, stout, unbranched bristles (*Figure 45*). .... ***Augochloropsis*** ♀

b. Thorax Tegula is oval in shape, with no indentations on the interior side.

Legs Basitibial plate is rounded, and clearly visible. Hind tibial spurs are simple, or finely serrated (*Figure 46*).

Abdomen There is no row of stout bristles on either T1 or T2. .... ▶ **Go to 29**

Figure 44

Figure 45

Figure 46

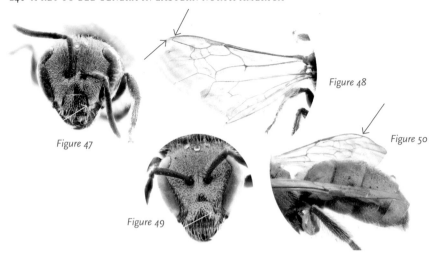

Figure 47

Figure 48

Figure 49

Figure 50

29 a. **Head** At the lower end of the paraocular area, there is a lobe (called the genal lobe) that extends down over the clypeus (*Figure 47*). The clypeus is green almost its whole length. The mandible has two apical teeth of about equal size.

   Wing Marginal cell is cut off at its apex, though a very narrow vein continues past the end of the marginal cell (*Figure 48*).

   Abdomen S1 with a ridge running down the middle, from its anterior to posterior margins. .... *Augochlora* ♀

   b. **Head** Paraocular area is not produced into the clypeus; the epistomal suture (the lateral margin of the clypeus) is gently angled or, at most, right-angled (*Figure 49*). The lower half of the clypeus is dark brown to black, but not metallic.

   Wing Marginal cell extends to the margin of the wing, with no truncation (*Figure 50*).

   Abdomen S1 without a central ridge running from the anterior to posterior margins. .... *Augochlorella* ♀

30 a. **Abdomen** T1–T4 with strong, clearly evident bands of hair running across the apex of each. In worn specimens, this may be most visible on the sides of each tergal segment (*Figure 51*).

   Wing The veins separating the first, second, and third submarginal cells from each other are always dark and strongly presented. .... *Halictus* ♀

   b. **Abdomen** T1–T4 either without any hair bands at all *or*, if hair bands are present, they are at the base of each tergal segment, emerging from under the apical margin of the tergal segment before (*Figure 52*).

   Wing The veins separating the first, second, and third submarginal cells from each other may be weak (*Figure 53*). .... *Lasioglossum* ♀

Figure 51   Figure 52   Figure 53

31   a. **Head** The antennal sockets are on the lower half of the face, below the
midpoint of the inner margin of the compound eyes, and only about the width
of one antennal socket above the top (base) of the clypeus (*Figure 54*). .... ***Dufourea*** ♀

     b. **Head** The antennal sockets are higher on the face, occurring above or at
the midpoint of the inner margin of the compound eyes, and appearing well
above the top of the clypeus. .... ▶ Go to 32

32   a. **Abdomen** Integument of tergal segments with iridescent, often pearlescent
apical margin that is completely lacking in punctation or hairs (*Figure 55*)............. ***Nomia*** ♀

     b. **Abdomen** Tergal segments may be lightly iridescent, but if so, there are also
hair bands. .... ▶ Go to 33

33   a. **Wings** Two submarginal cells. .... ▶ Go to 34

     b. **Wings** Three submarginal cells. .... ▶ Go to 36

34   a. **Size** Petite to small (4–10 mm).

     Integument Dark black bee with ivory joints, ivory pronotum, and usually
ivory markings on face, next to each compound eye. Body is almost entirely hairless.

     Head Facial foveae appear as long grooves on head, running beside each
compound eye (*Figure 56*). Tongue is bilobed or blunted. .... ***Hylaeus*** ♀

Figure 54   Figure 55   Figure 56

b. Size Medium-sized bees.

Integument Body may be sparsely haired, but not hairless; often with bands on the abdomen.

Head Facial foveae not as above. Tongue not bilobed or blunted. .... ▶ **Go to 35**

35 **a. Abdomen** Flattened.

Leg Hind basitarsus is thinner than the hind tibia, and also nearly as long as it (*Figure 57*).

Wing The second **submarginal** cell is shorter than the first. And the first submarginal crossvein makes a right angle with the bottom vein, and ends close to the first recurrent vein (*Figure 58*). .... *Hesperapis* ♀

b. Abdomen More robust, rounded.

Leg Hind basitarsus is the same width as the hind tibia, but shorter than it (*Figure 59*).

Wing The second submarginal cell is as long as or longer than the first. And the first submarginal crossvein is strongly angled, so that its junction is usually far away from the first recurrent vein (*Figure 60*). .... *Macropis* ♀

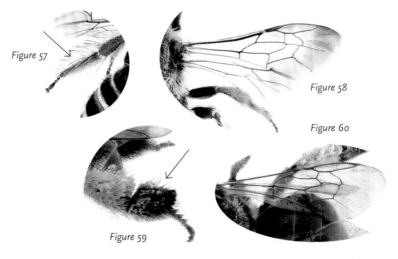

Figure 57

Figure 58

Figure 60

Figure 59

36 **a. Head** Genal area is thickened, as is the vertex, so that the head appears thick (*Figure 61*).

Abdomen First tergal segment is divided by a deep notch, so that its shape is V-like from above (*Figure 62*). On the sternal segments, dense tufts of hair (scopa) occur laterally on S2–S5, and then continue up the sides of the tergites. .... *Dieunomia* ♀

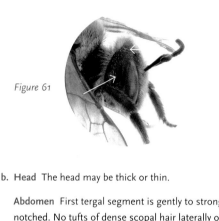

Figure 61

Figure 62

b. Head The head may be thick or thin.

Abdomen First tergal segment is gently to strongly concave, but not deeply notched. No tufts of dense scopal hair laterally on S2–S5. .... ▶ Go to 37

37 **a. Size** Extremely large bee with extensive and bristly scopal hairs, restricted to tibia (*Figure 63*).

Wing Smoky, and marginal cell long and thin, extended to long point that curves gently from the wing margin. Base of marginal cell extends over top of prestigma; there is no stigma. Second submarginal cell notably narrows as it approaches the marginal cell.

Abdomen Few hairs are seen, so that the polished black tergal segments are easily visible. No yellow hairs on females of this bee. .... *Xylocopa* ♀

b. Size Small to large bee of various coloration.

Wing On the wing, the marginal cell is not shaped as above, and a stigma is present.

Abdomen The abdomen is distinctly hairy. .... ▶ Go to 38

38 **a. Legs** Arolia absent (*Figure 64*). .... ▶ Go to 39

b. Legs Arolia present (*Figure 65*). .... ▶ Go to 40

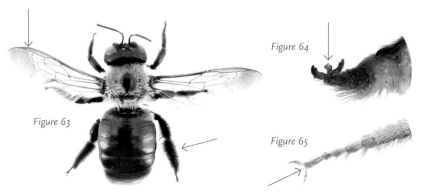

Figure 64

Figure 63

Figure 65

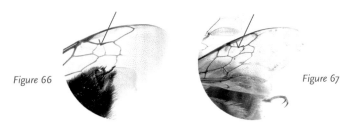

Figure 66   *Figure 67*

39   **a. Wings** Second submarginal cell much smaller than the first and third
(*Figure 66*). .... *Ptilothrix* ♀

    b. Wings Second submarginal cell same size as, or bigger than, the first and
third submarginal cells (*Figure 67*). .... *Centris* ♀

40   **a. Size** Petite bee, andreniform.

    Tongue Short-tongued, with all labial palpi of the same length, and glossa
pointed (*Figure 68*). .... *Melitta* ♀

    b. Size More robust bee with euceriform or anthophoriform shape.

    Tongue Long-tongued, with the first and second labial palpi much longer
than the third and fourth (*Figure 69*). .... ▶ Go to 41

Figure 68   *Figure 69*

41   **a. Head** When viewed from front, the vertex rounds gently, so that the ocelli are
all below the margin that is the top of the head (*Figure 70*). .... ▶ Go to 42

    b. Head When viewed from front, the vertex is concave to flat, so that the ocelli,
and even the compound eyes, stand out from the margin that is the top of
the head (*Figure 71*). .... ▶ Go to 43

Figure 70   *Figure 71*

Figure 72

Figure 73

Figure 74

Figure 75

42   a.   **Head**   Proboscis extends to the end of the thorax.

     Thorax   Hair patterns alternate light and dark (*Figure 72*), creating distinctive swirls.

     Scopae   Long and heavily branched (*Figure 73*). .... ***Melitoma*** ♀

    b.   **Head**   Proboscis does not extend to the end of the thorax.

     Thorax   Hair is thick, and even, and an off-white color (*Figure 74*).

     Scopae   Heavily branched, but much shorter (*Figure 75*). .... ***Diadasia*** ♀

43   a.   **Wing**   Cells of forewing almost entirely hairless (*Figure 76*). Toward the apex, and outside of the cells, the surface is hairless, too, but covered in small bumps that look like hair follicles. .... ▶ Go to 44

    b.   **Wing**   Entire forewing with numerous minute hairs; wing surface beyond veins not papillate (*Figure 77*) or, if so, with many pillae ending in hairs. .... ▶ Go to 45

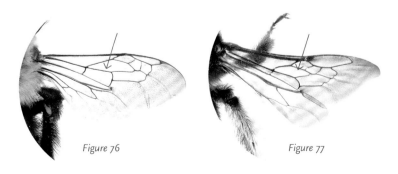

Figure 76

Figure 77

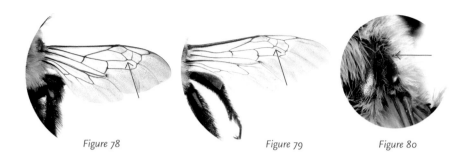

Figure 78   Figure 79   Figure 80

44 a. **Wing** The first recurrent vein ends very near middle of the second
submarginal cell (*Figure 78*). .... *Anthophora* ♀

   b. **Wing** The first recurrent vein ends near the junction of the second and third
submarginal cells (*Figure 79*). .... *Habropoda* ♀

45 a. **Thorax** Tegula narrowed at the front end (anterior) to a point (*Figure 80*).
The hair may need to be scraped from tegula for this to be clearly seen. .... *Melissodes* ♀

   b. **Thorax** Tegula round, not narrowed at all at the anterior end. .... ▶ Go to 46

46 a. **Abdomen** T1 and T2 with a metallic sheen. T4 and T5 have bright yellow or
white bands of hair running basally across them (*Figure 81*). .... *Florilegus* ♀

   b. **Abdomen** Notable hair bands, but never in the pattern described above
(*Figure 82*). .... ▶ Go to 47

47 a. **Head** Clypeus protrudes significantly from face (*Figure 83*).

   Abdomen On T2, hairs are plumose or simple, but never spatulate. .... *Eucera* ♀

   b. **Head** Clypeus more or less flat, protruding only slightly from face.

   Abdomen On T2, at least some of the hairs are branched at the base, and
spoon-shaped at the tip (*Figure 84*). .... *Svastra* ♀

Figure 81   Figure 82   Figure 83

Figure 84   *Figure 85*   *Figure 86*

48   a. **Wings** Three submarginal cells. .... ▶ **Go to 49**

     b. **Wings** Two submarginal cells. .... ▶ **Go to 80**

49   a. **Legs** Femur greatly enlarged, appearing inflated (*Figure 85*).

       Head Clypeus protrudes from face by about the width of one eye. Tongue
long, extending back to the posterior edge of the thorax.

       Distribution Bee rare, and currently found only in Florida. .... ***Euglossa dilemma*** ♂

     b. **Legs** Femur neither greatly enlarged nor appearing inflated.

       Head Clypeus flat: if protruding from face, not by the width of one eye.
Tongue short or long, but not extending as far back as the posterior edge of
the thorax.

       Distribution Widely distributed across North America. .... ▶ **Go to 50**

50   a. **Wing** Basal vein strongly arced, rather than running as a straight line to the
first submarginal cell (*Figure 39*). .... ▶ **Go to 51**

     b. **Wing** Basal vein straight, not strongly arcing in toward the wing base before
meeting the first submarginal cell. .... ▶ **Go to 58**

51   a. **Head** Usually with a yellow spot on the clypeus, often shaped like a top hat.
Tongue is long (*Figure 86*).

       Wing Second submarginal cell is triangular, distinctly narrowing at the end
nearest the wing margin.

       Abdomen Each tergal segment is slightly constricted, so that the abdomen
appears to have wavy edges (*Figure 41*). .... ***Ceratina*** ♂

     b. **Head** Never with yellow on the clypeus. Tongue is short, tapering to a point.

       Wing Second submarginal cell is more or less square.

       Abdomen Often with hair bands running across the abdomen. .... ▶ **Go to 52**

52 a. **Thorax** Bright polished green.

 Abdomen Green, or yellow and brown striped (*Figure 87*). .... ▶ Go to 53

 b. **Thorax** May be lightly metallic green or coppery, but not brilliantly so; more commonly brown or black.

 Abdomen Brown, red, metallic green, or black. .... ▶ Go to 56

53 a. **Head** Inner margin of compound eye without distinct notch; runs smoothly from bottom of face to the top. Clypeus with yellow stripe at apex.

 Thorax The posterior surface of the propodeum is completely outlined by a strong carina (*Figure 42*).

 Abdomen Yellow and brown striped. .... *Agapostemon* ♂

 b. **Head** Inner margin of compound eye with distinct notch, usually just above level of antennal sockets. Clypeus completely green.

 Thorax The propodeum gently curves to its lateral and dorsal surfaces, with no clear carina completely encircling the posterior surface (*Figure 43*).

 Abdomen Green. .... *Augochlorini* ♂ ▶ Go to 54

54 a. **Thorax** Tegula dented in on the interior side, forming a C-shape; not symmetric. Tegula metallic green, at least in part (*Figure 44*).

 Legs Hind tibia all green (*Figure 88*).

 Abdomen Apex of T1 and T2 lined with a row of short, stout, unbranched bristles (*Figure 45*). .... *Augochloropsis* ♂

 b. **Thorax** Tegula oval in shape, with no indentations on the interior side. Tegula brown.

 Legs Hind tibia yellow or red-brown, but not all green (*Figure 89*).

 Abdomen There is no row of stout bristles on either T1 or T2. .... ▶ Go to 55

Figure 87

Figure 88

55   **a. Head** At the lower end of the paraocular area, there is a lobe (called the genal lobe) that extends down over the clypeus (*Figure 47*). The clypeus is green almost its whole length. The mandible has two apical teeth of about equal size.

      Wing Marginal cell is cut off at its apex, though a very narrow vein continues past the end of the marginal cell (*Figure 48*).

      Abdomen Apical margin of S4 straight. .... ***Augochlora*** ♂

   b. Head Paraocular area is not produced into the clypeus; the epistomal suture (the lateral margin of the clypeus) is gently angled or, at most, right-angled (*Figure 49*). The lower half of the clypeus is dark brown to black, but not metallic.

      Wing Marginal cell extends to the margin of the wing, with no truncation (*Figure 50*).

      Abdomen Apical margin of S4 is concave. .... ***Augochlorella*** ♂

56   **a. Head** Much wider than long.

      Abdomen Usually deep blood red.

      Thorax Pits are wide and deep, so that the integument appears thickened (*Figure 90*). .... ***Sphecodes*** ♂

   b. Head As wide as or longer than wide.

      Abdomen Occasionally red, but usually black, brown, or lightly metallic green.

      Thorax Pitted, but not so that the integument appears substantially thickened. . ▶ Go to 57

57   **a. Head** The lower half of the clypeus is frequently yellow (*Figure 91*).

      Abdomen T1–T4 with strong, clearly evident bands of hair running across the apex of each. In worn specimens, this may be most visible laterally on each tergal segment (*Figure 51*).

      Wing The veins separating the first, second, and third submarginal cells from each other are always dark and strongly presented. .... ***Halictus*** ♂

Figure 89

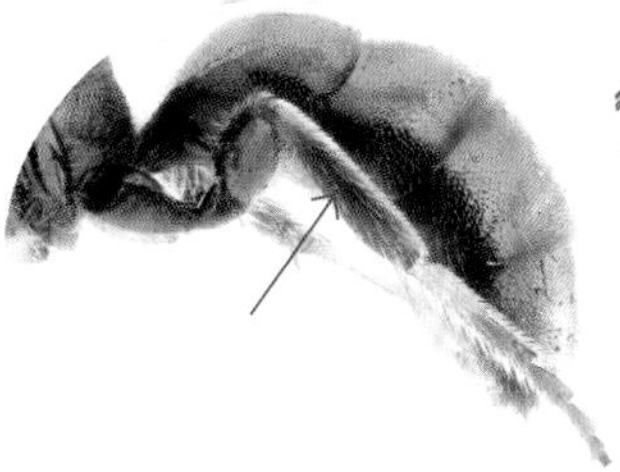

Figure 90

Figure 91

b. **Head** The lower half of the clypeus is not yellow.

Abdomen T1–T4 either without any hair bands at all *or*, if hair bands are present, they are at the base of each tergal segment, emerging from under the apical margin of the tergal segment before. This is best viewed at the lateral margins, rather than in the center (*Figure 52*).

Wing The veins separating the first, second, and third submarginal cells from each other may be weak (*Figure 53*). .... *Lasioglossum* ♂

58 a. **Head** Antennae extremely long, extending to the beginning of the abdomen (*Figure 92*). .... *Eucerini* ♂ ▶ **Go to 59**

b. **Head** Antennae short to modest, never extending to the beginning of the abdomen. .... ▶ **Go to 62**

59 a. **Abdomen** S6 with a large bump in the center (*Figure 93*).

Leg On the front leg, the femur is broadest near its middle (*Figure 94*).

Habitat Usually associated with wetlands in mid- to late summer. .... *Florilegus* ♂

b. **Abdomen** S6 has no large bump at the middle and is mostly flat, or slightly caved in.

Leg On the front leg, the femur is broadest near its base.

Habitat More widespread. .... ▶ **Go to 60**

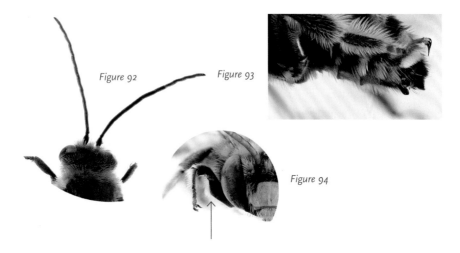

Figure 92 Figure 93

Figure 94

60 a. **Thorax** Tegula narrowed at the front end (anterior) to a point. The hair may need to be scraped from tegula for this to be clearly seen (*Figure 80*). ...... *Melissodes* ♂

b. **Thorax** Tegula round, not narrowed at all at the anterior end. .... ▶ **Go to 61**

Figure 95   Figure 96   Figure 97

61 a. **Head** With 4 maxillary palpi (*Figure 95*). One group of *Svastra* has 5 maxillary palpi; this group also has hairs on T2 that are plumose at the base, and spatulate at the ends. .... ***Svastra*** ♂ (less common of the two in this couplet, mostly summer)

    b. **Head** With 3, 5, or 6 maxillary palpi, but not 4. On the abdomen, T2 never has spatuloplumose hairs. .... ***Eucera*** ♂ (very common, mostly spring)

62 a. **Head** Two subantennal sutures run from each of the antennal sockets to the top of the clypeus. .... ***Andrena*** ♂
    Note: The bee genus Protandrena, *which is not featured in this book, will also key out here. It can be distinguished by the marginal cell, which is abruptly cut off, so that it appears as though the cell is angling away from the wing margin.*

    b. **Head** One subantennal suture runs from each of the antennal sockets to the top of the clypeus. .... ▶ Go to 63

63 a. **Hair** Hair across entire body is flattened, and appressed. In some cases almost scalelike. .... ▶ Go to 64

    b. **Hair** Erect, fluffy hair found widely across all parts of the body, or body nearly hairless and hair that is present stands up. .... ▶ Go to 66

64 a. **Integument** Thorax black, with red abdomen. Hair occurring in patches of appressed white hairs. .... ***Holcopasites*** ♂ (rare cleptoparasite)

    b. **Integument** Thorax and abdomen with patches of white and black; legs may be red, but never with a black thorax and red abdomen. .... ▶ Go to 65

65 a. **Abdomen** Pygidial plate is gently rounded, but flat when viewed from the side (*Figure 96*). .... ***Epeolus*** ♂

    b. **Abdomen** Pygidial plate is constricted at the middle when viewed from above (*Figure 97*). .... ***Triepeolus*** ♂

66 a. **Abdomen** First tergal segment is divided by a deep notch, so that its shape is V-like from above (*Figure 62*). Tergal segments are brown or black, but not iridescent.

    Legs Hind legs enlarged, with tibia and femur often flattened.

Figure 98

Figure 99

Head Genal area is thickened, as is the vertex, so that the head appears thick. The final antennal segment is flattened, and much broader than it is long (*Figure 98*). .... *Dieunomia* ♂

b. **Abdomen** First tergal segment is gently curved, or strongly concave, but not deeply notched.

Legs Hind legs not notably enlarged with femur or tibia flattened.

Head Genal area is not greatly thickened, and the final antennal segment is not modified in any way. .... ▶ Go to 67

67 a. **Abdomen** Tergal segments are strongly iridescent, almost pearlescent, and often with a margin of ivory as well, and completely lacking punctation or hairs (*Figure 55*). .... *Nomia* ♂

b. **Abdomen** Tergal segments black, brown, or hairy, but not strongly iridescent as described above. .... ▶ Go to 68

68 a. **Head** With yellow markings. May be on clypeus, near compound eyes, and/or on antennal scapes. .... ▶ Go to 69

b. **Head** Without any yellow markings on clypeus, near compound eyes, or on antennal scapes. .... ▶ Go to 73

69 a. **Integument** Body, especially abdomen but maybe also scutum, covered in yellow or red markings. .... *Nomada* ♂

b. **Integument** Body black or with yellow on face and joints, but thorax and abdomen not significantly covered in yellow or red markings. .... ▶ Go to 70

70 a. **Legs** No arolia between tarsal claws, though there may be a dense patch of hair. .... ▶ Go to 71

b. **Legs** Arolia clearly present between tarsal claws as a pad. .... *Anthoporini* ♂ ▶ Go to 72

71 a. **Wing** Marginal cell long and skinny, at least six times as long as it is wide. Stigma missing (*Figure 63*). Wings are smoky. .... *Xylocopa* ♂

  b. **Wing** Marginal cell elongated, but not so that it is 6 times as long as wide. Stigma may be small, but is definitely present. Wings are clear (*Figure 67*). .... *Centris* ♂

72 a. **Wing** The first recurrent vein ends very near middle of the second submarginal cell (*Figure 78*). .... *Anthophora* ♂

  b. **Wing** The first recurrent vein ends near the junction of the second and third submarginal cells (*Figure 79*). .... *Habropoda* ♂

73 a. **Head** Antennae emerge very low, less than one antennal socket above the top of the clypeus (*Figure 54*). .... *Dufourea* ♂

  b. **Head** On the head, antennae emerge variously, but are always more than the width of one antennal socket above the top of the clypeus. .... ▶ Go to 74

74 a. **Wing** Second recurrent vein is clearly curved (*Figure 37*). .... *Colletes* ♂

  b. **Wing** Second recurrent vein is very straight. .... ▶ Go to 75

75 a. **Hair** Typically bright yellow hair on head, thorax, and abdomen, with some black, red, or white stripes present on abdomen.

  Head Malar space long, usually at least as wide as width of compound eye.

  Wing Hindwing missing jugal lobe (*Figure 5*). .... *Bombus* ♂

  b. **Hair** May be hairy, but hair is not bright yellow, or otherwise as above.

  Head Malar space not as long as the width of the compound eye.

  Wing Hindwing with perfectly normal jugal lobe. .... ▶ Go to 76

76 a. **Head** Compound eyes hairy (*Figure 3*). .... *Apis* ♂

  b. **Head** Compound eyes not hairy. .... ▶ Go to 77

77 a. **Wing** Outer vein of third submarginal cell gently curving up to meet marginal cell (*Figure 99*). .... *Melitta* ♂

  b. **Wing** Outer vein of third submarginal cell with significant curve near midpoint, creating a lateral sigmoidal shape. .... ▶ Go to 78

78 a. **Legs** No arolia (*Figure 64*). .... *Ptilothrix* ♂

  b. **Legs** With arolia (*Figure 65*). .... ▶ Go to 79

79 a. **Head** Tongue extends just to the forelegs when stretched out below body. .... *Diadasia* ♂

  b. **Head** Tongue extends just beyond midlegs when stretched out below body. ... *Melitoma* ♂

80 a. **Head** Two subantennal sutures run from the clypeus to the antennal socket (*Figure 26*). .... *Panurginae* ♂ ▶ **Go to 81**

b. **Head** Just one subantennal suture runs from the clypeus to the antennal socket. ▶ **Go to 84**

81 a. **Wing** The marginal cell is often so truncate as to appear as a square. The stigma is enlarged, almost as big as the marginal cell (*Figure 30*).

   Size Minute: 4–8 mm. .... *Perdita* ♂

b. **Wing** The marginal cell is slightly truncated but is much longer than wide. Cell is angled off wing margin (*Figures 34, 36*).

   Size Small to medium: 6–10 mm. .... ▶ **Go to 82**

82 a. **Head** Anterior tentorial pit is along the outer subantennal suture (*Figure 31*). Extensive yellow or ivory markings that include the scape and other antennal segments, and areas next to each compound eye. Eyes, especially of live specimens, appear a light blue.

   Wing Marginal cell rounds gently off wing margin. Not immediately truncated. Stigma is small and often narrow, about the same size as the prestigma. ...... *Calliopsis* ♂

b. **Head** Anterior tentorial pit is along the epistomal suture, usually at the junction of the epistomal suture and the outer subantennal suture. There may be some yellow, but markings are not extensive. Eyes are dark gray to black.

   Wing Marginal cell is sharply truncated, as a straight line. Stigma is variable. . ▶ **Go to 83**

83 a. **Thorax** On side of body, pre-episternal groove is missing (*Figure 33*).

   Wing First recurrent vein exactly meets the first transverse cubital (the vein separating the two submarginal cells) (*Figure 34*).

   Abdomen T2–T5 are hairy along the margins. .... *Panurginus* ♂

b. **Thorax** On side of body, pre-episternal groove is visible (*Figure 35*).

   Wing First recurrent vein meets the middle of the second submarginal cell, not exactly meeting the first transverse cubital (*Figure 36*).

   Abdomen T2–T5 are not hairy along the margins. .... *Pseudopanurgus* ♂
   Note: Some Protandrena *species that have 2 submarginal cells will also key out here—this genus is not covered in our book.*

84 a. **Wings** Basal vein slightly arcuate. First submarginal cell about twice as long as second.

   Body Slender and elongated, often very small (5–12 mm). .... *Hylaeus* ♂

b. **Wings** Basal vein straight. First and second submarginal cells about the same length.

Body More robust and typically larger (9–16 mm). .... ▶ **Go to 85**

85 a. **Tongue** Short, with pointed glossa. First two segments of labial palpus short, about same length as others (*Figure 100*). .... *Melittidae ♂ (in part)* ▶ **Go to 86**

b. **Tongue** Long, with glossa long and tapering. First two segments of labial palpus longer than other palpi (*Figure 101*). .... *Megachilidae ♂* ▶ **Go to 87**

86 a. **Abdomen** Very flat, and softer than in other bees.

Leg Hind basitarsus is thinner than the hind tibia, and also nearly as long as it (*Figure 57*). .... *Hesperapis ♂*

b. **Abdomen** More robust, rounded, and not so soft.

Leg On the leg, the hind basitarsus is the same width as the hind tibia, but shorter than it (*Figure 58*). .... *Macropis ♂*

87 a. **Abdomen** Pygidial plate present (*Figure 102*). .... *Lithurgopsis ♂*

b. **Abdomen** Pygidial plate absent. .... ▶ **Go to 88**

88 a. **Legs** Arolia absent (*Figure 9*). .... ▶ **Go to 89**

b. **Legs** Arolia present (*Figure 18*). .... ▶ **Go to 91**

89 a. **Thorax** Axilla are produced, elongated into points that extend over the propodeum.

Abdomen Tapers dramatically from front to back, ending with a series of lateral spines on T5 and T6 (*Figure 103*). .... *Coelioxys ♂*

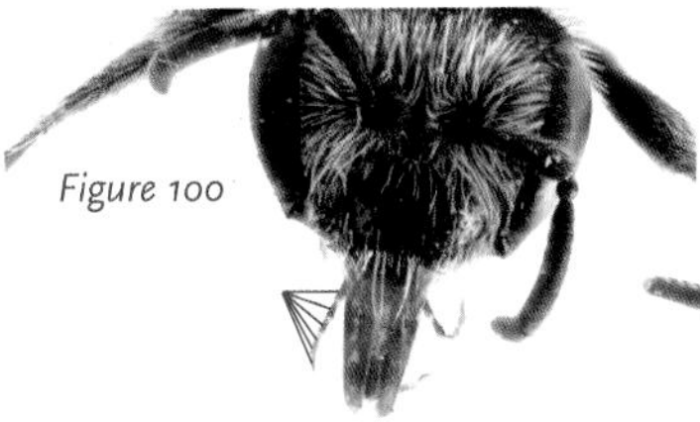

Figure 100

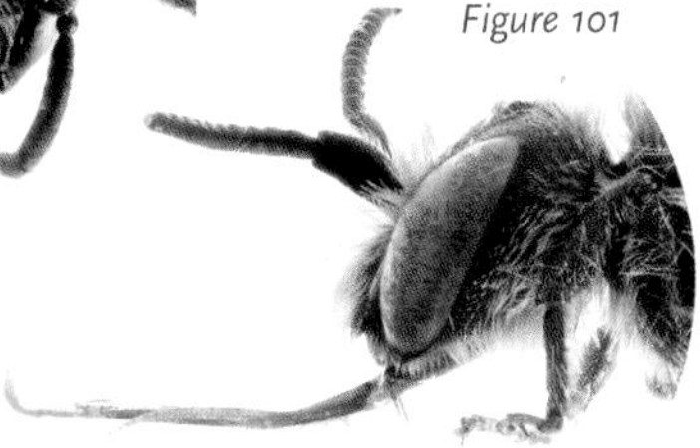

Figure 101

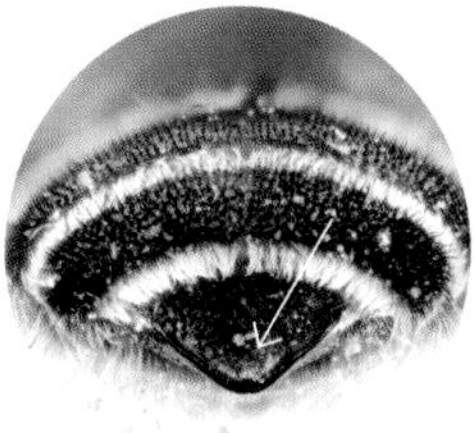

Figure 102

Figure 103

b. Thorax Axillae are rounded, and do not extend over the propodeum.

Abdomen Does not taper to a long point. .... ▶ **Go to 90**

90 **a. Integument** Head, thorax, and abdomen a combination of yellow and black
maculations. .... ***Anthidium*** ♂

b. Integument Head, thorax, and abdomen dark, though may be covered with
significant lighter-colored hair. Not widely marked with yellow and black. .... ***Megachile*** ♂

91 **a. Integument** Head, thorax, and abdomen dark, though may be covered with
significant lighter-colored hair. Not widely marked with yellow and black
maculations. May be metallic.

Wing Stigma and prestigma long. Second recurrent vein meeting second
submarginal cell before its distal edge. .... *Osmiini* ♂ ▶ **Go to 92**

b. Integument Head, thorax, and abdomen a combination of yellow and black
maculations. Never metallic.

Wing Stigma and prestigma short. Second recurrent vein meeting second
submarginal cell past its outer edge. .... *Anthidiini (in part)* ▶ **Go to 97**

92 **a. Legs** Middle tibia with two apical spines (*Figure 104*). .... ***Stelis*** ♂ *(rarer cleptoparasite)*

b. Legs Middle tibia with just one apical spine. .... ▶ **Go to 93**

Figure 104

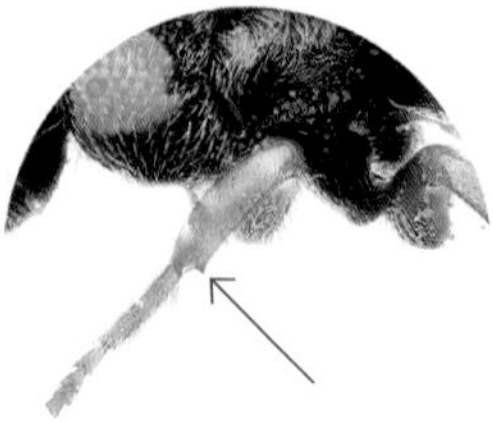

93 **a. Thorax** Propodeum is outlined by a carina that is made of a series of large
deep pits (*Figure 19*).

Abdomen Anterior (forward-facing) surface of T1 widely concave, with a
strong carina lining the edge (*Figure 20*). .... ***Heriades*** ♂

b. Thorax Propodeum does not have a carina made of deep pits outlining it.

Abdomen Anterior surface of T1 is less concave, and lacks carina. .... ▶ **Go to 94**

94 **a. Thorax** Parapsidal line is reduced to a small dot (*Figure 21*).

Integument The body is usually metallic. .... ***Osmia*** ♂

b. Thorax Parapsidal line is long, more than 3 times as long as it is wide (*Figure 22*).

   Integument The body is seldom metallic. .... ▶ **Go to 95**

95 **a. Thorax** Very elongated, so that the portion of the scutum anterior to the
   tegulae is as long as the portion posterior to them (*Figure 23*). .... *Chelostoma* ♂

   b. Thorax Not elongated; the portion of the scutum anterior to the tegula much
   less than the portion posterior to the tegula. .... ▶ **Go to 96**

96 **a. Thorax** The plate that makes up the side of the body (the mesepisternum) is
   split into two faces divided by a carina (*Figure 24*). The anterior (forward-
   facing) portion of this plate is shiny and polished, while the lateral (side-
   facing) portion is punctate. .... *Ashmeadiella* ♂

   b. Thorax The mesepisternum rounds gently from the anterior to the lateral
   faces, and both are punctate to the same degree (*Figure 25*). .... *Hoplitis* ♂

97 **a. Head** On the face, subantennal suture curves strongly outward before
   connecting to clypeus (*Figure 13*).

   Thorax Scutellum extends back (posteriorly) over the metanotum and
   pronotum as a broad shelf (*Figure 14*). .... *Anthidiellum* ♂

   b. Head On the face, the subantennal suture is a straight line between the
   antennal socket and the top of the clypeus.

   Thorax Scutellum ends before the metanotum and does not overhang the
   pronotum. .... ▶ **Go to 98**

98 **a. Abdomen** T7 has three lobes, with the middle lobe larger and longer than
   those on the sides (*Figure 105*). .... *Paranthidium* ♂ *(uncommon bee)*

   b. Abdomen T7 has no lobes. .... ▶ **Go to 99**

Figure 105

99   **a. Head** Preoccipital carina that separates its vertex and its posterior face is strong, so that the back of the head is not rounded.

    Thorax On the side of the body, the face that wraps from the side of the body around to the front (called the mesopleuron) is sharply angled, so that it looks like the outside corner of a cube (*Figure 11*). The front (anterior) margin of the scutum drops off quickly, and it bulges up significantly above the pronotal collar (*Figure 106*). .... *Dianthidium* ♂

  b. Head Preoccipital carina is not strongly carinate, but rounds gently from the vertex to the back of the head.

    Thorax On the side of the body, the mesopleuron is not sharply angled, but rounds gently. The anterior margin of the scutum tapers gently, not sloping steeply at its front (*Figure 107*). .... *Trachusa* ♂

100 **a. Wings** Three submarginal cells. .... ▶ Go to 101

  b. Wings Two submarginal cells. .... ▶ Go to 104

101 **a. Wings** Basal vein strongly arcuate (as in *Figure 39*). .... *Sphecodes* ♀

  b. Wings Basal vein straight, not strongly curved. .... ▶ Go to 102

102 **a. Wings** Marginal cell sharply pointed, and ending very near the apex of the wing (*Figure 108*). .... *Nomada* ♀

  b. Wings Marginal cell rounded, and not ending very near the apex of the wing.. ▶ Go to 103

Figure 106

Figure 107

Figure 108

Figure 109

Figure 110

103 a. **Abdomen** Pygidial plate is gently rounded, but flat when viewed from the side (*Figure 96*). .... *Epeolus* ♀

b. **Abdomen** Pygidial plate is constricted at the middle when viewed from above (*Figure 97*). .... *Triepeolus* ♀

104 a. **Abdomen** Very red, with small patches of appressed white hair (*Figure 109*). .. *Holcopasites* ♀

b. **Abdomen** Not red, with small patches of appressed white hair. .... ▶ Go to 105

105 a. **Legs** Tarsal claw cleft.

Wing Stigma short (*Figure 110*). .... *Stelis* ♀

Note: Dioxys, *a parasitic bee found in the Megachilidae bee family that we do not cover in this book, will also key to* Stelis, *based on the characters included here. It can be distinguished by the spine in the middle of the metanotum, which does not occur in* Stelis *specimens.*

b. **Legs** Tarsal claw simple.

Wing Stigma long. .... ▶ Go to 106

106 a. **Abdomen** Tapering to a very fine point. Each tergal segment with apical hair bands (*Figure 103*). .... *Coelioxys* ♀

b. **Abdomen** Tapering, but not to a distinct point. No abdominal hair bands. .... *Hylaeus* ♀

GLOSSARY

ABDOMEN: The last, most posterior, section of a bee. While it actually begins at the posterior end of the thorax in bees, for identification purposes here, it refers to the bee's last large body segment. See *metasoma*.

ANDRENIFORM: Having the general body form of an *Andrena*, with a thin head, round thorax, and slender oval-shaped abdomen.

ANTENNA (ANTENNAE): The two many-segmented appendages that extend outward from the center of a bee's face. Used for touch, taste, and smell.

ANTENNAL SOCKET: The holes from which the antennae emerge.

ANTERIOR: Situated near the front of the body, or end with the head.

ANTERIOR TENTORIAL PIT: A small pit located along the epistomal suture, one on either side of center. The location of this pit differs between genera.

ANTHOPHORIFORM: Having the general body form and habits of an *Anthophora*, with a larger head with large eyes, robust thorax, and thick abdomen. Fast-flying.

APICAL: Refers to the apex, or end, of a segment—farthest from where the segment begins.

ARCUATE: Curved, as opposed to straight.

AROLIUM (AROLIA): On the leg, padlike structure between the tarsal claws. Often easiest to see on the forelegs.

AXILLA (AXILLAE): On the thorax, a rounded or triangular point just posterior to and lateral of the scutum, behind the tegula. May project out from the body and hang over the metanotum. There is one on either side of the scutum.

BASAL: Refers to the beginning of a segment. May be written as *basad* to mean "just before."

BASAL VEIN: On the forewing, the vein that forms the end of the radial cell and the beginning of the first marginal cell.

BASITARSUS (BASITARSI): On the leg, the enlarged or elongated segment between the tibia and the tarsal segments; the segment of the tarsal segments nearest the bee's body. In bees, the basitarsi are often larger than other tarsal segments; in wasps this is usually not the case. Depending on the leg, may be the forebasitarsus, midbasitarsus, or hind basitarsus.

BASITIBIAL PLATE: A small plate at the base of the hind tibia; analogous to a human kneecap.

CARINA (CARINAE): A clearly defined, usually very thin ridge, like the keel on a boat. Can be as simple as a raised line, and may be more or less strong depending on the bee and the structure.

CARINATE: Having a carina.

CLEPTOPARASITE: A bee in which the female lays eggs inside the provisioned nest cell of another bee, in essence the cleptoparasitic larva "steals" pollen that was left for the host bee's own offspring. Female cleptoparasitic bees do not have *scopae*.

CLYPEUS (CLYPEI): The section of the face below the antennae, outlined by the *epistomal sutures*. May be extremely convex or protruding, or relatively flat. The apical margin may be straight, concave when looking straight on, lobed, or convex depending on the species. In males, is often colored.

COMPOUND EYE: The large eyes on either side of a bee's head, made up of many hexagonal facets.

CONCAVE: Curving inward; forming a broad indentation.

CONVEX: Curved outward; roundly protruding.

CORBICULA (CORBICULAE): A large hairless patch on the hind tibia of bumble bees, honey bees, and a few other species, and on the sides of the propodeum in *Andrena*. The hairless patch is surrounded by curved stiff hairs. The structure is used for carrying pollen.

COXA (COXAE): The basal-most segment of a bee's leg, between the thorax and the trochanter. Depending on the leg, may be the forecoxa, midcoxa, or hind coxa.

CISTAL: Relating to the outermost part; away from the center of the body.

DORSAL: Relating to the upper, or "back," side of an animal.

EPISTERNAL GROOVE: On the thorax, a groove on the side (the mesepisternum) that runs vertically, originating below the wing bases. The length of the episternal groove varies in many genera, and is absent in some.

EPISTOMAL SUTURE: On the head, the groove that outlines the edge of the clypeus, running from the edge of the mandible, around the top of the clypeus, and intersected by one or two subantennal sutures.

EUCERIFORM: Having the general body form and habits of a Eucerini, often with long antennae, a robust thorax, and a thick abdomen. Slimmer than anthophoriform bees, but also fast-flying.

FEMUR: On the leg, the third segment of the leg, between the trochanter and the tibia.

FIMBRIA (FIMBRIAE): A fringe of hairlike or comblike projections.

FIRST RECURRENT VEIN: On the wing, the vein that runs usually just behind the first or second submarginal cell. It is on the same "row" as the second recurrent vein and the basal vein. Where it meets with the submarginal cells can aid in identification.

FLAGELLOMERE: On the head, any segment of the antennae beyond (distal to) the scape and pedicel.

FLAGELLUM (FLAGELLA): The collection of all flagellomeres on the antennae.

FORELEG: The leg closest to the head.

FOREWING: The wing, one on either side of a bee's body, that is closest to its head, when the wings are laid flat so that they are parallel to the ground.

FOVEA (FOVEAE): A depressed area; in bees this most commonly refers to the depression beside each compound eye, which may be filled with hair.

FRONS: The central area above the antennal sockets and below the ocelli on a bee's head.

GALEA: On bee mouthparts, the bladelike structure, usually elongated. There is one on either side of the central proboscis.

GENA: On the head, the region between the back of the compound eye and the back of the head.

GENERALIST: See *polylectic*.

GENITALIA: On the abdomen, the collective term for the genital structures of a bee. Usually refers to male structures.

GLOSSA (GLOSSAE): The portion of a bee's tongue nestled between the galea, and nearest labial palpi. Analogous to the human tongue. In long-tongued bees, the glossa tends to be long and slender.

HEAD: The first, most anterior section of a bee's body containing the antennae, mouthparts, and eyes.

HIND LEG: The leg farthest from the head.

HINDWING: The wing, one on either side of a bee's body, that is closest to its abdomen, when the wings are laid flat so that they are parallel to the ground.

IMPUNCTATE: A region of the integument without any pits, often shiny.

INNER ORBITAL MARGINS: On the head, the inner margin of the compound eyes. May converge, be parallel, be notched, or be raised depending on the genus.

INTEGUMENT: The hardened external layer of a bee; analogous to human skin. May be roughened, pitted, hairy, or with ridges.

JUGAL LOBE: On the wing, the posterior-most lobe of the hindwing, demarcated by a notch in the distal margin. May be missing in some genera.

LABIAL PALPUS (PALPI): On the mouthparts, the jointed, segmented structures adjacent to the glossa. The number and relative length of the palpi may differ between genera, and even between families.

LABRUM: On the head, the hinged plate that hangs below the clypeus; can fold up or down in front of the mouthparts.

LAMELLATE: Referring to a structure that is thinned, platelike, and often translucent.

LATERAL: Relating to the sides.

LEGS: The three pairs of appendages that hang below a bee's body; all are attached to the thorax.

LOBE: A rounded protuberance on the body of a bee that seems separated from the other body parts.

MACULATION: A spot of lighter color on an otherwise dark integument.

MALAR SPACE: On the head, the area between the basal edge of the compound eye and the beginning of the mandible. When measuring, it is the shortest distance between the two.

MANDIBLE: On the head, large, hardened appendages (paired, one to either side) that hinge below each compound eye and cross or meet below the center of the clypeus. May contain points at the apical margin that are called "teeth." The whole structure is analogous to a human jaw.

MARGINAL CELL: On the wing, the distal-most cell, past the stigma. It rests on the anterior margin of the wing.

MAXILLARY PALPUS (PALPI): On the mouthparts, the jointed segmented structures attached to the base of the galea.

MEGACHILIFORM: Having the general body form and habits of Megachilidae; head, thorax, and abdomen all robust, and rounded—not elongate. Abdomen often as wide as thorax. Tendency to hover in front of flowers.

MESEPISTERNUM: On the thorax, the segment posterior to the pronotum, making up the majority of the side of the thorax, with the metepisternum beginning posterior to it. The midcoxae attach to it ventrally.

METANOTUM: On the thorax, the last dorsal segment. Just posterior to the scutellum.

METASOMA: The posterior portion of a bee's body, including the tergal and sternal segments, and the propodeum. In this book, the word *abdomen* is used instead of *metasoma*, and the propodeum is included as part of the thorax.

MIDLEGS: The middle set of legs on a bee, between the fore and hind legs.

MOUTHPARTS: The mandibles and proboscis of a bee.

OCELLUS (OCELLI): Three small, simple, round eyes on the top of a bee's head. Used for light detection.

OLIGOLECTIC: A bee that gathers pollen from a small suite of usually closely related flowers. Also known as a specialist bee.

OMAULUS: On the side of the thorax, the angle separating the forward face and lateral face of the mesepisternum.

OVIPOSITOR: The egg-laying structure on a female bee, modified to sting.

PARAOCULAR AREA: On the head, the area between the compound eye and the clypeus.

PARAPSIDAL LINE: On the thorax, a line (there are two, one on either side of center) on the scutum.

PEDICEL: On the head, the segment of the antenna between the scape and the flagellum.

PITS: Indentations on the integument of a bee. May be close together or widely spaced, and of various sizes. The integument in between the pits may be shiny or dull, completely separate from the pits.

PLUMOSE: Featherlike, referring to hairs on a bee's body.

POLYLECTIC: A bee that collects pollen from any number of flowering plants, not appearing to limit itself to some subset of what's available. Also known as generalists.

POSTERIOR: Toward the hind or rear portion of a bee's body.

PREPYGIDIAL FIMBRIA (FIMBRIAE): A brush of dense hairs on the apex margin of T5 in females. Not present in all females.

PREOCCIPITAL REGION: On the head, the area posterior to the preoccipital ridge that makes up the back of the head.

PREOCCIPITAL RIDGE: On the head, a carina that separates the vertex from the posterior portion.

PRESTIGMA: On the wing, the dark, usually very small area adjacent to the stigma, on the side closest to the body. Its size varies between genera.

PRONOTAL LOBE: On the thorax, a lobe on the posterior edge of the pronotum, toward the dorsal end.

PRONOTUM: The anterior-most segment of the thorax, just behind the head. It is collar-like, and extends from the dorsal surface down either side toward the forelegs.

PROPODEAL ENCLOSURE: On the thorax, the posterior face of the propodeum that is often concave; it might be surrounded by a carina, or modified hairs.

PROPODEAL PIT: On the thorax, at the center of the propodeal enclosure, ventral to where the abdomen joins the thorax, there is a deep pit that may be rounded or elongated depending on the species.

PROPODEUM: On the thorax, the last segment, includes both a dorsal and posterior face. This segment is technically the first segment of the abdomen.

PUBESCENCE: Hair on a bee's body. May be short or long, fine or thick.

PUNCTATION: The small pits often seen on a bee's body.

PYGIDIAL FIMBRIA: On the thorax, dense hairs to either side of the pygidial plate on T6; only in species that have a pygidial plate.

PYGIDIAL PLATE: On the abdomen, the flat plate found centrally on T6 of females and T7 on males. May be surrounded by a ridge and may extend beyond the end of the tergal segment on which it occurs. Not present in all bees.

SCAPE: The elongated very first segment of the antennae, emerging from the antennal socket.

SCOPA (SCOPAE): The long, thick, often plumose hairs on female bees used for collecting pollen. Usually on the hind legs, or on the ventral side of the abdomen.

SCROBAL GROOVE: On the thorax, a horizontal groove on the mesepisternum that intersects the episternal groove, below the tegula.

SCUTELLUM: On the thorax, the segment (plate) directly posterior to the scutum.

SCUTUM: On the thorax, the large dorsal plate between the wings and behind the head.

SECOND RECURRENT VEIN: On the forewing, the vein that delineates the outer edge of the second medial cell; occurs just below the outermost submarginal cell.

SPATULOPLUMOSE: Hairs that are branched, with the ends of each branch flattened.

SPECIALIST: See *oligolectic.*

STERNA: The plates making up the underside of the abdomen. Numbered from anterior to posterior as S1–S8. Sternal segments may have protrusions or tufts of hair running across them.

STIGMA: On the forewing, a dark-colored spot, just before the marginal cell.

STING: On the abdomen, the modified ovipositor possessed by female bees; used as a defensive mechanism.

SUBANTENNAL SUTURE: On the head, a groove (or grooves) that runs from the antennal socket to the epistomal suture around the clypeus.

SUBMARGINAL CELLS: On the forewing, the two or three cells that compose the row of cells below the marginal cell.

SUPRACLYPEAL AREA: On the head, the area between and below the antennal sockets and above the clypeus; below the frons, which occurs above the antennal sockets.

TARSAL CLAWS: Two fine points ("claws") at the apex of the leg in bees; may be cleft or simple. Used for clasping rough surfaces.

TARSUS (TARSI): On the leg, the segments distal to the tibia and basitarsus, usually small and more or less square. There are usually four segments.

TEGULA (TEGULAE): On the thorax, small plates that cover the bases of the forewings. Shape and color differ depending on the species.

TERGUM (TERGITES, TERGAL SEGMENTS, TERGA): On the abdomen, the plates composing the dorsal surface of the abdomen, numbered from anterior to posterior as T1–T7. The first tergal segment, T1, has both an anterior face and a dorsal face, and may have a carinate ridge separating the two. Tergal segments may have protrusions or bands of hair running across them.

THORAX: The middle body part of a bee, sandwiched between the head and the abdomen.

TIBIA: On the leg, the segment between the femur and the basitarsus.

TIBIAL SPINE: On the hind leg, a pointed projection that occurs on the apex of the tibia. It is not hinged and cannot move. Not all bees possess tibial spines, and they can be very small or blunted.

TIBIAL SPUR: On the hind leg, the spine or spines that extend from the distal end of the tibia. Tibial spurs are hinged and movable. On the foreleg and midleg there is one tibial spur, and in most bees the hind leg has two tibial spurs.

TROCHANTER: On the leg, the segment between the coxa and the femur.

TRUNCATE: Describing something that is cut off at the tip, rather than drawn out to a point.

VANNAL LOBE: On the wing, the lobe of the hindwing, just before the jugal lobe.

VENTRAL: Relating to the underneath or bottom of the bee.

VERTEX: On the head, the topmost portion of the head. Ocelli are located on the vertex.

WINGS: Structures on the sides of an organism's body responsible for flight. In bees they are thin, membranous, and translucent. There are two wings on each side of a bee's body: the forewing and the hindwing.

REFERENCES

INTRODUCTION

Cane, J. H., and Sipes, S. 2006. Floral specialization by bees: analytical methods and a revised lexicon for oligolecty. *In* N. M. Waser, J. Ollerton (eds.), *Plant-pollinator interactions: from specialization to generalization.* University of Chicago, pp. 99–122.

Danforth, B. N., Minckley, R. L., Neff, J. J., and Fawcett, F. 2019. *The Solitary Bees.* Princeton University Press.

Linsley, E. G. 1958. The ecology of solitary bees. *Hilgardia* 27(19): 543–599.

Michener, C. D. 2000. *The Bees of the World.* Johns Hopkins University Press.

Mitchell, T. B. 1960. *Bees of the eastern United States.* Vol. 1 and 2. North Carolina Agricultural Experiment Station, Raleigh. 557 pp.

Wilson, J. S., and Carril, O.J.M. 2015. *The Bees in Your Backyard: A Guide to North America's Bees.* Princeton University Press.

HALICTIDAE

Moure, J. S. and Hurd Jr., P. D. 1987. An annotated catalog of the halictid bees of the western hemisphere (Hymenoptera: Halictidae). *An annotated catalog of the halictid bees of the Western Hemisphere (Hymenoptera: Halictidae).* Smithsonian Institution Press.

AUGOCHLORA

Gibbs, J., Ascher, J. S., Rightmyer, M. G., and Isaacs, R. 2017. The bees of Michigan (Hymenoptera: Apoidea: Anthophila), with notes on distribution, taxonomy, pollination, and natural history. *Zootaxa* 4352(1): 1–160.

Stockhammer, K. A. 1966. Nesting habits and life cycle of a sweat bee, *Augochlora pura* (Hymenoptera: Halictidae). *Journal of the Kansas Entomological Society* 39: 157–192.

AUGOCHLORELLA

Coelho, B.W.T. 2004. A review of the bee genus *Augochlorella* (Hymenoptera: Halictidae: Augochlorini). *Systematic Entomology* 29(3): 282–323.

Mueller, U. G. 1996. Life history and social evolution of the primitively eusocial bee *Augochlorella striata* (Hymenoptera: Halictidae). *Journal of the Kansas Entomological Society* 69(4): 116–138.

Ordway, E. 1966a. The bionomics of *Augochlorella striata* and *A. persimilis* in eastern Kansas. *Journal of the Kansas Entomological Society* 39: 270–313.

Ordway, E. 1966b. Systematics of the genus *Augochlorella* (Hymenoptera, Halictidae) north of Mexico. *University of Kansas Science Bulletin* 46: 509–624.

Packer, L. 1990. Solitary and eusocial nests in a population of *Augochlorella striata* (Provancher) (Hymenoptera: Halictidae) at the northern edge of its range. *Behavioral Ecology and Sociobiology* 27: 339–344.

Sakagami, S. F., and Michener, C. D. 1962. *The Nest Architecture of the Sweat Bees (Halictinae), a Comparative Study.* University of Kansas Press, Lawrence, 135 pp.

AUGOCHLOROPSIS

Sandhouse, G. A. 1937. The bees of the genera *Augochlora*, *Augochloropsis*, and *Augochlorella* (Hymenoptera: Apoidea) occurring in the United States. *Journal of the Washington Academy of Sciences* 27(2): 65–79.

Gibbs, J. 2017. Notes on the nests of *Augochloropsis metallica fulgida* and *Megachile mucida* in Central Michigan (Hymenoptera: Halictidae, Megachilidae). *Great Lakes Entomologist* 50(1): 4.

AGAPOSTEMON

Eickwort, G. 1981. Aspects of the nesting biology of five Nearctic species of *Agapostemon* (Hymenoptera: Halictidae). *Journal of the Kansas Entomological Society* 54: 337–351.

Roberts, R. B. 1972. Revision of the bee genus *Agapostemon* (Hymenoptera: Halictidae). *University of Kansas Science Bulletin* 49: 437–590.

Roberts, R. B. 1973. *Bees of Northwestern America: Agapostemon*. Technical Bulletin 175. Oregon State University, Corvallis. 23 pp.

HALICTUS

Hogendoorn, K., and Leys, R. 1997. Life-cycle of *Halictus rubicundus* Christ (Hymenoptera: Halictidae) in the Netherlands: Comparison of two populations. *Journal of the Kansas Entomological Society* 70(4): 347–352.

Kim, J., Williams, N., and Kremen, C. 2006. Effects of cultivation and proximity to natural habitat on ground-nesting native bees in California sunflower fields. *Journal of the Kansas Entomological Society* 79(4): 309–320.

Packer, L., Gravel, A.-I. D., and Lebuhn, G. 2007. Phenology and social organization of *Halictus (Selodona) tripartitus* (Hymenoptera: Halictidae). *Journal of Hymenoptera Research* 16: 281–292.

Richards, M. H., and Packer, L. 1996. The socioecology of body size variation in the primitively eusocial sweat bee, *Halictus ligatus* (Hymenoptera: Halictidae). *Oikos* 77(1): 68–76.

Roberts, R. B. 1973. *Bees of Northwestern America:* Halictus *(Hymenoptera: Halictidae)*. Technical Bulletin 126. Oregon State University, Corvallis. 23 pp.

Yanega, D. 1993. Environmental influences on male production and social structure in *Halictus rubicundus* (Hymenoptera: Halictidae). *Insectes Sociaux* 40(2): 169–180.

LASIOGLOSSUM

Gibbs, J., Packer, L., Dumesh, S., and Danforth, B. N. 2013. Revision and reclassification of *Lasioglossum (Evylaeus)*, *L. (Hemihalictus)*, and *L. (Sphecodogastra)* in eastern North America (Hymenoptera: Apoidea: Halictidae). *Zootaxa* 3672(1): 1–117.

SPHECODES

Robertson, C. 1897. North American Bees—Description and Synonyms. *Transactions of the Academy of Science of St. Louis* 7(14): 315–356.

DIEUNOMIA

Minckley, R. L., Wcislo, W. T., Yanega, D., and Buchmann, S. L. 1994. Behavior and phenology of a specialist bee (*Dieunomia*) and sunflower (*Helianthus*) pollen availability. *Ecology* 75(5): 1406–1419.

Wcislo, W. T., and Buchmann, S. L. 1995. Mating behaviour in the bees, *Dieunomia heteropoda* and *Nomia tetrazonata*, with a review of courtship in Nomiinae (Hymenoptera: Halictidae). *Journal of Natural History* 29(4): 1015–1027.

Wcislo, W. T., and Engel, M. S. 1996. Social behavior and nest architecture of nomiinae bees (Hymenoptera: Halictidae: Nomiinae). *Journal of the Kansas Entomological Society* 69(4): 158–167.

NOMIA

Cockerell, T.D.A. 1910. The North American bees of the genus *Nomia*. *Proceedings of the United States National Museum* 38(1745): 289–298.

Parker, F. D., Griswold, T. L., and Botsford, J. H. 1996. Biological notes on *Nomia heteropoda* Say (Hymenoptera: Halictidae). *Pan-Pacific Entomologist* 62: 92.

Wcislo, W. T. 1993. Communal nesting in a North American pearly-banded bee, *Nomia tetrazonata*, with notes on nesting behavior of *Dieunomia heteropoda* (Hymenoptera: Halictidae: Nomiinae). *Annals of the Entomological Society of America* 86(6): 813–821.

DUFOUREA

Arduser, M. S. 1986. Records of *Dufourea maura* (Hymenoptera: Halictidae) from Isle Royale National Park, Michigan. *Great Lakes Entomologist* 19: 175–176.

Eickwort, G. C., Kukuk, P. F., and Wesley, F. R. 1986. The nesting biology of *Dufourea novaeangliae* (Hymenoptera: Halictidae) and the systematic position of the Dufoureinae based on behavior and development. *Journal of the Kansas Entomological Society* 59: 103–120.

Gibbs, J., Dumesh, S., and Griswold, T. L. 2014. Bees of the genera *Dufourea* and *Dieunomia* of Michigan (Hymenoptera: Apoidea: Halictidae), with a key to the *Dufourea* of eastern North America. *Journal of Melittology* 29: 1–15.

Kukuk, P. F., Eickwort, G. C., and Wesley, F. R. 1985. Mate-seeking behavior of *Dufourea novaeangliae* (Hymenoptera: Halictidae: Dufoureinae): the effects of resource distribution. *Journal of the Kansas Entomological Society* 58: 142–150.

COLLETIDAE

Almeida, E.A.B. 2008. Colletidae nesting biology (Hymenoptera: Apoidea). *Apidologie* 39: 16–29.

Almeida, E.A.B., and Danforth, B. N. 2009. Phylogeny of colletid bees (Hymenoptera: Colletidae) inferred from four nuclear genes. *Molecular Phylogenetics and Evolution* 50: 290–309.

Michener, C. D., and Deyrup, M. 2004. *Caupolicana* from Florida (Hymenoptera: Colletidae). *Journal of the Kansas Entomological Society* 77(4): 774–782.

COLLETES

Batra, S.W.T. 1980. Ecology, behavior, pheromones, parasites and management of the sympatric vernal bees *Colletes inaequalis, C. thoracicus* and *C. validus*. *Journal of the Kansas Entomological Society* 53: 509–538.

Gardner, K. E., and Ascher, J. S. 2006. Notes on the native bee pollinators in New York apple orchards. *Journal of the New York Entomological Society* 114(1): 86–91.

Stephen, W. P. 1954. A revision of the bee genus *Colletes* in America north of Mexico (Hymenoptera: Colletidae). *University of Kansas Science Bulletin* 36: 149–527.

Romankova, T. 2003. Bees of the genus *Colletes* of Ontario (Hymenoptera, Apoidea, Colletidae). *Journal of the Entomological Society of Ontario* 134: 91–106.

Rozen, J. G., Jr., and Favreau, M. S. 1968. Biological notes on *Colletes compactus compactus* and its cuckoo bee, *Epeolus pusillus* (Hymenoptera: Colletidae and Anthophoridae). *Journal of the New York Entomological Society* 76(2): 106–111.

HYLAEUS

Barrow, E. M. 1975. Occupancy by *Hylaeus* of subterranean halictid nests (Hymenoptera: Apoidea). *Psyche* 82: 74–77.

Daly, H. V., and Magnacca, K. V. 2003. *Insects of Hawaii: Hawaiian* Hylaeus (Nesoprosopis) *Bees (Hymenoptera: Apoidea)*. Vol. 17. University of Hawaii Press, 240 pp.

Rau, P. 1930. Nesting habits of the twig-dwelling bee, *Prosopis modestus* Say. *Psyche*. 37: 173–175.

Sheffield, C. S., Dumesh, S., and Cheryomina, M. 2011. *Hylaeus punctatus* (Hymenoptera: Colletidae), a bee species new to Canada, with notes on other non-native species. *Journal of the Entomological Society of Ontario* 142: 29–43.

Snelling, R. R. 1983. Studies on North American bees of the genus *Hylaeus*. 6. An adventive Palearctic species in southern California (Hymenoptera: Colletidae). *Bulletin of the Southern California Academy of Sciences* 82: 12–16.

ANDRENA

Barrows, E. M. 1978. Male behavior in *Andrena erigeniae* (Hymenoptera: Andrenidae) with comparative notes. *Journal of the Kansas Entomological Society* 51: 798–806.

Davis, L. W., and LaBerge, W. E. 1975. The nest biology of the bee *Andrena (Ptilandrena) erigeniae* Robertson (Hymenoptera: Andrenidae). *Illinois Natural History Survey Biological Notes* 95. 16 pp.

Donovan, B. J. 1977. A revision of North American bees of the subgenus *Cnemidandrena* (Hymenoptera: Andrenidae). University of California Publications in Entomology. 107 pp.

LaBerge, W. E. 1969. A revision of the bees of the genus *Andrena* of the Western Hemisphere. Part II. *Plastandrena, Aporandrena, Charitandrena*. *Transactions of the American Entomological Society* 95: 1–47.

LaBerge, W. E. 1980. A revision of the bees of the genus *Andrena* of the Western Hemisphere. Part X. Subgenus *Andrena*. *Transactions of the American Entomological Society* 106: 395–525.

LaBerge, W. E. 1985. A revision of the bees of the genus *Andrena* of the Western Hemisphere. Part XI. Minor subgenera and subgeneric key. *Transactions of the American Entomological Society* 111: 441–567.

LaBerge, W. E. 1987. A revision of the bees of the genus *Andrena* of the Western Hemisphere. Part XII. Subgenera *Leucandrena, Ptilandrena, Scoliandrena,* and *Melandrena. Transactions of the American Entomological Society* 112: 191–248.

LaBerge, W. E. 1989. A revision of the bees of the genus *Andrena* of the Western Hemisphere. Part XIII. Subgenera *Simandrena* and *Taeniandrena. Transactions of the American Entomological Society* 115: 1–56.

LaPlaca Reese, C. S., and Barrows, E. M. 1980. Co-evolution of *Claytonia virginica* (Portulacaceae) and its main native pollinator, *Andrena erigeniae* (Andrenidae). *Proceedings of the Entomological Society of Ontario* 82: 685–694.

Norden, B. B., and Scarbrough, A. G. 1979. Nesting biology of *Andrena (Larandrena) miserabilis* Cresson and description of the prepupa (Hymenoptera: Andrenidae). *Brimleyana* 2: 141–146.

Ribble, D. W. 1967. The monotypic North American subgenus *Larandrena* of *Andrena* (Hymenoptera: Apoidea). *Bulletin of the University of Nebraska State Museum* 6: 27–42.

Osgood, E. A. 1989. Biology of *Andrena crataegi* Robertson (Hymenoptera: Andrenidae), a communally nesting bee. *Journal of the New York Entomological Society* 97: 56–64.

CALLIOPSIS

Dyer, J. G., and Shinn, A. F. 1978. Pollen collected by *Calliopsis andreniformis* Smith in North America (Hymenoptera: Andrenidae). *Journal of the Kansas Entomological Society* 51: 787–795.

Shinn, A. F. 1967. A revision of the bee genus *Calliopsis* and the biology and ecology of *C. andreniformis. University of Kansas Science Bulletin* 46: 753–936.

PANURGINUS

Neff, J. L. 2003. Nest and provisioning biology of the bee *Panurginus polytrichus* Cockerell (Hymenoptera: Andrenidae), with a description of a new *Holcopasites* species (Hymenoptera: Apidae), its probable nest parasite. *Journal of the Kansas Entomological Society* 76(2): 203–216.

PERDITA

Graenicher, S. 1914. Wisconsin bees of the genus *Perdita. Canadian Entomologist* 46: 51–57.

Timberlake, P. H. 1960. A revisional study of the bees of the genus *Perdita* F. Smith, with special reference to the fauna of the Pacific coast (Hymenoptera, Apoidea). Part IV. University of California Publications in Entomology 17. 156 pp.

Torchio, P. F. 1975. The biology of *Perdita nuda* and descriptions of its immature forms and those of its *Sphecodes* parasite (Hymenoptera: Apoidea). *Journal of the Kansas Entomological Society* 48(3): 257–279.

PSEUDOPANURGUS

Timberlake, P. H. 1973. Revision of the genus *Pseudopanurgus* of North America. University of California Publications in Entomology 72: i–vi. 58 pp.

MELITTIDAE

Cane, J. H. 1997. Violent weather and bees: populations of the barrier island endemic, *Hesperapis oraria* (Hymenoptera: Melittidae) survive a Category 3 hurricane. *Journal of the Kansas Entomological Society* 70(1): 73–75.

Cane, J. H., Snelling, R. R., and Kervin, L. J. 1996. A new monolectic coastal bee, *Hesperapis oraria* Snelling and Stage (Hymenoptera: Melittidae), with a review of desert and Neotropical disjunctives in the southeastern U.S. *Journal of the Kansas Entomological Society* 69(4): 38–247.

Michez, D., Patiny, S., and Danforth, B. N. 2009. Phylogeny of the bee family Melittidae (Hymenoptera: Anthophila) based on combined molecular and morphological data. *Systematic Entomology* 34: 574–597.

Michez, D., and Patiny, S. 2005. World revision of the oil-collecting bee genus *Macropis* Panzer 1809 (Hymenoptera: Apoidea: Melittidae) with a description of a new species from Laos. *Annales de la Societe entomologique de France* 41(1): 15–28.

Payette, A. 2013. First record of the bee *Melitta americana* (Smith) (Hymenoptera: Melittidae) for Quebec and Canada. *Canadian Field Naturalist* 127(1): 60–63.

Stage, G. I. 1966. *Biology and systematics of the American species of the genus* Hesperapis *Cockerell*. University of California: Berkeley.

MEGACHILIDAE

Gonzalez, V. H., Griswold, T., Praz, C. D., and Danforth, B. N. 2012. Phylogeny of the bee family Megachilidae (Hymenoptera: Apoidea) based on adult morphology. *Systematic Entomology* 37(2): 261–286.

Praz, C. J., Muller, A., Danforth, B. N., Griswold, T. L., Widmer, A., and Dorn, S. 2008. Phylogeny and biogeography of bees of the tribe Osmiini (Hymenoptera: Megachilidae). *Molecular Phylogenetics and Evolution* 49: 185–197.

ASHMEADIELLA

Hurd, P. D., Jr., and Michener, C. D. 1955. The megachiline bees of California. *Bulletin of the California Insect Survey*. 3:1–248.

Krombein, K. V. 1967. *Trap-nesting wasps and bees: life histories, nests, and associates*. Smithsonian Publication 4670. Smithsonian Press, Washington, D.C. 590 pp.

CHELOSTOMA

Eickwort, G. C. 1980. Two European species of *Chelostoma* established in New York State (Hymenoptera: Megachilidae). *Psyche* 87(3–4): 315–323.

Michener, C. D. 1938. American bees of the genus Chelostoma. *Pan-Pacific Entomologist* 14: 36–45.

HERIADES

Michener, C. D. 1938. American bees of the genus *Heriades*. *Annals of the Entomological Society of America* 31: 514–531.

Matthews, R. W. 1965. *Biology of* Heriades carinata *Cresson (Hymenoptera, Megachilidae)*. American Ecological Institute. 126 pp.

HOPLITIS

Medler, J. T. 2012. A note on *Hoplitis producta* (Cresson) in Wisconsin (Hymenoptera: Megachilidae). *Canadian Entomologist* 93(7): 571–573.

Michener, C. D. 1947. A revision of the American species of *Hoplitis* (Hymenoptera, Megachilidae). *Bulletin of the American Museum of Natural History* 89(4): 263–319.

Michener, C. D. 1955. Some biological observations on *Hoplitis pilosifrons* and *Stelis lateralis* (Hymenoptera, Megachilidae). *Journal of the Kansas Entomological Society* 28(3): 81–87.

Sedivy, C., Dorn, S., and Muller, A. 2013. Molecular phylogeny of the bee genus *Hoplitis* (Megachilidae: Osmiini)—how does nesting biology affect biogeography? *Zoological Journal of the Linnean Society* 167(1): 28–42.

OSMIA

Bosch, J., and Kemp, W. P. 2002. *How to manage the Blue Orchard Bee*. Sustainable Agriculture Network. 87 pp.

Cane, J. H., Griswold, T., and Parker, F. D. 2007. Substrates and materials used for nesting by North American *Osmia* bees (Hymenoptera: Apiformes: Megachilidae). *Annals of the Entomological Society of America* 100(3): 350–358.

Rightmyer, M. G., Griswold, T., and Brady, S. G. 2013. Phylogeny and systematics of the bee genus *Osmia* (Hymenoptera: Megachilidae) with emphasis on North American *Melanosmia*: subgenera, synonymies, and nesting biology revisited. *Systematic Ecology* 35: 561–576.

Rust, R. W. 1974. The systematics and biology of the genus *Osmia*, subgenera *Osmia*, *Chalcosmia*, and *Cephalosmia*. *Wasmann Journal of Biology* 32: 1–93.

Sandhouse, G. A. 1939. The North American bees of the genus *Osmia*. *Memoirs of the Entomological Society of Washington* 1: 1–167.

Wu, Y. 2004. Ten new species of the tribe Osmiini from China (Apoidea, Megachilidae, Osmiini). *Acta Zootaxonomica Sinica* 29: 531–537.

Yoon, H. J., Lee, K. Y., Kim, S. Y., Lee, Y. B., Kim, N., and Jin, B. R. 2015. Effects of location, direction, altitude, and placement of trap nests on the rate of trap-nesting of *Osmia* solitary bees. *Journal of Asia-Pacific Entomology* 18(4): 695–700.

COELIOXYS

Baker, J. R. 1971. Development and sexual dimorphism of larvae of the bee genus *Coelioxys*. *Journal of the Kansas Entomological Society* 44(2): 225–235.

Baker, J. R. 1975. Taxonomy of five Nearctic subgenera of *Coelioxys* (Hymenoptera: Megachile). *University of Kansas Science Bulletin* 50(12): 649–730.

Bohart, G. E. 1970. The evolution of parasitism among bees. USU Faculty Honor Lectures, Paper 18. 30 pp.

MEGACHILE

Bzdyk, E. L. 2012. A revision of the *Megachile* subgenus *Litomegachile* Mitchell with an illustrated key and description of a new species (Hymenoptera, Megachilidae, Megachilini). *ZooKeys* 221: 31–61.

Eickwort, G. C., Matthews, R. W., and Carpenter, J. 1981. Observations of the nesting behavior of *Megachile rubi* and *M. texana* with a discussion of the significance of soil nesting in the evolution of megachilid bees (Hymenoptera: Megachilidae). *Journal of the Kansas Entomological Society* 54(3): 557–570.

Krombein, K. V. 1967. *Trap-Nesting Wasps and Bees: Life Histories, Nests, and Associates.* Smithsonian Press, Washington, D.C. 570 pp.

Magnum, W. A., and Sumner, S. 2003. A survey of the North American range of *Megachile (Callomegachile) sculpturalis*, an adventive species in North America. *Journal of the Kansas Entomological Society* 76(4): 658–662.

Michener, C. D. 1953. The biology of a leafcutter bee (*Megachile brevis*) and its associates. *University of Kansas Science Bulletin* 35: 1659–1748.

Pitts-Singer, T. L., and Cane, J. H. 2011. The alfalfa leafcutting bee, *Megachile rotundata*: the world's most intensively managed solitary bee. *Annual Review of Entomology* 56: 221–237.

Sheffield, C. S., Ratti, C., Packer, L., and Griswold, T. 2011. Leafcutter and mason bees of the genus *Megachile* Latrielle (Hymenoptera: Megachilidae) in Canada and Alaska. *Canadian Journal of Arthropod Identification.* doi:10.3752/cjai.2011.18.

Williams, H. J., Strand, M. R., Elzen, G. W., Bradleigh Vinson, S., and Merrit, S. J. 1986. Nesting behavior, nest architecture, and use of Dufour's gland lipids in nest provisioning by *Megachile integra* and *M. mendica mendica* (Hymenoptera: Megachilidae). *Journal of the Kansas Entomological Society* 59(4): 588–597.

ANTHIDIELLUM

Schwarz, H. F. 1926. North American *Dianthidium, Anthidiellum,* and *Paranthidium. American Museum Novitates* 226: 1–26.

Turrell, M. J. 1976. Observations on the mating behavior of *Anthidiellum notatum* and *Anthidiellum perplexum. Florida Entomologist* 59(1): 55–61.

Romankova, T. 2004. Ontario nest-building bees of the tribe Anthidiini (Hymenoptera, Megachilidae). *Journal of the Entomological Society of Ontario* 134: 85–89.

ANTHIDIUM

Gibbs, J., and Sheffield, S. 2009. Rapid range expansion of the wool-carder bee, *Anthidium manicatum* (Linnaeus) (Hymenoptera: Megachilidae), in North America. *Journal of the Kansas Entomological Society* 82(1): 21–29.

Gonzalez, V. H., and Griswold, T. L. 2013. Wool carder bees of the genus *Anthidium* in the Western Hemisphere (Hymenoptera: Megachilidae): diversity, host plant associations, phylogeny, and biogeography. *Zoological Journal of the Linnean Society* 168(2): 221–425.

Griswold, T., Gonzalez, V. H., and Ikerd, H. 2014. AnthWest, occurrence records for wool carder bees of the genus *Anthidium* (Hymenoptera, Megachilidae, Anthidiini) in the Western Hemisphere. *ZooKeys* 408: 31–49.

Hoebeke, E. R., and Wheeler, A. G., Jr. 1999. *Anthidium oblongatum* (Illiger): an Old World bee (Hymenoptera) new to North America, and new North American records for another adventive species, *A. manicatum* (L.). *University of Kansas Natural History Museum Special Publication* 24: 21–24.

Miller, S. R., Gaebel, R., Mitchell, R. J., and Arduser, M. 2002. Occurrence of two species of Old World bees, *Anthidium manicatum* and *A. oblongatum* (Apoidea: Megachilidae), in northern Ohio and southern Michigan. *Great Lakes Entomologist* 35(1): 65–69.

O'Brien, M. F., Swanson, D. R., and Monsma, J. 2012. *Anthidium oblongatum* (Apoidea: Megachilidae) confirmed as a Michigan resident, with notes on other Michigan *Anthidium* species. *Great Lakes Entomologist* 45(1–2): 99–101.

Payne, A., Schildroth, D. A., and Starks, P. T. 2011. Nest site selection in the European wool-carder bee, *Anthidium manicatum*, with methods for an emerging model species. *Apidologie* 42(2): 181–191.

Wirtz, P., Kopka, S., and Schmoll, G. 1992. Phenology of two territorial solitary bees, *Anthidium manicatum* and *A. florentinum* (Hymenoptera: Megachilidae). *Journal of Zoology* 228(4): 641–651.

DIANTHIDIUM

Krombein, K. V. 1967. *Trap-nesting wasps and bees. Life histories, nests and associates.* Smithsonian Press, Washington, D.C. 570 pp.

Michener, G. R., and Michener, C. D. 1999. Mating behavior of *Dianthidium curvatum* (Hymenoptera: Megachilidae) at a nest aggregation. *University of Kansas Natural History Museum Special Publication* 24: 37–43.

O'Brien, M. F. 2007. Notes on *Dianthidium simile* (Cresson) (Hymenoptera: Megachilidae) in Michigan. *Great Lakes Entomologist* 40: 23–28.

PARANTHIDIUM

Evans, H. E. 1993. Observations on the nests of *Paranthidium jugatorium perpictum* (Cockerell) (Hymenoptera: Megachilidae: Anthidiini). *Pan-Pacific Entomologist* 69(4): 319–322.

Griswold, T. L., and Michener, C. D. 1988. Taxonomic observations on Anthidiini of the Western Hemisphere (Hymenoptera: Megachilidae). *Journal of the Kansas Entomological Society* 61: 22–45.

Michener, C. D. 1975. Nests of *Paranthidium jugatorium* in association with *Melitoma taurea* (Hymenoptera: Megachilidae and Anthophoridae). *Journal of the Kansas Entomological Society* 48: 194–200.

STELIS

Bennett, F. D. 1966. Notes on the biology of *Stelis (Odontostelis) bilineolata* (Spinola), a parasite of *Euglossa cordata* (Linnaeus) (Hymenoptera: Apoidea: Megachilidae). *Journal of the New York Entomological Society* 74(2): 72–79.

TRACHUSA

Brooks, R. W., and Griswold, T. L. 1988. A key to the species of *Trachusa* subgenus *Heteranthidium* with descriptions of new species from Mexico (Hymenoptera: Megachilidae: Anthidiini). *Journal of the Kansas Entomological Society* 61(3): 332–346.

Michener, C. D. 1941. A synopsis of the genus *Trachusa* with notes on the nesting habits of *T. perdita* (Hymenoptera, Megachilidae). *Pan-Pacific Entomologist* 17: 119–125.

Rozen, J. G., and Hall, H. G. 2012. Nesting biology and immatures of the oligolectic bee *Trachusa larreae* (Apoidea: Megachilidae: Anthidiini). *American Museum Novitates* 3765: 1–24.

LITHURGOPSIS

Brach, V. 1979. Notes on the biology of *Lithurgus gibbosus* Smith in Florida (Hymenoptera: Megachilidae). *Bulletin of the Southern California Academy of Sciences* 77: 144–147.

Rozen, J. G., Hall, G. H. 2014. Nest site selection and nesting behavior in the bee *Lithurgopsis apicalis* (Megachilidae, Lithurginae). *American Museum Novitates* 3796: 1–24.

Snelling, R. R. 1983. The North American species of the bee genus *Lithurge* (Hymenoptera: Megachilidae). *Contributions in Science* 343: 1–11.

APIDAE

Michener, C. D. 1990. Classification of the Apidae (hymenoptera). *University of Kansas Science Bulletin* 54(4): 75–164.

Wilson, J. S., and Carril, O.J.M. 2015. *The Bees in Your Backyard: A Guide to North America's Bees.* Princeton University Press.

XYLOCOPA

Balduf, W. V. 1962. Life of the carpenter bee, *Xylocopa virginica* (Linn.). *Annals of the Entomological Society of America* 55: 263–271.

Barrows, E. M. 1983. Male territoriality in the carpenter bee *Xylocopa virginica virginica*. *Animal Behaviour* 31(3): 806–813.

Gerling, D., and Hermann, H. R. 1978. Biology and mating behavior of *Xylocopa virginica* L. (Hymenoptera, Anthophoridae). *Behavioral Ecology and Sociobiology* 3(2): 99–111.

CERATINA

Daly, H. V. 1973. *Bees of the genus* Ceratina *in America north of Mexico.* University of California Press, Berkeley. 114 pp.

Ginsberg, H. S. 1984. Foraging behavior of the bees *Halictus ligatus* (Hymenoptera: Halictidae) and *Ceratina calcarata* (Hymenoptera: Anthophoridae): foraging speed on early summer composite flowers. *Journal of the New York Entomological Society* 92: 162–168.

Grissell, E. E. 1976. The carpenter bees of Florida (Hymenoptera: Apidae: Xylocopinae). Florida Department of Agriculture and Consumer Services, Division of Plant Industry, Entomology Circular 167.

Rehan, S. M., and Sheffield, C. S. 2011. Morphological and molecular delineation of a new species in the *Ceratina dupla* species-group (Hymenoptera: Apidae: Xylocopinae) of eastern North America. *Zootaxa* 2873: 35–50.

DIADASIA

Adlakha, R. L. 1969. *A systematic revision of the bee genus* Diadasia *Patton in America north of Mexico (Hymenoptera, Anthophoridae)*. University of California, Davis. 376 pp.

Linsley, E. G., and MacSwain, J. W. 1958. The significance of floral constancy among bees of the genus *Diadasia* (Hymenoptera, Anthophoridae). *Evolution* 12: 219–223.

Sipes, S. D. 2001. Phylogenetic relationships, taxonomy, and evolution of host choice in *Diadasia* (Hymenoptera: Apidae). PhD Dissertation. Utah State University, Logan.

MELITOMA

Linsley, E. G., MacSwain, J. W., and Michener, C. D. 1980. *Nesting biology and associates of* Melitoma *(Hymenoptera, Anthophoridae)*. Vol. 90. University of California Press. 47 pp.

Michener, C. D. 1975. Nests of *Paranthidium jugatorium* in association with *Melitoma taurea* (Hymenoptera: Megachilidae and Anthophoridae). *Journal of the Kansas Entomological Society* 48: 194–200.

PTILOTHRIX

Rust, R. W. 1980. The biology of *Ptilothrix bombiformis* (Hymenoptera: Anthophoridae). *Journal of the Kansas Entomological Society* 53: 427–436.

Simpson, M. D. 2009. An evaluation of *Hibiscus moscheutos* ssp. *lasiocarpos* and *Ipomoea pandurata* as host plants of the specialist bee, *Ptilothrix bombiformis* (Apoidea: Emphorini) and the role of floral scent chemistry in host-selection. MSc. Thesis. Southern Illinois University Carbondale. 80 pp.

EUCERA

Carper, A. L., Schwanters, C. J., and Jamieson, M. A. 2019. A new state record of the rare bee, *Cemolobus ipomoeae* (Hymenoptera, Apidae), from Colorado, USA. *Journal of the Kansas Entomological Society* 91(2): 171–175.

Hurd, P. D., Jr., and Linsley, E. G. 1964. The squash and gourd bees *Peponapis* Robertson and *Xenoglossa* Smith inhabiting America north of Mexico. *Hilgardia* 35: 373–477.

Miliczky, E. R. 1985. Observations on the nesting biology of *Tetralonia hamata* Bradley with a description of its mature larva (Hymenoptera: Anthophoridae). *Journal of the Kansas Entomological Society* 58(4): 686–700.

Timberlake, P. H. 1969. A contribution to the systematics of North American species of *Synhalonia* (Hymenoptera, Apoidea). University of California Press, Berkeley. 82 pp.

FLORILEGUS

LaBerge, W. E. 1957. The genera of bees of the tribe Eucerini in North and Central America (Hymenoptera, Apoidea). *American Museum Novitates* 1837: 1–44.

Laberge, W. E., and Ribble, D. W. 1966. Biology of *Florilegus condignus* (Hymenoptera: Anthophoridae), with a description of its larva, and remarks on its importance in alfalfa pollination. *Annals of the Entomological Society of America* 59(5): 944–950.

MELISSODES

LaBerge, W. E. 1956. A revision of the bees of the genus *Melissodes* in North and Central America. Part I (Hymenoptera, Apidae). *University of Kansas Science Bulletin* 37(2): 911–1194.

LaBerge, W. E. 1956. A revision of the bees of the genus *Melissodes* in North and Central America. Part II (Hymenoptera, Apidae). *University of Kansas Science Bulletin* 38(1): 533–578.

LaBerge, W. E. 1961. A revision of the bees of the genus *Melissodes* in North and Central America. Part III (Hymenoptera, Apidae). *University of Kansas Science Bulletin* 42: 283–663.

Rau, P. 1938. Additional observations on the sleep of insects. *Annals of the Entomological Society of America* 31(4): 540–556.

Wright, K. W., Miller, K. B., and Song, H. 2020. A molecular phylogeny of the long-horned bees in the genus *Melissodes* Latreille (Hymenoptera: Apidae: Eucerinae). *Insect Systematics and Evolution*.

SVASTRA

LaBerge, W. E. 1956. A revision of the bees of the genus *Melissodes* in North and Central America. Part I (Hymenoptera, Apidae). *University of Kansas Science Bulletin* 37(18): 911–1194.

LaBerge, W. E. 1958. Notes on the North and Central American bees of the genus *Svastra* Holmberg (Hymenoptera: Apidae). *Journal of the Kansas Entomological Society* 31(4): 266–273.

Rozen, J. G. 1964. The biology of *Svastra obliqua obliqua* (Say), with a taxonomic description of its larvae (Apoidea, Anthophoridae). *American Museum of Natural History* 2170: 1–13.

ANTHOPHORA

Brooks, R. W. 1983. Systematics and bionomics of *Anthophora*: the Bomboides group and species groups of the New World. *University of California Publications in Entomology* 98: 1–86.

Frison, T. H. 1922. Notes on the life history, parasites and inquiline associates of *Anthophora abrupta* Say, and some comparisons with the habits of certain other Anthophorinae (Hymenoptera). *Transactions of the American Entomological Society* 48: 137–156.

Norden, B. B., and Scarbrough, A. G. 1982. Predators, parasites, and associates of *Anthophora abrupta* Say (Hymenoptera: Anthophoridae). *Journal of the New York Entomological Society* 90: 181–185.

Norden, B. B. 1984. Nesting biology of *Anthophora abrupta* (Hymenoptera: Anthophoridae). *Journal of the Kansas Entomological Society* 57: 243–262.

HABROPODA

Cane, J. H. 1994. Nesting biology and mating behavior of the Southeastern Blueberry bee, *Habropoda laboriosa* (Hymenoptera: Apoidea). *Journal of the Kansas Entomological Society* 67(3): 236–241.

Cane, J. H., and Payne, J. A. 1988. Foraging ecology of the bee *Habropoda laboriosa* (Hymenoptera: Anthophoridae), an oligolege of blueberries (Ericaceae: *Vaccinium*) in the southeastern United States. *Annals of the Entomological Society of America* 81: 419–427.

CENTRIS

Fox, W. J. 1899. Synopsis of the United States species of the hymenopterous genus *Centris* Fabr. with a description of a new species from Trinidad. *Proceedings of the Academy of Natural Sciences of Philadelphia* 51: 63–70.

Pemberton, R. W., and Liu, H. 2008. Naturalization of the oil collecting bee *Centris nitida* (Hymenoptera, Apidae, Centrini), a potential pollinator of selected native, ornamental, and invasive plants in Florida. *Florida Entomologist* 91(1): 101–110.

EUGLOSSA

Dressler, R. L. 1967. Pollination by euglossine bees. *Evolution* 22: 202–210.

Eltz, T., Fritzch, F., Pech, J. R., Aimmermann, Y., Ramirez, S. R., Quezada-Euan, J.J.G., and Bembe, B. 2011. Characterization of the orchid bee *Euglossa viridissima* (Apidae: Euglossini) and a novel cryptic sibling species, by morphological, chemical, and genetic characters. *Zoological Journal of the Linnean Society* 163: 1064–1076.

Pascarella, J. 2017. Range extension of the introduced bee species *Euglossa dilemma* (Hymenoptera: Apidae) in Monroe County, Florida, with notes of additional range extensions in southern Florida. *Florida Entomologist* 100(1): 209–210.

Pemberton, R. W., and Wheeler, G. S. 2006. Orchid bees don't need orchids: evidence from the naturalization of an orchid bee in Florida. *Ecology* 87: 1995–2001.

Roubik, D. W., and Hanson, P. E. 2004. *Orchid bees of tropical America. Biology and field guide.* Instituto Nacional de Biodiversidad. Santo Domingo de Heredia, Costa Rica. 370 pp.

Skov, C., and Wiley, J. 2005. Establishment of the Neotropical orchid bee *Euglossa viridissima* (Hymenoptera: Apidae) in Florida. *Florida Entomologist* 88: 225–227.

BOMBUS

Cameron, S. A., and Hines, H. M. 2007. A comprehensive phylogeny of the bumble bees (*Bombus*). *Biological Journal of the Linnean Society* 91(1): 161–188.

Colla, S., and Packer, L. 2008. Evidence for decline in eastern North American bumblebees (Hymenoptera: Apidae), with special focus on *Bombus affinis* Cresson. *Biodiversity and Conservation* 17(6): 1379–1391.

Colla, S., Richardson, L., and Williams, P. 2011. Bumble bees of the eastern United States. USDA.

Jandt, J. M., and Dornhaus, A. 2009. Spatial organization and division of labour in the bumblebee *Bombus impatiens*. *Animal Behaviour* 77(3): 641–651.

Williams, P. H., Thorp, R. W., Richardson, L. L., and Colla, S. R. 2014. *Bumble bees of North America: an identification guide.* Princeton University Press. 208 pp.

APIS

Seeley, T. D. 2010. *Honeybee democracy*. Princeton University Press.

Winston, M. L. 1991. *The biology of the honey bee*. Harvard University Press.

Ratnieks, F. L., and Carreck, N. L. 2010. Clarity on honey bee collapse? *Science* 327(5962): 152–153.

NOMADA

Mitchell, T. B. 1962. Bees of the eastern United States, volume 2. North Carolina Agricultural Experiment Station Technical Bulletin 152: 1–557.

EPEOLUS

Brumley, R. L. 1965. A revision of the bee genus *Epeolus* Latreille of western America north of Mexico. MS Thesis. Utah State University. 92 pp.

Onuferko, T. M. 2017. Cleptoparasitic bees of the genus *Epeolus* Latreille (Hymenoptera: Apidae) in Canada. *Canadian Journal of Arthropod Identification* 30: 1–62.

Onuferko, T. M. 2018. A revision of the cleptoparasitic bee genus *Epeolus* Latreille for Nearctic species, north of Mexico (Hymenoptera, Apidae). 755: 1–185.

Rozen, J. G., Jr., and Favreau, M. S. 1968. Biological notes on *Colletes compactus compactus* and its cuckoo bee, *Epeolus pusillus* (Hymenoptera: Colletidae and Anthophoridae). *Journal of the New York Entomological Society* 76(2): 106–111.

TRIEPEOLUS

Bohart, G. E. 1966. Notes on *Triepeolus remigatus* (Fabricius), a "cuckoo bee" parasite of the squash bee, *Xenoglossa strenua* (Cresson) (Hymenoptera: Apoidea). *Pan-Pacific Entomologist* 42: 255–262.

Rightmyer, M. G. 2008. *A review of the cleptoparasitic bee genus* Triepeolus *(Hymenoptera: Apidae).—Part 1*. Zootaxa 1710. Magnolia Press, Auckland. 170 pp.

Rozen, J. G., Jr. 1966. The larvae of the Anthophoridae (Hymenoptera, Apoidea). Part 2. The Nomadinae. *American Museum Novitates* 2170: 1–13.

HOLCOPASITES

Hurd, P. D., Jr., and Linsely, E. G. 1972. *Parasitic bees of the genus* Holcopasites Ashmead *(Hymenoptera: Apoidea)*. Smithsonian Contributions to Zoology 114, Washington, D.C.

INDEX

The pages in **bold** indicate a full species description.